MACROECONOMIC THEORY AND POLICY

CRITICAL ESSAYS ON THE DYNAMICS OF CAPITALISM

MACROECONOMIC THEORY AND POLICY

CRITICAL ESSAYS ON THE DYNAMICS OF CAPITALISM

AMIT BHADURI

SETU PRAKASHANI

Macroeconomic Theory and Policy : Critical Essays
on the Dynamics of Capitalism by Amit Bhaduri.
Cover Design : Dilip Ghosh, Sculpture : Sanjay Das
First Edition : January 2010
ISBN : 978-81-903272-2-0

Rupees Two hundred fifty Only

Published by Archana Das & Subrata Das on behalf of Setu Prakashani
12/A Shankar Ghosh Lane Kol-6 India Ph. 033-22190704 / 09433074548
setuprakashani@yahoo.co.in Type setting by Mudran Graphics 24 Raja Lane
Kol-9 Printed by Graphic Reproduction 8/3 Chintamoni Das Lane Kol-9.

ACKNOWLEDGMENT

1. Some Implications of Economic Openness with Special Reference to India (ECONOMIA POLITICA / a. XXV, n. 3, December 2008. This essay is also part of a wider research, Geosviluppo, innovazione e competitività: la posizione Italo-europea (D. 3.2., 2005), Department International Economics of Catholic University, Milan.

2. Structural Change and economic development: On the Relative roles of Effective Demand and the price Mechanism in a 'Dual' Economy (*Rethinking Development Economics,* ed by Ha-Joon Chang, London Anthem Press, 2003, pp. 220-235).

3. Increasing Returns and the Division of Labour in the Theory of Economic Development in *Economic Development and social Change* edited by G. Vaggi and G. Stathakis, Routledge , London and New York (Lecture at the European Society for the History of Economic Thought, Reythemno, Crete, March 2002).

4. Expanded Reproduction in the light of modern Growth theory (Elgar Companion to Classical Economics).

5. On the Dynamics of profit-led and wage-led Growth (*Cambridge Journal of Economics* 2008, 32, pp.147-160).

6. Predatory Growth (*Economic and Political Weekly* 19 April, 2008).

7. The Impact of Globalization on Indian Economic Development (Dr. John Mathai lecture, 2006).

8. A Failed World View (Foundation Day Lecture, Inter University Centre for Astronomy and Astrophysics, Pune, December, 2008).

9.Unemployment and the Real wage: the economic basis for contesting ideologies.

10. Capitalist Accumulation in Logical & Historical Time.The above two articles are published in *Unconventional Economic Essays,* OUP Delhi.

11. The Political Economy of Social Democracy is published in *On the Border of Economic Theory and History,* OUP Delhi.

12. Joblessness.

13. Making sense of the AD-AS model.

14. Short-period Macroeconomic Aspects of Foreign Aid. The above three articles are published in *Employment and Development : Essays from an Unorthodox Perspective,* OUP Delhi. (the above six articles are reproduced with permission from OUP Delhi).

CONTENTS

Section-I Dynamics of the Capitalist economy: Focus on the domestic market.

Section-II Dynamics of the Capitalist economy: Focus on foregin market.

Section-III Long run Dynamics: Economic growth and ideology.

AN INTRODUCTION TO THE PRINCIPLE OF EFFECTIVE DEMAND

Consider an idealized economy producing only two goods: one good like rice is needed for **immediate** consumption, and is called the **consumption good**. The other good is like a plough or a tractor which cannot be consumed immediately. The latter consists of various instruments needed to help current production, and to augment the future production capacity of the economy. These instruments of production are lumped together, and described as an **investment good**. Although this distinction between immediately consumable consumption goods and immediately non-consumable investment goods is being made here in terms of the physical characteristics of the goods, the physical distinction is not essential for the argument. As a matter of fact in real life any such distinction is often not clear cut, e.g. one can have rice seeds which can be consumed but become investment good in so far as they are used for investment to augment future production; similarly a tractor which is usually treated as an investment good, but can also be used for current transport, and therefore becomes partly a consumption good. The analytical distinction between the consumption and the investment good lies not in their physical characteristics, but in the fact that the former is meant only for present consumption, and the latter only for future consumption. It might be mentioned that abstract categories like consumption or investment goods usually do not correspond unambiguously to specific things in real life, but allow grouping things together by some of their essential characteristics needed for analytical purposes.

In an economy without many of the complications of money (to which we turn later), we assume each worker employed in the consumption goods sector produces 10 bags of rice per year, and is paid a **real** wage in 6 bags of rice per year, leaving a surplus of (10-6) = 4 bags of rice per worker. The importance of this surplus is twofold. **First,** it provides the source of profit for the employer or capitalist. **Second,** since workers producing investment goods like machines cannot live by eating machines, their real wage must also be paid in effect from this **surplus** of consumption goods or bags of rice. If the real wage is assumed to be the same in both the consumption and the invest goods sector i.e.6 bags , then the surplus produced by worker in the consumption sector must sustain the consumption by workers engaged in producing machines in the investment sector. To analyze the essence of this problem in the simplest possible way, assume workers consume the entire wage paid to them, and do not save anything at all. The capitalists on the other hand save everything and consume nothing.

Denoting, L_i = number of workers in the investment sector, and L_c = number of workers in the consumption sector, we can set up a market clearing balance equation for consumption goods, by which the demand for consumption goods by workers in the investment sector, i.e. $6L_i$ is equal to the supply of surplus consumption good (10-6) L_c. Note this surplus remains over and above the consumption by workers engaged directly in the production of consumption goods, and has to find a market for being sold for (monetary) profits. Otherwise it will remain as just physical surplus in the form of inventories.

Numerically the balance equation which entails the selling of the surplus in the market is given by,

$$6\,L_i = (10\text{-}6)\,L_c \tag{1}$$

Writing w = real wage rate per worker in terms of consumption goods, and x = net output or productivity per worker in the consumption goods sector, we have in symbols,

$$w\,L_i = (x\text{-}w)L_c \tag{2}$$

It would hardly be an exaggeration to say that this extraordinarily simple equation (2) provides us with one of the most fundamental insights into macroeconomics. A failure to interpret it correctly results in misunderstanding and confusion. The critical importance of this equation arises from a question it raises. Does the amount of surplus generated i.e. $(x\text{-}w)L_c$ determine how much investment i.e. wL_c can take place? Or is the amount of investment determined **independently** and, the amount of surplus available tends to adjust to it? If we claim that the level of surplus which is supplied by the consumption sector is exactly the amount demanded for investment, in effect we are saying that no adjustment is needed in so far as the economy maintains by assumption its market clearing balance. This indeed is the answer assumed by mainstream neo-classical economics which determines investment from the supply side in terms of given surplus. On the other hand, if we claim that investment is determined independently of the available surplus, say by expectations of future profits, we have to postulate the nature of adjustment which would follow. The **demand side** Keynesian economics focuses on such adjustments by postulating investment as an independent variable, irrespective of the available amount of surplus.

Written in terms of the proportion in which labour can be employed in the two sectors to ensure the balance between demand and supply of consumption goods, equation (1) becomes,

$$L_c/L_i = (10-6)/6 = 2/3 \qquad (3)$$

Or, orrespondingly in symbols,

$$L_i/L_c = (x-w)/w \qquad (4)$$

The proportionality states that labour cannot be employed arbitrarily in the two sectors without running the risk of either too much or too little (i.e. negative excess) demand for consumption goods in relation to the supply of its surplus. If this proportionality is violated, the demand supply imbalance fails to clear the market, and must set up changes or **adjustments** in the economy in one way or another. A good deal of macroeconomic theory is about the adjustments that might be set in motion

Take a specific example. Some economist might say, in a labour surplus country we should employ all unemployed people in the construction sector. In so far as this strategy produces non-consumable infrastructural goods like roads and irrigation dams, the construction workers have to be supported from the **surplus** of the consumption goods. With infrastructural expansion increasing the number of workers in the investment goods sector, suppose 18 (or 18 million, the unit does not matter in this case) **additional** workers denoted by $\Delta L_i = 18$ are employed. Provided we assume that productivity $x=10$ and real wage $w=6$ remain the same, we can calculate from (3) the additional employment needed in the consumption sector to maintain balance between demand and supply of consumption goods as,

$$\Delta L_c = (18)(3/2) = 27 \qquad (5)$$

Algebraically, the same calculation is rewritten from (4),

$$\Delta L_c = (\Delta L_i w/x-w) \qquad (6)$$

Equation (6) provides **both a theory of what determines the size of the market, and how production expands in response to larger market size.** The crux of the theory is that, the size of the market for the surplus over what is consumed directly by workers in the consumption sector is determined not in the consumption sector, but by the total wage bill of the workers in the investment goods sector as stated in (2) or (6). Thus, the increase in real investment measured by the additional number of workers ΔL_i in the investment sector employed at some given real wage w creates additional demand ($\Delta D = w\Delta L_i$) for the surplus consumption goods. As a result, if equilibrium is to be restored the number of workers in the consumption sector ,each producing a surplus (x-w) has to increase by ΔL_c , to restore the balance between additional demand and additional **surplus** of consumption goods. This determines L as the **dependent** variable on the supply side adjusting to an **independently** postulated increase of ΔL_i on the demand side in equation (6).

It appears to be a fairly obvious idea; and yet not so obvious. The conventionally trained economist has been in the habit of thinking that an increase in demand would lead mostly to an increase in price. And yet, in the above example, the increase in the demand for consumption goods due to greater employment in the investment sector by $w\Delta L_i$ leads to an increase in employment (ΔL_c) and output ($x\Delta L_c$) in the consumption sector rather than in the price of consumption goods. And, output expands to the point at which it produces an additional surplus $(x-w)\Delta L_c$ to match the additional demand for consumption goods ($w.\Delta L_i$) to satisfy equation (6).

The view that adjustment through expansion in output would take place to meet additional demand implies that quantity rather than price is the central adjusting variable. This is the distinguishing characteristic of Keynesian demand side approach to macroeconomics. It maintains that, except in rather special situations like near full employment or full capacity utilization, significant scope exists for **quantity rather than price adjustment to excess demand or supply,** and would be the general rule for adjustment in a capitalist market economy. This is almost certainly true in situations of deep recession due to extensive presence of under utilized capacity and unemployed labour. But it is true to only a lesser extent in more normal situations, because in a market economy some unemployment and underutilized capacity usually coexist. This contrasts sharply against the orthodox economic view which relies mostly on price rather than quantity adjustment at least in the short run in response to higher or lower demand. In turn, this reliance on price adjustment is based because of its implicit assumption of near full employment or capacity utilization which rules out quantity adjustment.

Interestingly, the theory of effective demand implies that the adjustment in the output of consumption goods have to be several times greater than the direct increase in demand created directly by the initial extra investment. In the above example the direct increase in demand for consumption goods is from the larger wage bill of the investment sector i.e. $w\Delta L_i$ = (6)(18) =108 bags of rice; whereas the output of consumption goods has to increase from (5) by $x\Delta L_c$ = (10) (27)=270 bags. This is because 27 workers in the consumption sector themselves consume (6)(27)= 162, and the **surplus** they produce over and above their own consumption, i.e. (270-162)= 108 matches exactly the demand for consumption goods from the investment sector. Because surplus is only a fraction of the output per worker, (x-w)/x = (10-6)/10=4/10=2/5, output has to expand 5/2= 2.5 times to produce each additional unit of surplus. This is the basic idea of **the multiplier**, which says that the increase in demand in the economy would be several times more than the initial increase in investment, depending on how large is the surplus as a fraction of the total output of the consumption sector.

The multiplier works as a **convergent process over time** through rounds of expenditure and income. It is captured conveniently by a **dwindling geometric series**. Note $1 > w/x > 0$ is the share of wage in each unit of out and it is entirely consumed by assumption while all profit (1-w/x) is saved. Consequently (w/x) defines the propensity to consume, and (1-w/x) the propensity to save in this economy. The denominator of the multiplier implied by (6) can be expanded in a convergent geometric series as,

$$m=(x/x-w) = 1/(1-w/x) = 1+(w/x)+(w/x)^2+(w/x)^3+\ldots\ldots \qquad (7)$$

The geometric series shows that initially one unit of demand is generated for surplus consumption goods through the injection of one additional unit of increased wage bill in the investment sector, represented by the first term of the series. This initial additional unit of **expenditure becomes the income** of those in the consumption sector on whom it is spent, and out of their share of this unit income workers receive and consume (w/x) while capitalists save their entire income (1-w/x). Workers expenditure (w/x) becomes the income of the next round for wage and profit recipients in the consumption sector leading to further expenditure $(w/x)^2$ and so on giving rise to the convergent geometric series in (7).

All profit is saved and all wage consumed merely simplifies the exposition, but the assumption is not essential. For instance, if workers consume c_w and save the rest of each unit of income received, i.e. $c_w = (1-s_w)$, and capitalists earning profit have consumption and saving propensities similarly related by, $c_p = (1-s_p)$, we can generalize the above multiplier analysis to get an overall consumption propensity c , which is a **weighted average** of the consumption propensities of the two classes with the distribution of income between profit(1-w/x) and wage(w/x) determining the weights, i.e.

$$c = c_p\,(1-w/x)+c_w\,(w/x)= (1-s_p)(1-w/x)+(1-s_w)(w/x) \qquad (8)$$

In this case c in (8) replaces w/x in (7) as the propensity of consumption per unit of output **taking into account the class distribution of income.** On simplification the multiplier becomes,

$$m = 1/(1-c) = 1/\{s_p h + s_w (1-h)\} \quad (9)$$

where h=(1-w/x), i.e. the share of profit in income, and the multiplier is the inverse of the weighted average of the saving propensities of the two classes.

A special case known as the 'classical savings function' assumes that all wages are consumed i.e. $s_w=0$, but some constant fraction $1>s_p>0$ of profit is saved. On this assumption, (9) reduces to,

$$m=1/s_p h \quad (10)$$

Since no wage is saved by assumption, and (1-w/x) = h is the share of profit of which s_p is saved, $s_p h$ defines the saving propensity of the economy.

Another frequently made assumption is that all classes have the same consumption propensity, i.e. $s_p = s_w = s$, to yield from (9) the multiplier as,

$$m = 1/s \quad (11)$$

The economic picture underlying this multiplier process is the simple idea of a **circular flow** of income and expenditure. Demand, created at each round of expenditure by some becomes the income of some others in the economy; and from each round of income received a fraction is consumed but the rest is saved. Since the fraction saved is withdrawal from the expenditure stream in each round, the income expenditure balance in the economy requires the withdrawals through saving through various rounds of the multiplier to be balanced by the original injection of expenditure through investment. Thus the multiplier implies investment saving balance. This is immediately seen from equation (11). Since s is the fraction saved out of each unit of income in (11), income has to increase by a factor of (1/s) units to match an additional unit of investment. Similar interpretations hold for all other versions of the multiplier like (9) and (10).

Therefore the market clearing equilibrium or balance we set out originally in equations (1) or (2), or its more complicated versions involving consumption and saving by capitalists and workers in (8) can be represented equivalently as saving investment equality. In the simple case of equation (2),

$$(x-w)L_c = S_c = wL_i = W_i = \Pi_c \quad (12)$$

In (12) the physical surplus S_c of consumption goods finds a market equal to the wage bill of the investment sector W_i and is realized into profits

$\prod_c$ of the consumption sector. This represents a balance through inter sectoral exchange between demand generated by the consumption sector and the supply of surplus by the consumption sector. On both sides of this **inter sectoral balance equation** (12), we add the profit $\prod_i$ of the investment sector to obtain,

$$(W_i + \prod_i) = (\prod_c + \prod_i) \tag{13}$$

This is another way of writing,

$$I = \prod = S \tag{14}$$

On the left hand side, the total value added or net output I of the investment sector is profit $\prod_i$ plus wage W_i of that sector, while total profit $\prod$ equals total savings S of the economy because by assumption, no wage and all profit is saved in this case.

When capitalists consume some fraction c_p of their profit, we could extend the argument corresponding to equation (10) by noting that consumption out of profit C_p is also supported from the surplus of the consumption sector. Thus the physical surplus of consumption goods S_c is realized into profits of that sector through the market provided by both the wage bill of the investment sector W_i and capitalists consumption out of profits C_p to yield,

$$C_p = c_p \prod \tag{15}$$

And an extended version of the balance equation (12) becomes,

$$W_i + C_p = W_i + c_p \prod = S_c = \prod_c \tag{16}$$

Again adding on both sides and simplifying,

$$I + c_p \prod = \prod \tag{17}$$

which reduces to,

$$I = (1-c_p) \prod = s_p \prod = s_p \, hY = S \tag{18}$$

where $h = \prod / Y$ is the share of profit in income, $Y = W + \prod$. In this case, since all wage is assumed to be consumed, the entire saving becomes a fraction s_p of profits .

If we make the assumption corresponding to (11) that, all classes save a uniform proportion s of their income then workers save and withdraw from their expenditure sW, while capitalists withdraw $s\prod$ as saving. Consequently, instead of(12) or (16) the balance equation becomes,

$$W_i - sW + \prod - s\prod = S_c = \prod_c \tag{19}$$

As before, adding Π on both sides and simplifying,

$$(W_i + \Pi_i) + \Pi\text{-s}\,(W+\Pi) = (\Pi_c + \Pi_i) = \Pi \qquad (20)$$

Cancelling total profit Π on both sides, we obtain the investment saving equality as,

$$I = s(W+\Pi) = sY. \qquad (21)$$

Thus in each case the profit realization equation (12), (16) or (19) is seen to be equivalent to the corresponding investment saving equality equation (14), (18) or (21).

A frequent source of confusion arises from the accounting procedures of **double entry** format followed in all modern systems of national income accounts. Double entry records each item both as an asset and as a liability of equal value on two sides of the format. Therefore assets and liabilities are matched in a strictly **accounting** sense, and cannot diverge by definition, and denoted by an **identity** like x (assets) x (liabilities) for **all** possible values of x. In contrast, an **equation** is true only for some **particular** value of the same relevant variable x, e.g.
$x+2=5$ which is true only for $x=3$ or a slightly more complicated example $x^2 = 4$, true for multiple values of x= =2,-2.

Since different versions of the consumer goods market clearing equations stated above, (12), (16) or (19), say basically the same thing, namely that the entire surplus produced by the consumption sector S_c finds a market of **exactly** matching size through the wage bill of the workers in the investment goods sector and capitalists consumption out of profits, this means no surplus remains unexpectedly unsold. Consequently, there is no unplanned change inventories (A). This corresponds to the notion of an equation which is only true when unplanned inventory change in the consumption sector is zero ($A_c = 0$). The identity (22) becomes an equation (12) only for a particular value of $A_c = 0$, meaning no unexpected build up or running down of inventories. Thus equation (12) depicts **equilibrium in so far as all sales expectations of businessmen are satisfied.** On the other hand, if we allow for the possibility of unplanned (positive or negative) change in inventories, (12), (16) or (19) would become identities true for all values of the surplus S_c. For instance, we could rewrite (12) in the double entry format as an identity,

$$(x-w)\,L_c \equiv S_c \equiv wL_i + A_c \equiv W + A_c \equiv \Pi_c + \Pi_{c'} \qquad (22)$$

which must always hold for **all** values of the unplanned change in inventories A_c. It says for example the surplus produced S_c is either sold as wage bill to workers in the investment sector W_i or remains unsold (or over sold) as addition to (or subtraction from) the existing stock of inventories. To make the other side of the double entry format balance, this unplanned addition to inventories enters as unrealized profits $\prod_c$.

Adding on both sides of (22) a similar identity for the investment goods sector showing unsold investment goods inventories A_i become the unrealized profit of that sector $\prod'_i$, this yields the identity for the whole economy,

$$(W_i + A_c) + (\prod_i + A_i) \equiv (\prod_c + \prod_c') + (\prod_i + \prod_i') \quad (23)$$

and becomes,

$$I + A \equiv \prod + \prod' \equiv S, \quad (24)$$

where **investment includes all unplanned inventory accumulation** A on the left hand side, while profits shown in the middle are realized as well as unrealized, depending on whether goods have been sold $\prod$ or remain unsold $\prod'$. Finally, with all profits saved by assumption, **saving equals profit realized and unrealized**. On these definitions, unplanned changes in inventory are included as investment on the one hand, while savings include both realized and unrealized profit on the other, to turn the equality between investment and saving into an accounting identity. The same interpretation holds for all other cases of saving investment equality like (18) or (21). In each case it necessarily holds for **all values** of A irrespective of whether sales expectations are realized or not, and becomes an equation only when sales expectations are exactly realized, which means no unplanned change in inventories at the **particular value** of A=0.

The macroeconomic principle of effective demand is probably the most striking example of "uncommon common sense" in macroeconomics. What it says is indeed common sense and yet, its implications go against what most men and women of 'practical affairs' consider as common sense! Therefore it poses a challenge to conventional wisdom in economic thinking. Most importantly **it breaks the analogy between the individual and the society.** It demonstrates how using microeconomic arguments for one individual can mislead in macroeconomic reasoning. Macroeconomics is not simply microeconomics of one individual magnified many times. The most celebrated example illustrating this point is the role of savings (or surplus in the above exposition), known as the **'paradox of thrift'**. If everyone consumes less and saves more in (21) the demand slackens and the market for the realization of surplus into profits becomes smaller. This is hardly beneficial for a capitalist market economy, where production for the market is driven by the profit motive. As a thought experiment we can consider the extreme situation where everyone saves all their income. With no demand for goods, the market economy cannot survive!

It also shows what we call a similar **paradox of exploitation**. If each worker is paid a lower real wage, surplus as well as **potential** profit per worker increases, and total surplus would also increase at any given level of employment in the consumption sector. However, without higher investment this surplus cannot be realized into actual profit, while the problem might even be exacerbated by a lower wage bill in the investment sector due to lower real wage per worker. This line of reasoning, known as **the wage cut controversy,** led many economists to argue that a reduction in real wage rate, even if politically possible, might not be an effective in fighting unemployment as it would further exacerbate the overall deficiency of demand. The conventional Marxist argument that capitalists can increase their profit simply by exploiting workers more to increase surplus per worker is also problematic for the same reason. By increasing surplus per worker, more profit is not made in the **aggregate** unless the size of the market for realizing the surplus into monetary profits expands sufficiently.

The implications of the paradox of thrift upset conventional wisdom in many ways. The conventionally accepted **individual virtue** of saving can become a **public vice**. It also upsets the conventional logic of corporate management by pointing out that **what is good for an individual business corporation is not necessarily good for the economy.** And yet, it is a common fallacy in which politicians often indulge by claiming that the economy should behave like an efficient corporation. This is false. For instance, if one company may manage to reduce cost, say by cutting the wage or 'downsizing' its labour force so that its labour productivity increases at the same wage rate. This might in turn increase its competitive edge, and augment its profits. However, if all firms and companies cut wages or downsize their labour force, aggregate demand will fall. As a result, the bigger surplus generated per worker (x-w) by higher productivity(x) or lower wage (w) may not find an adequate market to be realized into profit; instead it might just remain unsold goods as unplanned accumulation of inventories.

Equation (16) highlights yet another paradoxical aspect of the role of saving in a capitalist economy. **Socially useless, even harmful expenditure can become useful** in a capitalist market economy by providing a market for the realization of surplus into profit. For instance, any leisure class, capitalists or landlords by simply consuming(C_p) become useful in so far as they expand the market for selling surplus consumption goods. For instance, a **financial bubble** may be created to stimulate consumption by the rich speculating in the stock market. Similarly investments in military expenditure or "digging holes in the ground to fill them up again" can become useful.

The negative impact of saving on demand is implied by the multiplier formula itself. For instance, note that higher savings propensities in (9), (10) or (11) reduce the value of the multiplier, because the extent of demand generated per unit of investment becomes lower with higher savings propensity. However, this paradoxical idea that more saving can be harmful to the economy becomes easy to understand once we realize that the act of saving is simply a withdrawal of purchasing power, and cannot help a market economy unless savings find an expenditure outlet through investment.. For saving to become beneficial, it has to convert itself necessarily into the act of investing, and that does not happen automatically within any given period of time. The role of saving looks paradoxical only if the act of investment and saving are considered one and the same. In terms of the analysis set out above, say in (12), it means that whatever is the surplus S_c of the consumption sector, it would **identically** be the same as wage bill W_i of the investment sector. This means investment cannot be decided independently by the capitalists or the government to generate more demand and output through quantity adjustment, which in turn would generate more saving. Instead, an independently given level of saving from a given level of output is assumed to constrain the level of investment. This has led to many false arguments especially in the realm of public finance to claim that more public investment **crowds out** private investment, government budget deficit cannot increase total demand because the total level of investment is fixed and many other arguments in similar vein. Thus, whether we assume investment is independent of saving or not influences strongly our views on economic policy.

Ideologically the principle of effective demand cuts both ways. It is an analytical principle which can show up the defect of both left and right wing orthodox thinking. For instance, it shows how a conventional argument that capitalists can increase their profit simply by exploiting workers more to increase surplus **per worker** is problematic, because by increasing surplus per worker more profit is not made in the **aggregate** unless the size of the market for realizing the surplus into monetary profits expands sufficiently Similarly, technical progress like say the introduction of computers can run into the road block of inadequate demand, if it increases productivity too fast without corresponding expansion of the market. As a result the system will suffer from the symptoms of **over production**. Obversely if the growth in wage is kept too low in relation to the growth in productivity, the system might suffer from **under consumption**.

The market size needed for the realization of surplus into profit comes from several different sources in a capitalist economy. It can come from (a) higher wage per worker,w or (b) higher investment, I_1 which might even overcompensate a lower wage or (c) higher consumption by the capitalists. Each of these possibilities are shown, for example, in equation (16). This allows for politically very different stances of economic policy, all consistent with the principle of effective demand. Trade Unions for example might rightly claim that higher wages are good for capitalism as it leads to an expansion of the market. It can be called the path of **wage-led expansion** that has provided the intellectual basis for the welfare state which typically favours higher wage either directly or indirectly through various welfare measures for health, education, old age pension etc. A diametrically opposite pro chamber of commerce policy would be to claim that wages should be restrained to increase the profitability of investment. If investment responds sufficiently strongly to this lower wage and higher profit policy, a case can be made intellectually for a path of **profit-led expansion**. Indeed this has been the main contention of pro-business economic conservatism. Since wage restraint means that the market expands slowly in the short run, a special problem arises with profit led expansion. With the volume of sales expanding slowly investment usually tends to be inhibited despite higher profit per unit of sale brought about by wage restraint. To help profit led growth strategy especially in a globalizing economy, it is often claimed that the additional surplus can be sold in the world market as exports. However, the attempt to convert or supplement profit-led into **export-led expansion** typically faces similar difficulties. Expansion of exports through cost cutting measures like wage restraint or productivity growth through downsizing of the labour force shrinks domestic demand which might out weigh the expansion of export demand. Moreover, in an economy open to international trade both export and import would typically increase. While export would be an addition to aggregate demand, import would be a subtraction from it. On the whole a country can hope to add to its aggregate demand through export-led expansion only if its export exceeds its import, i.e. an **export surplus** country. However, this immediately points to the inherent limitation for generalizing this strategy for all countries, because export surplus of some countries must mean corresponding import surplus of other countries. Hence if the strategy works for some countries, it must fail for others in what might be called a zero sum game of international trade.

Both effective demand and production are governed by the market principle. Goods and services are produced only if there is sufficient demand in the market, while production for the market attributes to the physical goods and services the social character of '**commodities**'. Thus the essential characteristic is not derived from their specific physical characteristics, but from the overwhelming presence of the market in production, distribution and consumption. As a result even non-producible natural resources like land, water, forest, even clean air ,and of course increasingly all types of labour services, gradually become '**commoditized**' to be bought and sold in the markets. It is hardly surprising therefore that, both demand and supply side economics try to conceptualize the market, but in significantly different ways.

At the most fundamental level, all demand side economics based on the principle of effective demand aims at providing a theory of the **extent** to which commodity production can proceed at a particular time. The binding constraint in this scheme is identified as the level of aggregate demand. In conceptualizing the market place, supply side economics on the other hand identifies rising cost as the binding constrains. In this view profit-maximizing output is restricted by rising marginal cost, and demand presents no serious problem. This circumvention of the aggregate demand problem arises because supply side neo-classical macroeconomic or general equilibrium analysis restricts itself mostly to a theory of **exchange** between goods and services without considering the extent to which exchanges can proceed in a market economy. This means that main avenue for adjustment becomes the **relative price** or the exchange rate between two commodities. The price of commodity in relative excess supply rises while that of the commodity in relative excess demand falls in a **self-regulating market** to eliminate excess demand or supply. This happens for all commodities including the price of labour which is real wage. Thus the cause for unemployment in supply side economics is too high a real wage rate, and lowering real wage is the remedy. Similarly, saving and investment are seen as loanable funds with the rate of interest as the price eliminating the inequality between investment and saving. In such a world there is little possibility of a general failure of aggregate demand, because flexible relative prices do their work to keep resources fully employed. Thus, except in the case of an insufficiently flexible interest rate, investment and savings are equated through the interest rate at full employment, just as there exists no possibility of unemployment unless the real wage rate is insufficiently flexible. This is the unifying world view that rules neo-classical economics of all varieties, moderate ones trying to explain why particular prices are not sufficiently flexible and the price mechanism fails, and in more extreme cases particular markets do not even get formed to permit exchanges(they are called neo-Keynesians of various shades),. The more extreme neo-classical versions either claim that the market never fails to clear by balancing demand with supply almost instantaneously, or if it fails, the failure is temporary and is corrected in the longer run (called new Classical, rational expectation and monetarist theories of all variety).

The principle of effective demand can be understood from two rather different perspectives. The conventional view would be that Keynesian economics is a special case, some might say a very important special case, of the failure of the price mechanism to clear the labour market, or the market for loanable funds related to investment and saving. The less conventional view would be to claim that commodity production in a market economy is more structurally flawed It fail because the major economic actors have different objectives, information and even economic power, and the price mechanism is simply insufficient to deal with them coherently. The structural flaw was identified in the above analysis as arising from investment being determined autonomously by businessmen necessarily on the prospects of uncertain future profit stream.. Banks and other financial institutions lend to business against profit streams yet to materialize. Thus the finance advanced for business has almost nothing to do with the amount of money deposited as savings from the current income of households as savers. It might be added that the extent to which hire purchase, housing mortgage etc become important the distinction becomes less clear in a modern maket economy, just as corporate savings reduce the gap between corporations as investors and savers. Nevertheless, in the more stylized picture of capitalism the separation between investment and saving remains structural in the sense that the existing price system, e.g. the interest rate is not even meant to bridge this gap. Indeed Keynes needed his theory of 'liquidity preference' to assign a different role to the interest rate than that of equating investment with saving

The equality between investment and saving comes through a novel route in the theory of effective demand. Investment could be equated to saving, and markets for commodities get cleared not because of the working of the price mechanism, rather despite it. As elaborated above, higher investment stimulates higher utilization of existing production capacities, and paradoxically such expansion of production is usually easier the less efficient the market is by leaving large productive capacities unutilized. The resulting quantity adjustment translates into a Keynesian "income effect" that generates a higher level of saving to match higher investment through the multiplier mechanism. In this scheme of analysis **saving is not given because income is not given**, but varies with capacity utilization. Since saving can be generated through demand, **investment becomes a self-financing process**. Perhaps in this sense investment becomes self regulating in a capitalist market economy. This goes against the neo-classical notion of how the income effect impacts on market clearing through the operation of the price mechanism. When people are free to trade at prices which do not necessarily clear the market, the 'income effect' of exchange arises from the income which the demanders pay and the suppliers receive for particular commodities. Such income effects in general are arbitrary, and can be destabilizing. In other words, when neo-classical theory tries to reckon with income, things become problematic, while saving generated through the Keynesian income effect is stabilizing in the context of investment saving equality. Altogether different mechanisms for income generation, through capacity utilization and though shift in relative prices, provide the basis for these two different views.

A related aspect stems from the fact that neo-classical theory considers that prices are the **only signals** carrying information about relative scarcity in the market. In contrast, the principle of effective demand accommodates other types of signals like accumulation or running down of inventories, length of the order books of firms which are basically **quantity not price signals**, and gives Keynesian economics a wider scope.

Since Keynesian demand side economics does not place exclusive emphasis on adjustment through prices, it is often misinterpreted as operating under **fixed** prices. And yet, the very mechanism of saving investment equality leading to the multiplier analysis is sufficiently general to reckon with **flexible** prices. The essential idea is simple. Changing relative prices due to an exogenous change in demand would normally change the distribution of income (also the basis of the neo-classical 'income effect' in general equilibrium theory mentioned above), and if the distribution of income changes, total savings would be affected in so far as different social groups have different propensities to save. This opens up quite a different route for equating investment with saving through the working of the multiplier mechanism. Returning to the basic equations (2), (3) and (4), suppose, the proportion of labour is higher in the investment sector; instead of (L_i/L_c) being 2/3, let it be 4/5. In the latter case the proportion of balance between the surplus of the consumption goods and its demand as the wage bill of the investment sector (recall equation 12) is satisfied through a lowering of the real wage rate from 6 to 5., with labour productivity x in the consumption sector remaining constant at x=10.

How such reduction in the real wage rate with flexible prices take place can be illustrated in the context of the two class society of capitalists and workers, with different savings propensities. Making the classical assumption that all wage is consumed and a constant fraction s_p of profit is saved (recall equations 10 and 18), a higher level of investment can be matched by a higher level saving if adjustment in prices leads to the required fall in the real wage rate. This is possible **if the general price level rises faster the money wage rate in percentage terms to reduce the real wage.** Note in this model too flexible relative prices play a crucial role, but it is the ratio of the general price level and the money wage rate. As the profit margin per unit of sale rises,with the resulting redistribution of income in favour of profit earners who save more than workers, total savings increase sufficiently to match the higher level of investment, and eliminate the excess demand for consumption goods caused by initial higher investment. As the increased income of the profit earners shows itself in a higher share of profit, h in national income, the magnitude of the multiplier in (18) takes a lower value. This is another way of saying that the expansion of demand for consumption goods caused by a higher level of investment is lowered through the redistribution of income in favour of the class which has a higher propensity to save.

It has usually been argued that full employment or full capacity utilization is the dividing line that separates the regime of quantity from that of price adjustment in Keynesian economics. Thus the multiplier mechanism works either through quantity adjustment when excess productive capacity exists; alternatively, it works through price adjustment when no excess capacity exists. And yet, this is no more than a simplification. In more general cases, due to higher demand generated by higher investment real wage might even rise, if the money wage rate rises faster than price level to raise the real wage rate. While such redistribution in favor of wage would depress saving, higher demand from higher investment would stimulate capacity utilization to increase income and saving. With the two opposite effects working on the level of saving, the equality between investment and saving might still be restored if the **net** effect on saving of capacity expansion(quantity adjustment) and redistribution (price adjustment) is positive. This gives rise to a more generalized application of the multiplier mechanism which does not rule out price adjustment, but assigns to it the dual role of determining both the level and the distribution of income.

MAKING SENSE OF THE AGGREGATE DEMAND-SUPPLY MODEL

INTRODUCTION

In almost all recent textbooks on macroeconomics, the Keynesian theory of effective demand is sought to be generalized by explicitly incorporating the supply side. This results in a convenient macroeconomic construction which is familiar from its partial equilibrium counterpart: a falling aggregate demand *(AD)* and a rising aggregate supply *(AS)* curve intersect in the price-quantity space to determine simultaneously the equilibrium levels of price and output *(e.g.* Baumol and Blinder, 1991, pp. 181-182, Felderer and Homburg, 1992, pp. 97-101,109-112, Sachs and Larrain, 1993, pp. 66-68, Stiglitz, 1993, p. 694, Dornbusch and Fischer, 1994, pp. 202-208). This construction also serves in many empirically oriented research papers to distinguish especially a supply-shock from a demand-shock. This amounts to keeping either the AD or AS curve unchanged, while shifting the other curve to examine the comparative static properties of the shift on price and output *(e.g.* Bruno, 1986, Blanchard, 1989, Bernanke, 1994).

A central purpose of this paper is to show that neither the usual AD/AS generalization of Keynesian economics nor its comparative static applications in more applied work can be considered legitime from a logical point of view.[1] The construction is fundamentally flawed, as it leads to logical inconsistencies when applied to out-of-equilibrium situations (section 1). Consequently, despite the claims by the above-mentioned textbook authors and researchers, the AD/AS analysis cannot be used to visualize any kind of price or quantity adjustment process towards equilibrium; nor can it be used for deriving comparative static results, since the 'stability' of the system cannot even be discussed meaning-fully.[2] The AD/AS apparatus has to be reformulated before it can be used in any logically coherent sense. As section 2 of this paper shows,

The two co-authors who have contributed in the above article are Emeritus Professor Kazimierz Laski & Associate Professor Martin Riese. Both are from Kepler University, Linz, Austria.

there are two different routes to making this analysis logically consistent. Section 3 relates our reformulated approach to disequilibrium theory based on the 'short side' of the market principle. The last section sums lip the analysis with some comments on its implications.

A Logical Inconsistency

The construction of the AD/AS curve relates price P to that level of reall output y which would produce, demand-side equilibrium, *i.e.* generate just enough demand to match output at that price. This entails income-expenditure equilibrium of Keynesian analysis via the multiplier mechanism which underlies the usual formulation of the AD curve along either the familiar 45°-diagram or the Hicksian *IS* curve. To keep the exposition at its simplest, we treat real investment as autonomous at $I=\bar{I}$ in a closed economy without a government sector Thus, aggregate demand consists only of private consumption and autonomous investment, both in real terms. Moreover, assuming uniform propensities to consume for both wage-earners and profit-earners, consumption C may be postulated as proportional to output Y, namely, cY(l > c > O). The negative response of demand to the price level is captured through the real balance effect, by allowing another part of private consumption C to be a decreasing function of the price level. Consequently the demand-side equilibrium, derived from the usual multiplier analysis, is

$$Y_d = \bar{I} + \tilde{C}(P) + cY_d \quad [1]$$

implying

$$\frac{dY_d}{dP} = \frac{1}{s}\frac{d\tilde{C}(P)}{dP} \leq 0 \text{ where } s = (1-c) \quad [2]$$

While [2] establishes the negatively sloped conventional AD curve, owing to the real balance effect, the income-expenditure equilibrium through the multiplier mechanism along the AD curve entails that aggregate demand determines the level of output actually produced. However, the question arises as to whether firms would actually produce that level of output in accordance with their supply behaviour.

The supply side is usually constructed on the postulate of profit maximization under diminishing returns to labour as the only variable factor of production in the short run. Thus, at nominal wage w, price equals rising marginal cost under competitive conditions to yield

$$P = \frac{w}{f'} \quad [3]$$

where $f(L)$ represents the short-period production function with labour as the only factor subject to diminishing return, *i.e.*

$$Y_s = f(L),\ f' > 0,\ f'' < 0 \qquad [4]$$

At any given money wage $w = \bar{w}$, [3] and [4] imply,[4]

$$\left.\frac{dYs}{dP}\right|_{w=\bar{w}} = (f') \bullet \frac{dL}{dP} > 0 \qquad [5]$$

In other words, from [5] AS increases with price at a given nominal wage $\bar{w}$, because real wage falls to induce more employment and output at profit-maximizing equilibrium.

Figure 1 reformulates geometrically the *AD/AS* framework familiar from many textbooks. For a specified nominal wage w and a certain price, say P_1 the corresponding real wage $\bar{w}/P_1$ represented by the slope of the tangent to $f(L)$ at point A, determines via profit maximization a certain amount of employment L_a on the right-hand side. On the lefthand side of the diagram this corresponds to aggregate supply P_1 A' Parametric variation of P at given nominal wage w traces out the $AS(P)$ curve in accordance with [5].

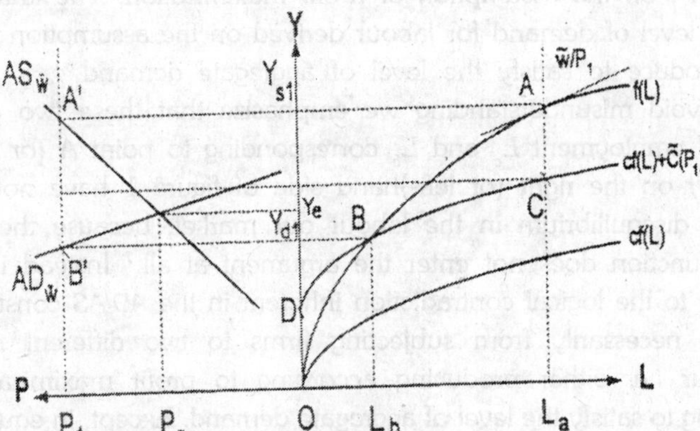

FIGURE 1.

Turning to the demand side, the individual components of aggregate demand in [1] are exhibited on the right-hand side of figure 1. Aggregate real consumption cY becomes just a scaled-down version of the utilization function. By adding the constant term $\bar{I} + \bar{C}$ (P_1) at price P_1 we derive total demand at price P_1 along the curve DBC.

Consequently, on the right-hand side of figure 1 for price level P_1, $Y_{dl}=f(L_b)$ where L_b denotes the amount of employment determined via the multiplier, which brings total expenditure and output into equilibrium. Again, by varying p parametrically the negatively sloped *AD(P)curve* may be traced out, in accordance with equations [1] and [2]. However , unlike the *AS(P)* curve, the *AD(P)* curve is traced out without any reference to any specific nominal wage rate. This implies that the real wage rate does not enter directly in defining AD.[5]

Nevertheless, for consistency of comparisons, we need to assume that the nominal wage in the construction of *AD* is the same as that for *AS*, viz. *w*. It is evident from the right-hand side of figure 1 that the profit maximization at real wage w/P_1 implies point *A*, but at the same real wage w/P_1 demand-determined equilibrium is achieved at point *B*. On the left-hand side of figure 1, this out-of-equilibrium position is shown explicitly: while aggregate demand *(AD)* at *B*' is less than aggregate supply *(AS)* at *A*' these two positions *A*' and *B*' cannot be meaningfully compared because they entail two inconsistent levels of employment L_a and L_b respectively. The former L_a is the derived demand for labour at real wage w/P_1 on the assumption of profit maximization. The latter, L_b is another level of demand for labour derived on the assumption that the firms produce to satisfy the level of aggregate demand.[6]

To avoid misunderstanding we emphasize that these two different levels of employment L_a and L_b corresponding to point *A (or A')* and *B (or B')* on the right (or left-)hand side of figure 1 have nothing to do with disequilibrium in the labour our market, because the labour supply function does not enter the argument at all.[7] Instead it points precisely to the logical contradiction inherent in the *AD/AS* construction. It arises necessarily from subjecting firms to two different rules of behaviour *i.e.* either producing according to profit maximization or producing to satisfy the level of aggregate demand. Except, in equilibrium where the distinction between the two rules is blurred, the same economic agent, namely the firm cannot obey both rules! This inconsistency becomes all the more apparent when the consequences of a price change are investigated. Assume that the initial situation of the economy is represented by the coordinates of the equilibrium point *E*. At price, P_e and output Y_e income-expenditure equilibrium (along curve *AD)* is achieved by firms which are also maximizing profit (along curve *AS)*. At the constant money wage *w*, if the price level increases (decreases) from P_e, then profit-maximizing firms are expected to increase (decrease) employment along the supply curve *AS*, while the same firms are expected to decrease (increase) employment along the demand curve *AD* to satisfy demand! This demonstrates how the two rules for the firms, profit maximization along *AS* and satisfying demand along *AD*, become self-contradictory outside equilibrium.

The economic fallacy in using the *AD/AS* framework as a macroeconomic apparatus to analyse out-of-equilibrium positions should now be apparent. In partial-equilibrium analysis of demand and supply, as a first approximation it may be plausible to posit two separate economic agents in the product markets —households as consuming units whose demand responds negatively, and firms as producing units whose supply responds positively, to higher price. This separation becomes untenable in aggregate demand-supply analysis, because firms are not only producers, but also —through their derived demand for labour— providers of employment to households which, in turn, determines the level of consumption expenditure. Viewed from this angle the problem with the *AD/AS* analysis lies in the inconsistency of postulating the level of aggregate demand independently of the level of employment actually offered by the firms. The two levels of employment or derived demand for labour in out-of-equilibrium situations emphasizes precisely this absurdity underlying the construction.

A class of macroeconomic models *(e.g.* Mankiw, 1992, chapter 8, pp. 214-234) tries to escape the problem arising from the circularity of the income-expenditure flow by taking resort to the quantity theory of money for providing the *AD* locus. With the quantity of money *M* and its velocity of circulation v constant, the quantity equation $Mv = PY$ is used to trace an inverse relation between *P* and Y, which is treated as the *AD* curve. The underlying idea that the quantity of money determines the level of nominal income and through a generalized real-balance effect also the level of aggregate demand, means that it is the exogenous supply of money which determines the demand for goods. This idea postulates again that aggregate demand has nothing to do with the actual level of employment offered by firms. To deny this link between the level of employment and the level of expenditure is to ignore the circular nature of the flow of income —the central innovation of macroeconomics since Keynes.[8]

Two Routes To Consistency

Since the logical inconsistency of the *AD/AS* analysis arises essentially from subjecting the same economic agent, namely the firm to two different rules of behaviour —profit-maximization along *AS* versus satisfying aggregate demand along *AD*— this also suggests naturally two routes to resolving this logical difficulty. Firms may be assumed either to maximize profits and remain always on their supply curve *AS* with aggregate demand derived from *AS*. Alternatively, the firms may be assumed to satisfy aggregate demand on the basis of some principie of 'bounded rationality' and remain always on the *AD* curve with aggregate supply derived from *AD*.

These two routes correspond to two well-established models in macroeconomics, the former termed 'neo-classical' and the latter termed Kaleckian, after the name of its innovator (Kalecki, 1933; 1971). The model of Keynes in the General Theory (1936) is a more complex hybrid case lying between these two extremes, on which we comment later in this section.

With profit maximization as the ruling principle in the neo-classical model, conditions [3] to [5] are always satisfied to yield profit-maximizing output Y_s at each price (given nominal wage *w)* and this level of output Y_s enters to determine the derived aggregate demand schedule (DAD). Formally, this satisfies,

$$Y_{dd} = \bar{I} + \tilde{C}(P) + cYs \qquad [6]$$

in place of former AD equation [1].

So long as the real-balance effect is relatively weak. Y_{dd} can be seen to be less responsive than Y_s to variations in the price level. Because, from [6],

$$\frac{dY_{dd}}{dP} = \frac{d\tilde{C}(P)}{dP} + c\frac{dY_s}{dP} \qquad [7]$$

so that $d\tilde{C}$ *(P)/dP* as a relatively small (negative) term is dominated by the (positive) term *c(dYs/dP)* to make the right hand side of [7] positive, while l>c>o ensures

$$\frac{dY_s}{dP} > \frac{dY_{dd}}{dP} > 0 \qquad [8]$$

or equivalently (in terms of inverse functions),

$$\frac{dP}{dY_{dd}} > \frac{dP}{dY_s} > 0 \qquad [9]$$

where customarily price is measured on the vertical axis, as in figure 2.[9]

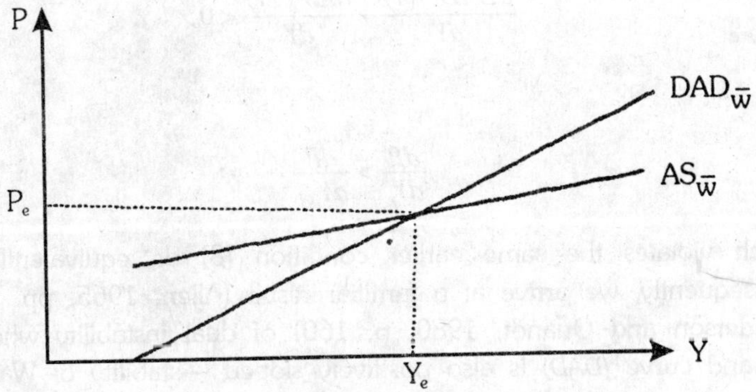

Figure 2

The fact that the DAD curve is an increasing function of price has important consequences for the stability equilibrium. So long as the *DAD* curve crosses the *AS* curve from below, price adjustment, imagined to be conducted by a Walrasian auctioneer, leads to equilibrium —because, as figure 2 shows, below (above) the equilibrium price P_e there is excess demand (supply) raising (lowering) price. In contrast, quantity adjustment, now imagined to be conducted by a Marshallian auctioneer, would lead away from equilibrium —because, below (above) the equilibrium output Y_e demand price quoted by the auctioneer is lower (higher) than the supply price, inducing firms to contract (expand) output further. More formally, the Walrasian price adjustment guided by the equation

$$\frac{dP}{dt} = a[DAD(P) - AS(P)], a > 0 \qquad [10]$$

is locally stable, if the relevant derivatives evaluated at equilibrium P_e satisfy,

$$DAD'(Pe) - AS'(Pe) < 0$$

$$\frac{dY_s}{dP} > \frac{dY_{dd}}{dP}$$

which is our earlier condition [8]. However, Marshallian quantity adjustment, guided by the equation involving inverse functions,

$$\frac{dY}{dt} = b[DAD^{-1}(Y) - AS^{-1}(P)], b > 0 \qquad [11]$$

is locally stable if the relevant derivatives evaluated at equilibrium Y_e satisfy,

$$\frac{dDAD^{-1}(Y)}{dY} - \frac{dAS^{-1}(Y)}{dY} < 0$$

i.e.,

$$\frac{dP}{dY_s} > \frac{dP}{dY_{dd}}$$

which violates the same earlier condition [8] or, equivalently, [9]. Consequently, we arrive at a familiar result (Allen, 1965, pp. 19-23; Henderson and Quandt, 1980, p. 160) of dual instability when the demand curve *(DAD)* is also positively sloped —stability of Walrasian price adjustment implies instability of Marshallian quantity adjustment and vice versa.

The second route to consistency comes from the primary role assigned to aggregate demand. In its starkest schematization, Kalecki assumed a 'conventional' profit margin on the basis of mark-up pricing which allows firms to respond to aggregate demand by expanding or contracting the quantity of output without any effect on price, so long as firms have significantly underutilized capacity. In this case, the relevant supply curve is a flat, horizontal line, where each price level is defined in relation to a different mark-up on constant unit variable (= marginal) cost, on the assumption of given labour productivity and money wage. Consequently, any shift in aggregate demand leads to correspondingly greater production along this perfectly elastic supply curve, through the usual rounds of the multiplier mechanism.[10]

This assumption of mark-up pricing establishes the primacy of aggregate demand in determining the level of output by departing from the neo-classical rule of precise profit maximization. Its justification in terms of 'satisficing behaviour' based on 'bounded rationality' is well-known *(e.g.* Bhaduri and Falkinger. 1990; Simon, 1979). However, unlike Kalecki, Keynes accepted precise profit maximization as the 'first postulate of Classical Economics' (1936, pp. 17-31). Nevertheless, despite accepting this postulate, he elaborated on a framework of analysis where the level of output is determined by the level of aggregate demand, and not by the real wage rate from the supply side through profit maximization. His argument follows a line of economic causation in which investment determines effective demand which leads correspondingly to a higher level of output through the multiplier mechanism. Nevertheless, as our preceding discussion shows, implied in this view is the assumption that firms follow the rule of satisfying higher aggregate demand, even if it means departing, at least temporarily, from the rule of precise profit maximization. The higher level of output subsequently leads to upward revision in price to restore profit maximizing equilibrium. This means upward revision in price by equating the lower marginal product of labour at that higher level of output with a lower real wage rate. Schematically,

$$\begin{pmatrix}\text{autonomous}\\ \text{investment}\end{pmatrix}\xrightarrow[\text{step1(multiplier)}]{\text{quantity adjustment}}\begin{pmatrix}\text{effective}\\ \text{demand}\end{pmatrix}=$$

$$\begin{pmatrix}\text{real output at}\\ \text{initial price level}\end{pmatrix}\xrightarrow[\text{step2(profit maximization)}]{\text{price adjustment}}\begin{pmatrix}\text{real}\\ \text{wage rate}\end{pmatrix}=\begin{pmatrix}\text{marginal product}\\ \text{of labour}\end{pmatrix}$$

Therefore, in the Keynesian theory the real wage rate is determined by, but is not a determinant of the level of employment. It is an endogenous variable determined through relative movements of price and money wage to satisfy the 'first postulate of Classical Theory'. This suggests both the important difference and the similarity between the Kaleckian and the Keynesian scheme. In the former case, the constancy of the conventional profit margin implies a constant real wage which permits price only to move in strict proportion to money wage (at given labour productivity). However, in the Keynesian case, price has to rise more than proportionally in relation to money wage so that real wage is depressed at a higher level of output. But despite this difference, both models recognize the dominant influence of aggregate demand on output through the multiplier with (Keynes) or without (Kalecki) the postulate of precise profit maximization, as encapsulated in figure 3. In conformity with our preceding discussion the shift from AD_1 to AD_2 (in both cases aggregate demand represented without real balance effect), brought about by an exogenous increase in real investment, results in increased output at fixed price P_a from Y_a to Yb in accordance with the multiplier. Thus, point B represents the Kalecki-Keynes quantity adjustment at given price. However, Keynes postulates a further adjustment, as firms increase prices (given nominal wage) along ***BE*** to restore profit-maximizing equilibrium by equating marginal value product of labour with the nominal wage rate.

In-figure 3, only by assigning a subsidiary role to the rule of profit maximization, the Kalecki-Keynes theory of demand-determined output escapes the neo-classical strait-jacket of output being determined from the supply side through profit maximization with real wage as the autonomous causal variable.

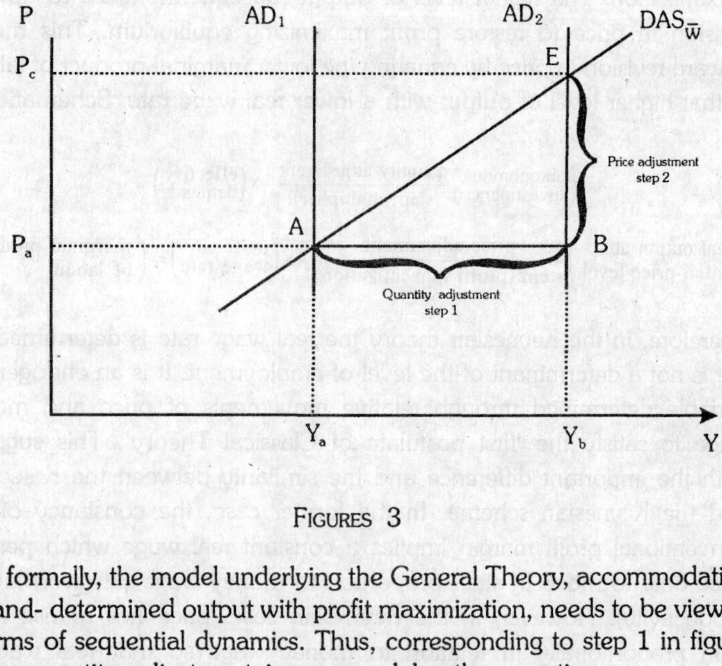

FIGURES 3

More formally, the model underlying the General Theory, accommodating demand- determined output with profit maximization, needs to be viewed in terms of sequential dynamics. Thus, corresponding to step 1 in figure 3, the quantity adjustment is governed by the equation

$$\frac{dY}{dt} = f'(L)\bullet\frac{dL}{dt} = a\bullet P[\bar{I} - sf(L)], a > 0 \qquad [12]$$

Note, price adjustment can play no role in [12] for closing the gap between real investment and real savings. It can only be closed via adjustment in real income and employment, assuming that reserve labour force is available. This system is locally stable if,

$$s>0 \qquad [13]$$

so that higher savings out of higher output always matches higher investment.

Price adjustment takes place in the subsequent sequence to restore profit maximization, with output and employment already in equilibrium, by equating real savings with real investment. Higher demand (investment) causing higher output lowers the marginal (and average) product of labour, so that firms raise their price even at a given nominal wage, $w = \bar{w}$ to restore profit-maximizing equilibrium. This price adjustment, corresponding to step 2 in figure 3, is governed by the equation,

$$\frac{dP}{dt} = \beta[\overline{w} - Pf'(L)], \beta > 0 \qquad [14]$$

where the relevant derivative is evaluated at $L= Le$ which has already attained equilibrium value (in step 1); consequently local stability of the system is guaranteed if.[11]

$$f' > 0$$

The revolutionary novelty of the model of the General Theory is often lost sight of by insisting that Keynes had also accepted the inverse relation between real wage and employment through profit maximization. Our formalization should make it clear that the methodological novelty lay in postulating a sequential dynamics, where output adjustment precedes (or has a faster speed of) price adjustment, in total contradiction to conventional wisdom of Marshallian short-period analysis (*cf.* Leijonhufvud, 1968). And, it is precisely on this point that the neo-classical interpretation of Keynes differs, since it requires price rise (due to higher demand/ investment or money supply) to precede in order to reduce real wage for profit-maximizing firms to be induced to produce more (*cf.* Blanchard, 1990, especially pp. 782-784, 803).[12]

Reinterpreting Disequilibrium Analysis

The sequential dynamics of the General Theory, where quantity adjustment precedes (or is faster than) price adjustment, suggests a way of removing the logical inconsistencies in the *AD/AS* framework. In a temporal sense, it implies that firms 'first' produce to satisfy higher aggregate demand, and 'then' (more slowly) raise price to restore profit-maximizing equilibrium (figure 3). This temporal division, aimed at reconciling the two apparently contradictory rules of satisfying aggregate demand and maximizing profit, has reappeared in a different way in modem disequilibrium theory (Clower, 1965; Malinvaud, 1977). In this latter formulation, two different economic states are distinguished according to which particular rule operates. Thus, whether firms pursue the satisfaction of demand or maximization of profit depends on the binding macroeconomic constraint characterizing the economy.

Viewed from this angle, the logical inconsistencies in the *AD/AS* apparatus seem to disappear at first sight, especially because this interpretation does not insist that spontaneous market forces drive the system towards equilibrium. Instead, in its simplest version it posits that the 'short side' of the market determines the rule to be followed to determine the actual outcome. Nevertheless, this does not escape the problem of inconsistency, because actual employment is still guided either by the rule of profit maximization by the firms or by their meeting aggregate demand. If actual employment is guided by the rule of profit maximization by firms along the *AS* curve then desired expenditure at this level of employment can not correspond meaningfully to the *AD* curve in figure 4 in so far as it is determined in isolation from the income received by the households, and thus violates the principle of the 'circular flow' of income. Alternatively, if actual employment is guided by the rule of satisfying aggregate demand by firms along the *AD* curve then the implied supply curve can no longer correspond to the *AD* curve for the same reason.

However, in terms of our preceding discussion of the two routes to consistency, we obtain a more transparent macroeconomic characterization

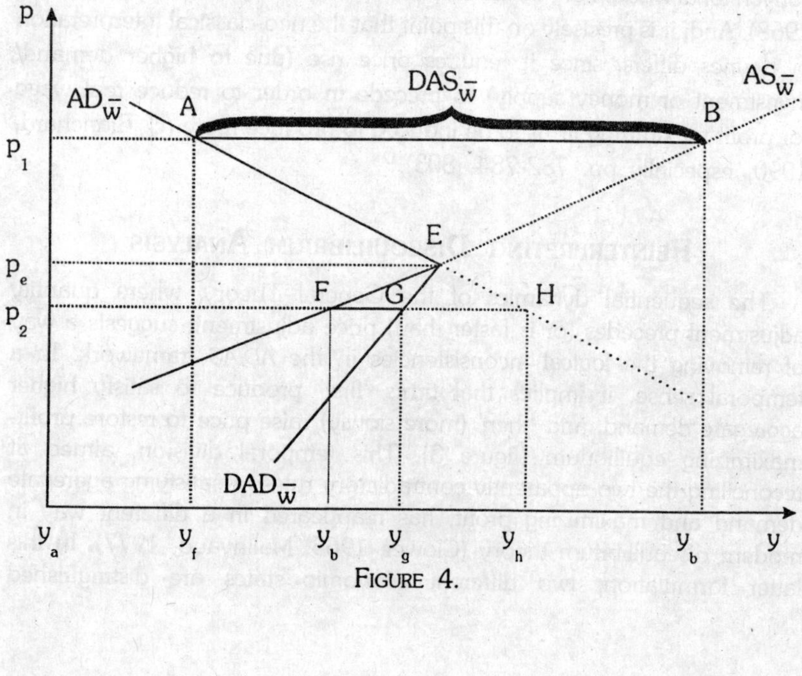

FIGURE 4.

of the nature of 'rationing' under disequilibrium. If the price level happens to be below the equilibrium, at level $P_2 < P_e$ (figure 4) aggregate supply is the shorter side of the market and equals Y_f while the notional aggregate demand is equal to Y_h. Since the latter is determined in complete isolation from the actual employment. Y_f and Y_h can be compared only in a very hypothetical way. This makes the notion of 'quantity rationing' outside equilibrium so problematic. However, previous analysis suggests the simpler solution, that at actual aggregate supply Y_f the actual derived aggregate demand (DAD) would be Y_g. Consequently, an actual (not notional) excess demand equal to the distance *FG*; in figure 4 obtains which would make the persistence of the price level P_2 below P_e rather difficult in a market economy.

On the other hand, if the price level is above equilibrium at $P_l > P_e$ the conventional AD/AS construction tells us that output determined by actual aggregate demand is Y_a while notional aggregate supply that would maximize profit is Y_b. This situation, interpreted in terms of our second (Kalecki) route to consistency, corresponds to *AB*, representing simply the actual derived supply curve. So long as the aggregate demand increases (not beyond Y_b) aggregate supply would passively adjust at the given price. The horizontal derived aggregate supply curve *AB* corresponds fully to the Kaleckian framework with the *AS* curve playing no other role than providing a boundary constraint to demand-determined output.

Concluding Observations

Our aim in this paper has been to demonstrate the logical inconsistency which arises in the *AD/AS* framework in all out-of-equilibrium positions, as the same economic agent, the firm, is assumed to be governed by two different rules —maximization of profits along *AS* and satisfaction of aggregate demand (without profit maximization) along *AD* (section 1). When this logical inconsistency is removed by subjecting firms to either of the rules, but not both, two distinct models with very different policy implications are obtained. In the neo-classical model, real wage is the exogenous variable determining profit-maximizing supply of output along *AS* from which aggregate demand *DAD* is derived. In this model aggregate demand has no independent existence and the model is not 'Keynesian' in any sense. In the contrasting model of Kalecki and Keynes, aggregate demand is assigned the dominant role in determining output, with (Keynes) or without (Kalecki) precise profit maximization (section 2). The *AD/AS* model interpreted in terms of a disequilibrium theory is seen to correspond precisely to the case of derived demand or derived supply. In the former case, the persistence of the disequilibrium situation in so far as price has to persist below its equilibrium level despite excess demand seems implausible. In the latter case, the disequilibrium theory can be reduced to the case of aggregate demand playina the governing role without profit maximization, as in Kalecki's model (section 3).

Our argument suggests that the conventional *AD/AS* framework is not only logically faulty but *economically* misleading as well. Perhaps the most awkward assumption of the *AD/AS* framework is that variations in the price level in a modern industrial economy can take place without significant repercussions on nominal wages (equations [3] to [5]). This assumption is not merely unrealistic, but also misleading in a theoretical sense -because it misrepresents the role assigned to the 'price mechanism' in the Keynesian model. The relative movements between prices and money wages are assigned the specific role of restoring profit-maximizing equilibrium in the Keynesian model through endogenous movement of the real wage, while output continues to be determined by the level of demand (section 2). This message is not merely lost in the conventional *AD/AS* framework. It also misleads by pretending that the price level simply equates demand with supply even in the macroeconomic context.

Notes :

1. Hall and Treadgold (1982) were among the first to hint at the difficulty resulting from various feedbacks between AD and AS, but failed to pinpoint the logical inconsistency. Since then other authors have also recognized independently the problematic nature of this construction, as was brought to our attention while the first version of our paper *(Bhaduri et ai,* 1994) was in circulation *(cf.* Barro. 1994: Fields and Hart, 1990: Colander, 1994).
2. Via Samuelson's 'Correspondence Principle' (1947) which requires the stability property of a system to be used to derive comparative static results. However, the AD/AS apparatus is used as a rule to analyse out-of-equilibrium price adjustment.
3. The model could be complicated by making investment a function of the interest rate price level etc eg. in the 1S/LM framework.

However, these complications are unnecessary for our present purpose, since none of these complications—in contrast to the real-balance—effect provides unambiguous argument in favour of a negatively sloped AD curve.

4. *Since,* $\left.\frac{dL}{dP}\right|_{w=\overline{w}} = [(f)^2 / wf''] > 0$

5. This is due to the assumption of uniform savings propensity for both profit -and wage-earners. —Note also that in figure 1, the level of production and employment are explicitly shown. When demand depends on distribution, e.g. in the form of a classical savings function making consumption equal to the wage bill, multiple equilibria may emerge naturally in this diagram, so that the conventional *AD* curve is no longer unique. This can be seen from the right-hand side of figure 1 when a straight line with intercept equal to investment plus the price-sensitive component of consumption, has a slope equal to the given real wage, *e.g.* at (w/P_1). For prices above equilibrium this straight line may intersect the utilization function twice.
6. Indeed, the Kahn-Keynes multiplier process generating round by round demand operates on the assumption that employment increases with each round of demand to generate further demand and employment in a convergent geometric series (Kahn, 1931).
7. Nor is there any presumption about full-employment at the equilibrium point where AD and AS intersect.
8. Contrary to chapter 8, in chapters 9-10 Mankiw (1992) takes into account the circular nature of the flow of income. In these chapters it is the level of production which determines the demand for goods and —in turn—for money. This demand for money in relation to the supply of money determines the equilibrium rate of interest. Note that the quantity theory of money is used here (ch. 9-10) essentially as a theory of transaction demand for money, but not for goods (unlike in ch. 8).
9. More precisely, the price elasticity of $\widetilde{C}$ *(P)* would have to be considerably larger than that of *Ys(P)* to produce a negatively sloped DAD curve. It is worth emphasizing that condition [8] or. equivalently [9] is economically the most plausible outcome, since *c(dYs/dP)* is usually considerably larger in magnitude than $[d\widetilde{C}(P)/dP]$.
10. See also footnote 6.
11. It is a common misconception to believe that nominal wages are constant in the Keynesian system. The system needs a relatively slower movement in nominal wage compared to price to attain stability, *e.g.* [14] is stable so long as,

$$\frac{dw}{dP} - f'(L) < 0$$

or, evaluated at full equilibrium (*i.e.* setting [12] and [14] both at stationary value)

$$\frac{dw}{w} < \frac{dP}{P}$$

12. Indeed, this view seems to be widely accepted following Friedman's (1977) interpretation of Keynes. However, as Keynes (1939) himself argued against Pigou, the 'good effect of an expansionist investment policy on employment' worked through demand expansion, and not through lower real wages. In addition, Keynes also revised his assumption that real wage moves contracyclically (Skarstein, 1992).

References

Allen, R. G. D., *Mathematical Economics,* London, Macmillan, 2nd edition, 1965.

Barro. R. J., 'TheAggregate-Supply/Aggregate-Demand Model'. *Eastern Economic Journal,* vol. 20. num.1. Winter, pp. 1-6, 1994.

Baumol, W. J. and Blinder, A. S., *Economics,* San Diego, Harcourt Brace, Jovanovich, 5th edition, 1991.

Bemanke, B. S., 'The Macroeconomics of the Great Depression: A Comparative Approach', National Bureau of Economic Research, *NBER Working Paper,* num. 4814, August, 1994.

Bhaduri, A. and Falkinger, 'Optimal price adjustment under incomplete information', *European Economic Review,* vol. 34, 1990, pp. 941-952.

Bhaduri, A., Laski. K. and Riese, M., 'Fallacies in Aggregate Demand/ Supply Analysis', The Vienna Institute for Comparative Economic Studies, *WIIIV Working* Papers, num. 4, July, 1994.

Blanchard, O. J., 'A Traditional Interpretation of Macroeconomic Fluctuations', *American Economic Review,* vol. 79, 1989, pp.1146-1164.

—'Why does money affect output? A Survey', chapter 15 in: *Handbook of Monetary Economics,* edited by Friedman. B. M. and Hahn. F. H., Elsevier, 1990.

Bruno, M., 'Aggregate Supply and Demand Factors in OECD Unemployment: An Update', *Economica,* num. 53, 1986, pp. S35-S52.

Colander, *D.,* 'The Stories We Tell: A Reconsideration of AD/AD Analysis', Middleburry College, mimeographed, 1994.

Clower, R.W., 'The Keynesian Counter-Revolution: A Theoretical Appraisal', in: *The Theory of Interest Rates,* London, edited by Hahn, F. H. and Brechling, F., 1965.

Dornbusch, R. and Fischer, S., *Macroeconomics*. New York. McGraw-Hill. 6th edition, 1994.

Felderer, B. and Homburg, S., *Macroeconomics and New Macroeconomics*, BerlinSpringer-Verlag, 2nd edition, 1992.

Fields. T. W. and Hart. W. R., 'Some Pitfalls in the Conventional Treatment of Aggregate Demand', *Southern Economic Journal*, vol. 56. num. 3. January. 1990, pp. 676-685.

Friedman, M., 'Comments on the Critics', in: Robert, J. G., *Milton Friedman's Monetary Framework. A Debate with his Critics*, The University of Chicago Press, 1977, pp. 132-177.

Hall, P. H. and Treadgold, M. L., 'Aggregate demand curve: a guide to use and abuse', *Australian Economic Papers*, vol.21, June, 1982, pp. 37-48.

Henderson, J. and Quandt, R., *Microeconomic Theory: A Mathematical Approach*, New York, McGraw-Hill, 3rd edition, 1980.

Kahn, R. F., 'The relation of home investment to unemployment'. *Economic Journal*, vol. 41, 1931, pp. 173-198.

Kalecki, M. *Selected Essays on the Dynamics of the Capitalist Economy*, Cambridge University Press, Cambridge, 1971 (1933).

Leijonhufvud. A. *On Keynesian economics & the Economics of Keynes*, Oxford University Press, Oxford, 1968.

Keynes. J. M., *The General Theory of Employment, Interest and Money*. London, Macmillan. (Page reference to Harbinger Edition, New York 1964), 1936.

—, 'Relative movements of real wages and output', *The Economic Journal*, vol. 49, March, 1939, pp. 34-51.

Malinvaud. E., *The Theory of Unemployment Reconsidered*, Oxford. 1977.

Mankiw. M. G., *Macroeconomics*, New York, Worth Publishers, 1992.

Sachs. J. D. and Larrain, F., *Macroeconomics in the Global Economy*, New York, Harvester/Wheatsheaf, 1993.

Samuelson, P. A., *The Foundations of Economic Analysis*, Harvard University Press, Cambridge, Massachusetts, 1947.

Simon. H. A., 'Rational decision making in business organizations'. *American Economic Review*, vol. 69, 1979, pp. 493-513.

Skarstein. R., 'The Shaky Supply Side. On Neoclassical Anomalies in Macroeconomic Theory', *Banca Nazionale del Lavoro Quarterly Review*, núm.183. December, 1992, pp. 407-430.

Stiglitz. J. E., *Economics*, New York, W. W. Norton, 1993.

UNEMPLOYMENT AND THE REAL WAGE
THE ECONOMIC BASIS FOR CONTESTING POLITICAL IDEOLOGIES

INTRODUCTION

Variations in wages have their two-sided role in industrial capitalism. Higher wages mean higher costs of manufacturing, but by providing more purchasing power to the workers they also stimulate demand. In its contradictory roles as the main element of (variable) production cost and as a major source of demand, movement in the wage rate has a complex, even ambiguous, effect on the level of empolyment and output. This accounts for the existence of contesting points of view on the relationship between wages and unemployment and, at the same time, also provides an economic basis for sustaining different political ideologies regarding the management of the capitalist economy. The central objective of this paper is to develop a macroeconomic framework in terms of which the issue of the relationship between wages and unemployment can be analysed with reference to these contesting political ideologies.

Our analysis is conducted from a broad Keynesian perspective which recognizes the central importance of effective demand. We reformulate Hicks' well know apparatus of the *IS*-curve (Hicks, 1937) to trace out the locus of aggregate demand through equality between investment and saving by postulating *exogenous* variations in the *real* wage rate. This differs from the models of the closed economy postulated by Keynes (1936) or by Kalecki (1939, 1971). In the model of *The General Theory*, the real wage rate is an *endogenous* variable : autonomous investment determines effective demand through the multiplier mechanism; effective demand determines the level of output and the level of output determines the real wage rate, in so far as the marginal product of labour at that particular level of output has to equal the real wage rate in order to satisfy profit miximising firms (Keynes, 1936, pp. 5, 17, 29, 23). Since the real wage rate is co-determined with, but is not a determinant of, the level of output and employment, it makes no sense to treat the real wage rate as an exogenous, policy variable in the model underlying *The General Theory* (E.g. Solow, 1987). Similarly, Kalecki's cost-determined prices leave little scope for exogenous variations in the real wage rate, in so far as the price level and the money wage level maintain a roughly proportional relationship, through the postulate of what Hicks (1974) called 'the wage theorem'.

In this paper, we depart from this tradition of treating the real wage rate as an endogenous variable for two reasons. **First,** in order to examine the connection between real wage and unemployment it is necessary to perform at least 'thought experiments' based on exogenous variations in the real wage rate. **Second,** as we shall later argue (in Section 3), in an open economy exogenous variations in the real wage rate may become feasible through such policies as adjustment in the exchange rate. Thus, in Section 2 of this paper, we set out the basic model of exogenous real wage variation in the context of a closed economy. Section 3 extends this model to the more plausible context of an open economy. The final Section 4 provides some concluding comments and observations on both the limitations and the potentialities of the present analysis in the course of summarising the main argument.

THE CLOSED ECONOMY

In an economy without significant foreign trade and economic activity by the government, private final expenditure on consumption and on investment are the two main components of aggregate demand. Consequentlty, there are two distinct ways to expand aggregate demand and output—through expanding private consumption and by stimulating private investment. The 'underconsumptionist' view, which predates even Marx, emphasised the need to maintain adequate private consumption expenditure through a policy of high (real) wages.[1]

Keynes (1936) distanced himself from the strictly underconsumptionist position in so far as he recognized that stimulating investment, especially public investment, could provide an alternative method of expanding aggregate demand and output. Contrasting his own views from those of the earlier underconsumptionists like Malthus and Sismondi, he writes :

> Practically I only differ from these schools of thought in thinking that they may lay a little too much emphasis on increased

> consumption at a time when there is still much social advantage to be obtained from increased investment. Theoretically, however, they are open to the criticism of neglecting the fact that there are *two* ways to expand output (Keynes, 1936, p. 325; emphasis in original).

Our first analytical task in this paper is to show how these 'two ways to expand output' emerge quite naturally through a reconstruction of the *IS*-curve, if exogenous variations in the real wage are permitted. The algebraic argument is kept simple by assuming that a constant fraction ($1>s>0$) of profit and no wage is saved. In this primitive model workers own no property and the entire property income goes to the capitalists in the form of profit.[2] These assumptions permit us to capture the underconsumptionist argument in a simple manner; any redistribution of income from profit to wage through higher real wage increases consumption and decreases saving according to the formula.

$$S = sR = s(R/Y)(Y/Y^*)Y^*$$

where, R = profit, Y = income (output) and, Y^* = full-capacity potential income (output). Since full-capacity output (Y^*) can be treated as constant in each short period, we normalise saving as well as all other relevant variables as proportions of full-capacity output. Hence, setting $Y^* = 1$, the normalised value of saving becomes.

$$S = shz, \; Y^* = 1 \tag{1}$$

where, $h = R/Y$ = share of profit, $1 > h > 0$ and $z = Y/Y^*$ = degree of capacity utilisation, $1 > z > 0$.[3]

In the closed economy all purchases and sales of intermediate raw materials cancel out, and we can think of the representative firm as vertically integrated using directly and indirectly a constant amount of labour per unit of final output.[4] However, this assumption of *constant* labour input per unit of output has two implications. **First,** it rules out all complexities of the labour process at the level of the firm, e.g. considerations of 'efficiency wage' where labour productivity itself may be influenced by the level of real wage (see Bowles, 1985). It also ignores the problem of 'permanent' administrative staff in the labour force in so far as such permanent staff constitutes a part of the firm's overhead cost. Thus, average labour productivity rises as more output is produced through higher capacity utilisation with the same level of permanent staff (cf. Baran and Sweezy, 1966; Kelecki, 1971; Rowthorn, 1981). Instead, we assume that all workers are 'operatives', i.e. their number varies directly with the level of output. This means that both marginal and average (variable) cost are constant at any given money wage rate, so long as labour is the only variable input (directly and indirectly) reqired in production. Assuming firms set a given profit margin on their constant marginal and average (variable) cost, the mark-up price equation is written as—

$$p = (1 + m)\ bw \tag{2}$$

where, p = price level, w = money wage rate, b = labour (directly and indirectly) needed per unit of final output, i.e. $1/b$ is labour productivity and m is profit margin as percentage mark-up on unit labour (prime) cost.

Equation (2) implies, on the one hand a positive functional relation between profit margin and profit share,[5] i.e.

$$h = m/(1+m),\ dh/dm > 0 \tag{3}$$

On the other, it exhibits the distributional conflict between profit margin/share and real wage at given labour productivity, i.e.

$$(1 + m)(w/p) = (1 - h)^{-1}(w/p) = (1/b) \tag{4}$$

Any increase in real wage rate, depressing profit margin and profit share (equation 4), must decrease savings (equation 1) and increase consumption to validate the under-consumptionist thesis in our model. Nevertheless, aggregate demand ($C + I$) may still rise or fall depending on what impact that lower profit margin/share has on investment. Since it is plausible to argue that, other things being equal, a lower profir margin/share would weaken the incentive to invest, the contradictory effects of any exogenous variation in the real wage on the level of aggregate demand become apparent. A higher real wage increases consumption, but reduces investment, in so far as investment depends on the profit margin. More formally, assuming the level of investment (as a proportion of full-capacity output due to normalisation, $Y^* = 1$) to be an increasing function of profit margin/share (see equation 3), i.e.

$$I = I\ (h),\ Y^* = 1 \tag{5}$$

the equality between saving and investment from (1) and (5) implies,

$$shz = I(h)$$

and the local slope of the *IS*-curve is given as

$$dz/dh = (I_h - sz)/sh, \quad I_h = (dI/dh) > 0 \qquad (6)$$

Since, the denominator on the right hand side of (6) is positive, the slope of the *IS*-curve is negative or positive depending on whether *sz* is greater or less than I_h i.e. whether savings responds more or less strongly than investment with respect to changes in the profit share (and margin).

Equation (6), describing the (local) properties of the *IS*-curve, explains why the under-consumptionist thesis may or may not be validated in a closed economy. When investment responds relatively weakly to changes in the profit margin/share (i.e. $I_h < sz$), the decrease in consumption demand due to a lower real wage and higher profit share (see equation 4) is not compensated entirely by the increase in investment demand. Consequently, aggregate demand ($C + I$) decreases as the real wage rate decreases (i.e. the profit share increases), resulting in an inverse relation between the profit share (h) and the degree of capacity utilisation (z). The under-consumptionist view that a lower real wage decreases the level of economic activity by reducing aggregate demand is valid in this case of mass consumption-based, wage-leg expansion. However, exactly the opposite argument holds when investment responds relatively strongly to variations in the profit share (i.e. $I_h > sz$). The fall in consumption due to a lower real wage (and higher profit share) is overcompensated by the increase in investment in this case of investment-based, profit-led expansion to invalidate the underconsumptionist thesis. The 'two ways to expand output' suggested by Keynes become analytically linked in our model through exogenous variation in the real wage and distribution of income between the classes.

Two observations are in order regarding the foregoing analysis. **First,** the conventional result of an inverse relation between the level of output (i.e. capacity utilisation, z) and the real wage rate, prepounded by Keynes in *The General Theory* (pp. 5, 17-18, 42, 289, 301) and also by neo-classical economists, is obtained only in the particular case of profit-led expansion. However, our result is obtained through a different route which does not depend on the assumption of profit maximisation, but recognizes the centrality of effective demand. Output expands at a lower real wage in this profit-led case simply because aggregate demand is higher owing to the strong response of investment to the higher profit margin/share brought about by a lower real wage rate. This is also the reason why we can obtain precisely the opposite result which contradicts the neo-classical Keynesian case. This is the case of wage-led expansion where a lower real wage leads to a contraction in the level of output owing to the relatively weak response of investment to a higher profit margin/share.[6]

Second, the investment demand function in equation (5) may be considered (rightly) to be implausible in so far as the rate of profit, and not the profit margin, is normally assumed to be a crucial determinant of investment. Given the accountants' book value of capital in the short period, the average rate of profit (r) depends definitionally, on both the profit margin/share and the degree of capacity utilisation, i.e.

$$r = R/K = (R/Y)(Y/Y^*)(Y^*/K) = hza \tag{7}$$

where, K = accountants' book value of capital, assumed given in the short period, and, $(Y^*/K) = a \equiv$ output capital ratio at full capacity, assumed given in the short period. Equation (7) shows how both profit share/margin and the degree of capacity utilisation (i.e. the 'acceleration' effect) enter jointly as arguments in the investment function through their influence on the rate of profit. However, although it has been a common practice to make the rate of investment depend simply on the rate of profit (e.g. Robinson, 1962; Marglin, 1984), this is theoreticaly unsatisfactory, because it does not go behind the rate of profit to its individual constituents. For instance, it is simply assumed that a given rate of profit will produce the same level of investment as results from high capacity utilisation and a low profit margin or from low capacity utilisation and a high profit margin. An investment function which depends simply on the rate of profit is insensitive to the influence of the existing degree of capacity utilisation, e.g. it neglects the possibility that, despite a high profit margin, investors may not be inclined to invest in additional capacity if massive excess capacity already exists.[7]

Observe that this influence of existing capacity on investment cannot be captured satisfactorily by simply introducing a term for capacity utilisation (z) along with the rate of profit (r) as the arguments in the investment function (see Rowthorn, 1981; Dutt, 1984; Taylor, 1985). The problem with this procedure is that it imposes unwarranted restrictions on the relative response of investment to the two constituents of the profit rate, h and z, with the result that the possibility of profit-led expansion is ruled out (why this is so is discussed in Appendix A). These problems are avoidable by treating profit share/margin and capacity utilisation as independent and separate arguments in an investment function, i.e. in place of our earlier equation (5) we have

$$I = I\ (h,\ z);\ Y^* = 1; \quad I_h > 0,\ I_z > 0 \tag{8}$$

The investment behaviour in (8) may be imagined to be based on static expectations where, current *average* profitabillity (*m* and *h*) and *average* degree of capacity utilisation (*z*) are used by investors as predictors of *marginal* profitability on new investment and the future state of demand respectively.

Although no investment function can be defended beyond a point, the investment function in (8) has the analytical advantage of clearly separating the 'demand side' impact on investment operating through the acceleration effect of higher capacity utilization from the 'supply side' impact operating through the cost-reducing effect of a lower real wage and higher profit margin/share. Since, these two variables, *z* and *h*, also enter in determining the rate of saving in (1), we can capture the dual effects of real wage variation through a reconstruction of *IS*-curve. Equating saving in (1) with investment in (8), the *IS*-curve is generated in the (*z, h*) space as—

$$shz = I(h,z) \tag{9}$$

which has the (local) slope,

$$dz/dh = (I_h - sz)\ /\ (sh - I_z) \tag{10}$$

Again, the slope of the *IS*-curve in (10) can be negative or positive, depending on the relative response of investment and saving to profit share in the numerator and to capacity utilisation in the denominator.

The standard textbook assumption, that at the margin saving is more responsive than investment to changes in capacity utilisation for making the Keynesian income adjustment process stable, imposes a sign restriction on the denominator in equation (10) namely,

$$sh - I_z > 0 \tag{11}$$

Since, the expression in the numerator for the slope of the *IS*-curve remains unchanged in (6) and (10), our previous economic interpretation holds (in view of inequality 11). With relatively weak response of investment to profitability (i.e. $I_h < sz$), consumption necessarily assumes the dominant role in effective demand. In this case of wage-led expansion, a lower profit share or equivalently, a higher real wage rate leads to higher aggregate demand as well as capacity utilization. This is shown in Fig. 1 as the *stagnationist regime.*

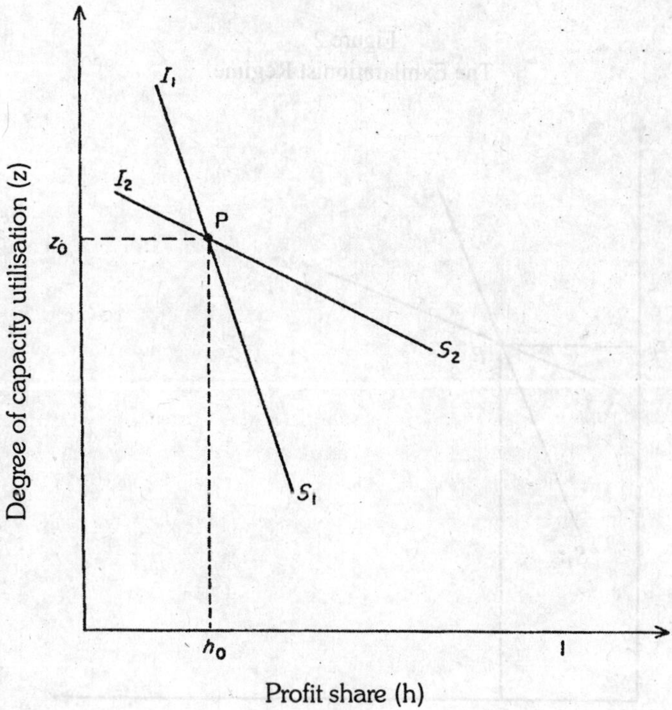

Fig 1 : *The stagnationist regime [with* (I_1S_1) or *without* (I_2S_2) *cooperation between labour and capital, depending on whether elasticity in absolute value at the initial point P* (h_0, z_0) *is greater (in* I_1S_1) or less *(in* I_2S_2) *than unity.*

An antithesis to this stagnationist regime emerges when the capitalist class is energetic and private investment responds vigorously to a higher profit margin/share. This means that the coefficient I_h is sufficiently large to ensure $I_h > sz$ which, in conjunction with (11), makes the *IS*-curve positively sloped.[8] In this case, profit and investment play the dominant role in expanding aggregate demand in so far as any reduction in consumption due to a lower real wage is more than compensated for by the enthusiastic response of private investmetn to that lower real wage. Counterposed against the stagnationist regime of Figure 1, this is shown as the *exhilarationist regime* in Figure 2.

The distinction between the stagnationist and the exhilarationist regimes brings into sharp focus the possibility that economic expansion may benefit the two classes very differently. Everywhere along the

Figure 2
The Exhilarationist Regime

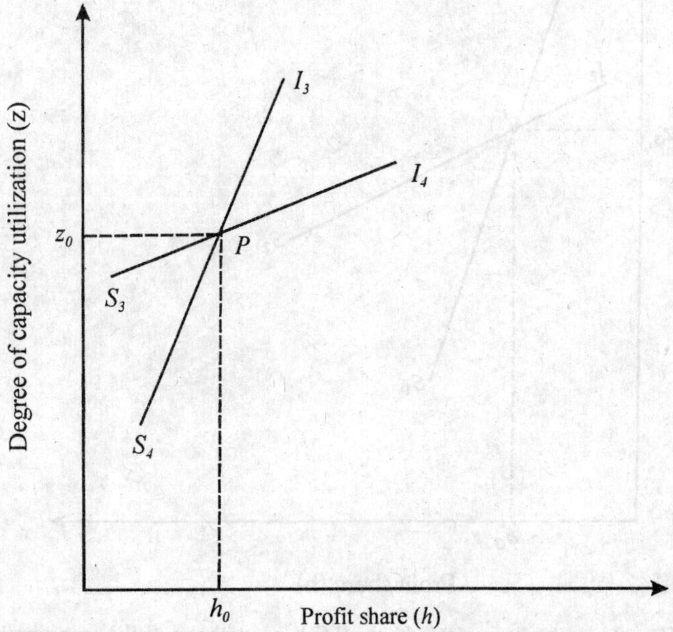

The exhilarationist regime (with I_3, S_3) or without (I_4S_4) cooperation between labour and capital, depending on whether elasticity at the initial point $P(h_0, z_0)$ is greater in (I_3S_3) *or less in* (I_4S_4) *than the relative share of profit to wage,* $h_0(1-h_0)$ at P.

negatively sloped *IS*-curve of the stagnationist regime, a higher real wage rate produces higher capacity utilization and higher employment. This means an unambiguous gain to the working class in terms of both a higher real wage *rate* and a higher real wage *bill*. Nevertheless, a fundamental tenet of the social democratic ideology, articulated with considerable intellectual force by the 'left Key-nesians', has been to stress that such all round gain to the workers need not imply unambiguous loss to the capitalists. Capitalism is not necessarily a zero-sum game. Despite a higher real wage rate and a lower profit margin/share, capitalists may continue to make a higher total profit in the stagnationist regime as they more than recoup on the volume of sales what they lose on profit margin per unit of sale. Given the accountant's book value of capital in the short period, a higher total profit would also mean a higher profit rate despite the lower profit margin/share. Therefore, the critical analytical condition for the successful working of this model of *co-operative capitalism* is that the normalized value of total profit, $R/Y^*) = (R/Y)\ (Y/Y^*) = hz$, must decrease as the real wage rate decreases and the profit share increases correspondingly, i.e.

$$d(hz)/dh < 0 \text{ or } -(h/z)(dz/dh) > 1 \qquad (12)$$

In other words, a co-operative relationship can be established between capital and labour in the stagnationist regime if the negatively-sloped *IS*-curve is elastic, as whown by I_1S_2 in Figure 1. Note that, by virtue of (10) and (11), this elasticity condition (12) is ensured if

$$zI_z > hI_h \qquad (13)$$

which implies that the investors must respond more strongly (measured by respective elasticities) to a variation in capacity utilization than in profit margin/share.

Economic co-operation between the classes envisaged in the social democratic ideology becomes problematic even in the stagnationist regime as condition (12) or, equivalently, (13) fails. A decline in the profit share brings about a small increase in capacity utilization along an inelastic *IS*-curve, shown by I_2S_2 in Figure 1, which is insufficient to compensate for the decline in profit margin per unit of sale. Consequently, both the total and the rate of profit decline as the real wage rate increases. The resulting model of *profit squeeze* (Glyn and Sutcliff, 1972; Goodwin, 1967) indicates the limit to co-operation in the stagnationist regime, despite the stimulating effect of a higher real wage on economic activity.

A profit squeeze due to a higher real wage rate is essentially a reinterpretation of the under-consumptionist argument from a radical point of view. Empirically, it is an appealing argument in the light of the experience of some OECD countries during the 1970s (Armstrong, Glyn, and Harrison, 1984; Glyn, Hughes, Lipietz, and Singh, 1988). Its analytical attraction lies in reconciling apparently incompatible theories. The left-Keynesian social democratic position takes its clue from the under-consumptionist argument that a high real wage is good for both labour and capital because it keeps effective demand buoyant. This can be reconciled with the radical Marxist view that class interests are necessarily conflictual, when a higher real wage fails to stimulate aggregate demand and capacity utilization sufficiently to accommodte the interests of both the classes (i.e. condition 12 and, equivalently, condition 13 are violated). The resulting squeeze on profit manifests conflictual class interests despite accepting the Keynesian logic of demand-determined output (Marglin and Bhaduri, 1990).

The limit to co-operative capitalism based on a high wage policy in the stagnationist regime may manifest itself in two rather different ways. In the short run, the squeeze on total profits could result in a lack of cohesion of economic interest *within* the capitalist class itself, especially if the loss in profit is very unevenly distributed, e.g. some sections of capitalists lose disproportionately while others may even earn higher profits. The political difficulty of pursuing a high wage policy may then lie not so much in attaining co-operation between capital and labour, as between the capitalists themselves.

In the longer run, maintaining economic expansion and higher capacity utilization through higher consumption and a lower profit margin/share in the stagnationist regime could breed trouble for social democratic co-operative economic policies. There is the danger that wage-led growth will lead to an inadequte rate of expansion in productive capacity over time. A 'crisis of underaccumulation' may occur if productive capacity persistently fails to keep pace with growth in the labour force. This would show up in structural unemployment which arises from a disproportionately large labour force in relation to existing capacity, rather than Keynesian deficiency of aggregate demand.[9]

From this longer-term perspective, even the social democratic strategy of wage-led expansion would require some restraint on the rate of growth of the real wage rate (in relation to labour productivity growth) so as to generate the required growth in productive capacity over time. It may indeed be argued that the 'social democratic consensus' rested historically on the double-edged assumption that, while the real wage should grow fast enough to keep up with the growth in productive capacity, it should not grow so fast as to endanger the required growth in productive capacity (Rowthorn, 1981). However, systematic analysis of these longer-term implication of wage-led economic expansion lies outside the scope of the present paper. Our focus here is entirely on the short period.

The stagnationist regime has its mirror image in the exhilarationist regime. Along the positively sloped *IS*-curve of the exhilarationist regime (Fig. 2) capitalists gain unambiguously in terms of both a higher profit margin/share as well as a higher total profit at higher capacity utilisation.

Contrary to the underconsumptionist argument and in confirmity with 'supply-side' logic, a higher level of capacity utilisation and employment becomes possible only at a lower real wage rate. But, despite a lower real wage rate, the working class as a whole would gain a higher real wage bill through higher capacity utilisation and employment if

$$de(W/Y^*)/dh = d\ (1 - h)z\ /dh > 0, \quad Y^* = 1$$

that is, if the (positive) elasticity of the *IS*-curve in the exhilarationist regime exceeds the relative share of profit to wage,

$$(h/z)(dz/dh) > h/(1 - h) \qquad (14)$$

Under condition (14), a given decrease (increase) in the real wage rate (profit share) stimulates the level of demand and capacity utilisation sufficiently to increase aggregate employment and the wage *bill*. as show by I_3S_3 in Fig. 2. This provides favourable ground for cooperation between the two classes in the exhilarationist regime. Nevertheless, since the increase in aggregate employment and the wage bill is achieved through lowering the real wage rate of the already employed (typically unionised 'inside' workers) this may also generate tensions within the working class, between the already employed 'insiders' and the newly employed 'outsiders'. However, even without condition (14) being satisfied, a reduction in the real wage rate of the 'insiders' would increase employment opportunities for the 'outsiders', albeit to a somewhat lesser extent along a relatively flat positively sloped I_4S_4 curve in Fig. 2. The exhilarationist regime is therefore *not* merely a situation of conflict between the capitalists and the 'inside' trade union members over distributive shares; it may be beset with intra-working class tension, which could help the capitalists to 'devide and rule'.

In the longer run, a sustained high rate of expansion of productive capacity through a high rate (and share) of investment required for maintaining adequate effective demand in the exhilirationist regime may create the opposite type of disproportionality. A 'crisis of overaccumulation' may develop gradually, as the productive capacity of the economy becomes disproportionately large in relation to the existing labour force. Structural excess capacity which does not originate in the Keynesian problem of deficient effective demand could become increasingly pervasive to heighten intra-capitalist rivalry. However, like the crisis of underaccumulation in the stagnationist regime, this overaccumulation crisis of the exhilarationist regime is a long-run problem, lying beyond the focus of this paper.

The Open Economy

The preceding analysis assumes greater relevance in the context of an open economy or two quite different reasons. **First,** we assumed in the context of a closed economy that a lower real wage rate would depress consumption, but stimulate investment by raising the profit margin/share within the short period. However, this is problematic in so far as investment, particularly in long-lived fixed capital equipment, is likely to respond more cautiously to a change in profit margin/share compared to consumption. Thus, the depressing effect of a lower real wage rate on consumption may be felt within the short period without its stimulating effect on investment materialising within the same period, owing to the widely different 'speeds of adjustment' of the two relevant variables. To the extent that exports and imports have faster speeds of adjustment (to price changes) compared to investment, the static short-term *IS*-curve analysis presented in this paper may be less misleading in the context of an open economy.[10]

Second, the assumption of exogenous variation in profit share, *h*, through exchange rate variation is easier to justify in an open economy (cf. Kalecki, 1939, ch. 3). Depreciation of the home currency would reduce the profit margin by increasing the cost of imported raw materials, while increasing the price of imported consumption goods would increase the cost-of-living index of domestic workers. As a result, there would be upward pressure on both prices and *money* wages. However, depending on the extent to which an open economy is subject to international price discipline, the proportional link between the money wage rate and the price level may become weakened (cf. Glyn and Sutcliff, 1972). For maintaining price competitiveness in the world market, a price-taker, 'small' open economy may not raise its export (and domestic) price level in proportion to the increase in domestic money wage rate with the result that the domestic profit margin/share is squeezed owing to a rising money wage as well as the higher cost of imported raw materials. In this way, an exogenous squeeze of the profit margin/share through devaluation becomes more easily justifiable in an open economy which is subject to international price discipline. However, this may be countered by raising the price level in home currency without 'spoiling' the foreign market significantly, as devaluation also makes home goods cheaper. More formally, international price competitivenes may be denoted by θ,

$$\theta = (vp_f)/p \tag{15}$$

and

$$(d\theta/\theta) = (dv/v)-(dp/p) \tag{16}$$

where, v = the rate of exchange of domestic currency per unit of foreign currency, p_f = price level of finished goods in foreign currency of the trade rivals which is assumed constant, and p = domestic as well as export price level of finished goods.

Thus, so long as devaluation in proportional terms, $d\theta/\theta$, exceeds the domestic rate of price increase, dp/p (given p_f), the international price competitiveness of the domestic economy would be enhanced. However, whether this enhanced price competitiveness can improve the home country's trade balance will depend on the responsiveness of the volume of export and import to prices, measured by the usual 'trade elasticities'.

If some raw materials are imported, the price equation (2) for an open economy becomes

$$p=(1+m)(bw+kp_f'v) \tag{17}$$

Where k=imported raw material per unit of output, assumed constant in the short period, and p_f'=imported price of raw material in foreign currency, also assumed constant.

Profit share, *net* of imported material cost is given as

$$h=[p-(wb+kp_f'v)]/p$$

which implies from (17), $h=m/I(1+m)$ as in equation (3). This ensures that profit margin (m) and net profit share (h) move in the same direction. Total differentiation of equation (17) yields on simplification the variation in total profit share as

$$dh=\lambda-h)[(dp/p)-\lambda(dw/w)-(1-\lambda)(dv/v)] \tag{18}$$

where $\lambda=(bw)/(bw+kp_f'v)$, i.e. the share of wage cost in unit prime cost. Thus, the impact of devaluation on international price competitiveness and profit share are captured by equations (16) and (18), respectively.

Export and import expenditure in domestic currency, again normalized as proportions of full-capacity imcome $I(Y^*=1)$, are given as

$$E=pX_e \text{ and } M=\upsilon\bar{p}_f X_m \tag{19}$$

where $\bar{p}_f$=constant average international price level of imported raw materials (p_f') and finished goods (p_f)[11].

The volume of export (X_e) has (total) elasticity with respect to international price competitiveness defined as

$$(\theta/X_e)\ (dX_e/d\theta)=n_e,\ n_e>0 \tag{20}$$

The volume of import (X_m), consisting of both raw materials and finished goods, depends both on international price competitiveness and on the activity level (z) of the domestic economy, i.e.

$$X_m=X_m\ (\theta,z);\ \partial X_m/\partial\theta<0,\ \partial X_m/\partial z>0 \tag{21}$$

with the corresponding (partial) elasticities of the volume of import given as

$$(\theta/X_m)\ (\partial X_m/\partial\theta)=-n_m \text{ and } (z/X_m)\ (\partial X_m/\partial z)=u,\quad n_m,\ u>0) \tag{22}$$

Assuming for algebraic simplicity an initial trade balance $(E_0=M_0)$, manipulation of equations (19) to (22) yield the familiar formula combining the 'price effect' with the 'income effect' of devaluation on marginal trade balance, i.e.

$$(dE-dM)=zg(n_e+n_m-1)(d\theta/\theta)-ugdz \tag{23}$$

where g=initial share of import and export in income.

The balance between income and expenditure in an open economy is restated from (1), (8) and (19) as

$$shz+M=I(h,z)+E \tag{24}$$

Totally differentiating (24) and substituting (23), the effect of devaluation on capacity utilization is obtained as

$$dz = [D^{-1}(I_h-sz)dh]+[D^{-1}gz\ \ (n_e+n_m-1)(d\theta/\theta)] \tag{25}$$

where the positivity of D = (gu + sh – 1_z) is sufficiently guaranteed by (11).

The first square-bracketed term on the right-hand side of (25) shows how devaluation affects capacity utilization through changes in profit share h and thus corresponds directly to the case of the closed economy (see (10)). The second square-bracketed term is the familiar effect of devaluation on the trade balance through changes in international price competitiveness. If international price competitiveness increases as a result of the rate of devaluation exceeding domestic inflation rate in percentage terms (equation 16), the overall 'trade effect' would be positive so long as the combined trade elasticities exceed unity, $n_e + n_m > 1$, to satisfy the Marshal-Lerner condition.

However, the 'income distribution effect' of devaluation operating through changes in profit share captured by the first square-bracketed term of (25) remains ambiguous. Devaluation may or may not increase the profit share, *h*, depending on the relative increase of domestic price and money wage, as shown by (18). Nevertheless, if devaluation results in improved international price competitiveness $(d\theta>0)$, as well as a higher profit share $(dh>0)$, then (16) and (18) together would imply $(dv/v) > (dp/p) > (dw/w)$, i.e. a lower *real* wage rate as a result of devaluation.[12] In this case, a direct analogy with the *closed* economy is easy to draw.

Devaluation resulting in a lower real wage and higher profit margin would raise the degree of capacity utilization by stimulating effective demand at home in the exhilarationist regime. This would make the first square-bracketed term on the right-hand side of (25) positive. This second term capturing the trade effect is also positive so long as the Marshall-Lerner condition is satisfied. Therefore, a strategy of lowering the real wage through devaluation to increase international price competitiveness (θ) and profit share (*h*) can stimulate capacity utilization *unambiguously* if the economy is in the exhilarationist regime. Otherwise, in a stagnationist regime the effect of this strategy on domestic activity remains ambiguous.

Nevertheless, the greater the trade 'openness' of the economy, indicated by a higher initial share of trade in income (*g*) as well as larger (absolute) values of the trade elasticities n_e and n_m, the more important the trade effect becomes. And if the positive trade effect dominates quantitatively the negative term in the first square bracket of (25) in a stagnationist regime, the open economy assumes an exhilarationist character.

In other words, a dominant trade effect tends of make the stagnationist logic increasingly irrelevant in a world characterised by high trade interdependence. The left social democratic emphasis on wage-led expansion derived from the stagnationist logic may be given up in the pursuit of export surplus by following restrictive macroeconomic policies to keep down real wages (and inflation) for greater international price competitiveness. Further, so long as successful export performance maintains a high enough level of employment to overcompensate a relatively low real wage rate, cooperation between labour and capital may continue to be fesible (condition 14). The only problem with this strategy is that it is impossible for all countries to achieve a trade surplus simultaneously. And yet, the lure of this impossibility has contributed substantially to the disintegration of the traditional social democratic ideology without any coherent alternative taking its place.

Summary And Concluding Observations

This paper has been motivated by our attempt to demonstrate that the Keynesian theory, which emphasizes the centrality of effective demand rather than 'supply-side' problems, has a far wider theoretical as well as political range than is usually recognized. Particular *models* such as that of 'cooperative capitalism' enunciated by the left Keynesian social democrats, the Marxian model of 'profit squeeze' or even the conservative model relying on 'supply-side' stimulus through high profitability and a low real wage, fit into the more general Keynesian theoretical scheme. They become particular *variants* of the theoretical framework presented here.

The framework is developed by counterposing the underconsumptionist idea that a high real wage is beneficial as it generates high effective demand against the orthodox view that high labour cost discourages production. In order to assign central importance to effective demand in determining the level of economic activity *(z)*, we reconstructed the familiar *IS*-curve, showing different commodity market-clearing levels of economic activity at a different real wage rate (which are inversely related to profit margin and share *h*, see equation 4). This resulted in the emergence of two economic regimes, depending on the *sign* of the (local) slope of the *IS*-curve (equation 10). When the *IS*-schedule is downward-sloping in the *(z.h)* space, the underconsumptionist idea emphasizing the beneficial 'demand effect' of a higher real wage is validated in what was described as the stagnationist regime of mass-consumption-based, wage-led expansion (Fig. 1). Obversely, if the *IS*-schedule is upward-sloping in that same space, an investment-based, profit-led exhilarationist regime obtains (Fig. 2).The latter regime contradicts the underconsumptionist view to lend support to the orthodox position that the 'cost effect' of a high real wage rate depresses economic activity.

In contrast to the sign of the slope of the *IS*-curve which is critical for characterizing the two regimes, its elasticity in absolute value is an indicator of the limits to co-operation between capital and labour. This can be summarized by imagining an *IS*-curve (linear for simplicity) which rotates gradually from the vertical position I_0S_0 to the horizontal position $I^{I}S^{I}$ in Fig. 3. The anti-clockwise and clockwise rotation of I_0P in the neighbourhood of the initial configuration (h_0,z_0) represented by point P spans the stagnationist and the exhilarationist regime respectively. So long as the elasticity of the *IS*-curve in absolute value exceeds unity in its anti-clockwise rotation from the vertical position I_0P, a higher *total* as well as a higher *rate* of profit despite a higher real wage rate makes co-operative capitalism feasible in the stagnationist regime (conditions 12 and 13). Similarly, clockwise rotation of I_0P from its vertical position, until the critical value of its elasticity $h/(1-h)$ is reached, spans a zone of feasible co-operation in the exhilarationist regime as employment and the *total* wage bill expand in spite of a lower real wage rate (condition 14). Co-operation gives way to conflict when these elasticity conditions (12) and (14) are violated in the stagnationist and in the exhilarationist regime respectively. It also needs emphasis that in either regime the feasibility of co-operation between the two contending classes does *not* rule out the possibility of intra-class conflict over the distribution of the total profit among the capitalists or of the total wage between the already employed 'insiders' and the newly employed 'outsiders'.

By showing that inter-class cooperation (or conflict) is possible in *either* regime, our analysis dispels a common misconception that the co-operative view of capitalism derives *exclusively* from the stagnationist logic of under-consumption. This observation becomes especially relevant in an open economy which is highly dependent on foreign trade and is sensitive to international price competition. Any positive 'demand effect' of a higher domestic real wage envisaged in the stagnationist logic tends to be outweighed by its negative 'cost effect' on international price competitiveness owing to greater reliance on the foreign market. Therefore, in its search for export surplus, an open economy could be driven increasingly towards the conservative, exhilarationist logic emphasizing the desirability of low labour costs. However, cooperation between the classes is still possible if a large enough export surplus is achieved to keep employment and the wage bill high despite the relatively low domestic real wage rate. Nevertheless, the impossibility of all countries achieving export surplus simultaneously makes this strategy inherently flawed.

For maintaining a direct analogy with the traditional (Hicksian) *IS*-

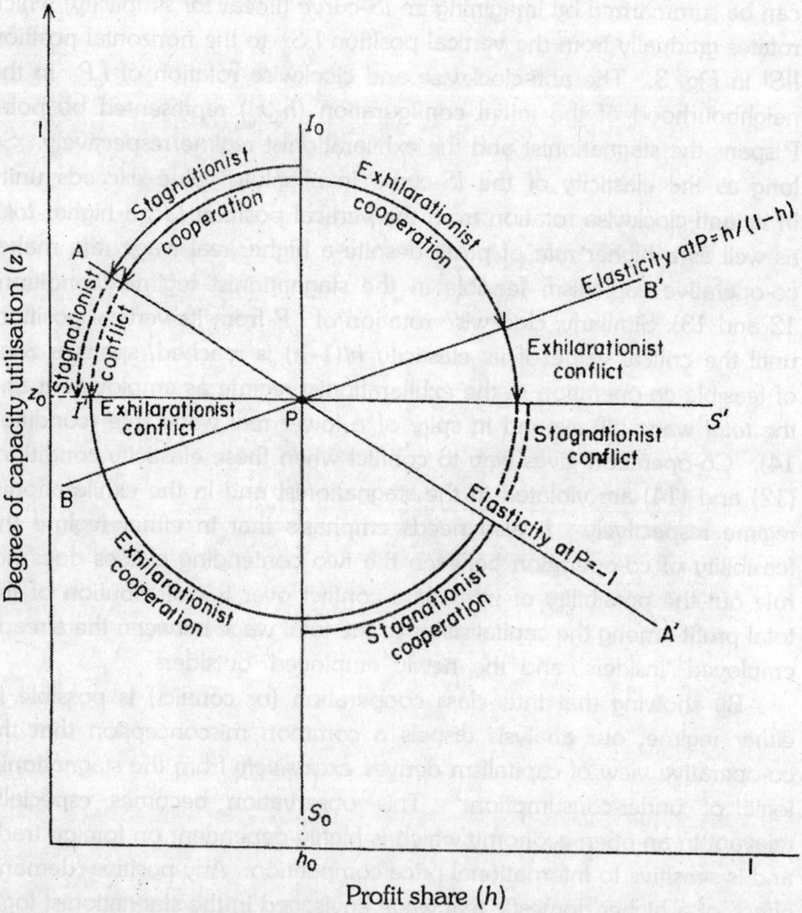

Fig. 3. *Zones of cooperation and conflict in the two regimes [zone I_0PA = S_0PA' = stagnationist cooperation (condition 12 satisfied); zone API' = $A'PS'$ = stagnationist conflict (condition 12 fails); zone I_0PB' = S_0PB = exhilarationist cooperation (condition 14 satisfied); zone $B'PS'$ = BPI' = exhilarationist conflict (condition 14 fails)].*

curve analysis as well as for expositional simplicity, our discussion was focused mainly on the short period, with only casual excursions into the longer-run problems of 'disproportionality' arising from under or over-accumulation. Lack of space also forced us to ignore all dynamic considerations.[13] Nevertheless, two central problems concerning dynamic analysis deserve comment for appreciating the limitation of our present static framework. **First,** a word of caution : the familiar 'stability condition' of inequality (11) turns out to be less compelling in a more general dynamic framework in which both capacity utilization (quantity) and profit share/real wage (price) are endogenously adjustable variables.[14] The familiar one-variable 'stability condition' (11) turns out to be neither necessary nor sufficient in the more general dynamic analysis, involving simultaneously adjustments in quantity *and* price variables. Note also that the stability properties could be affected by the non-linearity of the *IS*-schedule (unlike in Figs. 1-3). Even assuming (11), the value of its slope is only *locally* defined from (10) by the response of investment to the profit margin/share, I_h. It is plausible that I_h is influenced by the existing degree of capacity utilisation (z) to make the slope of the *IS*-curve different at different values of z (this is discussed in greater detail in Appendix B). This could introduce significant non-linearity into the *IS*-curve to make local stability analysis, based on linear approximation, an insufficient or even misleading guide to the actual stability properties of the system.

The recognition that quantities (capacity utilisation) and prices (the real wage) may adjust simultaneously in a more general dynamic model raises a deeper conceptual issue regarding the interpretation of the *IS*-curve itself. It can be treated *either* as the locus of stationary capacity utilisation, i.e., $\dot{z} = 0$, as has been implicity assumed in our (and Hicks') analysis, or as the locus of stationary price level, i.e., $\dot{p} = 0$, as we believe, is implied in Keynes' *General Theory* (especially pp. 17-18, 289, 301). Ultimately it boils down to one of the most important unsettled questions of modern macroeconomics: does excess demand for commodities lead primarily to quantity or to price adjustment? We cannot pretend to have an answer; but dynamic analysis cannot be undertaken without addressing this important, and as yet unsettled, question.

Notes :

1. We give one example, a resolution of 1817 by Leicester framework-knitters, predating the publication of Marx's first volume of *Capital* (1867) by fifty years : 'That in proportion as the Reduction of Wages makes the great Body of People poor and wretched, in the same proportion must the consumption of our manufacturers be lessened.

   That if liberal wages were given to the Mechanics in general throughout the Country, the Home Consumption of our Manufacturers would be immediately more than doubled and consequently every hand would soon find full employment.

   That to Reduce the Wage of the Mechanic of the Country so low that he cannot live by his labour, in order to undersell Foreign Manufacturers in a Foreign Market, is to gain one customer abroad and lose two at home...' (quoted in Thompson, 1963, p. 206).
2. Although this model is cast in the framework of the 'classical' savings function, it could be extended to the case of 'corporate capitalism', e.g. 's' can be interpreted as the constant fraction of corporate profit retained, and all distributed profit and wages would be assumed to be consumed by households. However, such 'extensions' would be trivial unless the financial determinants of corporate investments, especially the influence of the stock exchange market on invetment, are also introduced into the analysis. In the present paper, we deliberately abstract from all such financial complications, including the rate of interest, because this is not our immediate purpose.
3. The measure of capacity utilisation—actual output as a fraction of potential output—is a problematic concept. For those accustomed to thinking in terms of the production function and factor substitution leading to rising marginal cost, z is well defined so long as the elasticity of substitution is less than unity. Although the simplest assumption is to postulate constant labour productivity up to full-capacity output, this requires us to abandon either the notion of a competitive product market or profit-maximising equalibrium (Kalecki, 1971). The time-intensity of use of the capital stock, measured by the fraction of hours per period over which the equipment is in use, could provide a practical index of capacity utilisation, as proposed by Maris (1964) and used by Lucas (1970).
4. See Pasinetti (1981, ch. 6) on the link between inter-industry and vertically integrated analysis. The reader may be reminded here that the method works only so long as raw materials are also

produced (processed) within the inter-industrial structure, but are not primary commodities or exhaustible natural resources with 'demand-determined' prices (Kalecki, 1971).

5. With permanent staff incorporated in the analysis and assuming a uniform wage rate for all workers, profit share can be derived (cf. Rowthorn, 1981) as $h = (mz - f)/z(1 + m)$, instead of (3) in the text where, f = the ratio of (a constant number of) permanent staff to operative workers at full capacity output. Hence, unlike in the simpler case of the text (equation 3), profit share increase with capacity utilisation, i.e. $(\partial h/\partial m) > 0$, but in conformity with equation (3), the profit share increases with the profit margin, i.e. $(\partial h/\partial m) > 0$, other things remaining the same.
6. While in the profit-led case, the real wage rate would behave contra-cyclically, in the wage-led case, the real wage would move pro-cyclically. This isue has been debated empirically for the last fifty years, since the publication of *The General Theory*. Schor (1985) provides an excellent survey with an analysis of recent (1955-1980) evidence.
7. This may influence the shape of the *IS*-curve, as discussed further in Appendix B.
8. Recall that inequality (11) makes the slope of Hicks's traditional *IS*-curve unambiguously negative because in his construction a higher interest rate decreases *both* consumption and investment, so that aggregate demand is always lower at a higher interest rate. The variable comparable to the interst rate in our present construction is the real wages rate which is inversely related to the profit margin/share through (4). The ambiguity of the slope of our *IS*-curve stems from the contradictory effects of the real wage on consumption and on investment. The former increases (see 1) but the latter decreases (see 8) at a higher real wage rate. These contradictory effects also underlie part of the difficulty in justifying analytically stability conditon (11), if both z and h adjust in a general dynamic model, as emphasized at the end of the paper.
9. Malinvaud (1982) provides an alternative analysis of how a high real wage could lead to such structural enemployment, through a slower pace of accumulation as well as through factor substitution against labour, resulting in what we describe as the crisis of underaccumulation (plus over-mechanization induced by a high real wage).
10. The familiar J-curve phenomenon in the balance of trade associated with the depreciation of currency arises precisely when exports and/

or imports have relatively slow speeds of adjustment and low price elasticities in the short period. But, even in this case, they are likely to have faster speeds of adjustment compared to investment in fixed capital.

11. The import price index ($\bar{p}_f$) is a weighted average of imported raw material price (p_f'), and price of finished product (p_f), which changes owing to changes in the composition of raw material to finished product import. This 'composition effect' is ignored here by assuming the import composition to be roughly constant in the short period.
12. From (18), $(d\theta/\theta)>0$ implies $(dv/v) > (dp/p)$. From (16) and (18), $dh>0$ implies $\lambda > [(dv/v)-(dp/p)]/[(dv/v)-(dw/w)]$. Since, by definition, $1>\lambda>0$, it is easy to see $(dp/p)>(dw/w)$.
13. Marglin and Bhaduri (1986) provides some preliminary dynamic analysis (in terms of *local* stability) of a range of models only some of which have been discussed hear. However, see Appendix B which indicates why *local* analysis may be misleading.
14. For this reason, we began by showing the essential economic logic of the two regimes in the simpler case of equation (6) which does not involve condition (11).

References :

Armstrong, P., Glyn, A. and Harrison, J. 1984. *Capitalism since World War II*, London, Fontana

Baran, P. and Sweezy, P. 1966. *Monopoly Capital*, New York, Monthly Review Press.

Bowels, S. 1985. The production process in a competitive economy : Walrasian, neo-Hobbesian and Marxian models, *American Economic Review*, Vol. 75, March.

Dutt, A. K. 1984. Stagnation, income distribution and monopoly power, *Cambridge Journal of Economics*, vol. 8, no. 1.

Glyn, A. and Sutcliff, R. 1972. *British Capitalism, workers and the Profit Squeeze*, Harmondsworth, Penguin.

Glyn, a., Hughes, A., Lipietz, A. and Singh, A. 1990. The rise and fall of the Golden Age, in Marglin, S. A. (ed.), *Golden Age of Capitalism*.

Goodwin, R. M. 1967. Growth cycles, in Feinstein, C. H. (ed.), *Socialism, Capitalism and Economic Growth*, Essays presented to Maurice Dobb, Cambridge : Cambridge University Press.

Hicks J. R. 1937. Mr Keynes and the classics : a suggested interpretation. *Econometrica,* April.

—1974. *The Crisis in Keynesian Economics,* Oxford, Basil Blackwell

Kalecki, M. 1939. *Essays in the Theory of Economic Fluctuations,* London, George Allen & Unwin

Kalecki, M. 1971. Selected Essays on the Dynamics of the Capitalist Economy, Cambridge : Cambridge University Press.

Keynes, J. M. 1936. *The General Theory of Employment, Interest and Money,* London, Macmillan

Lucas, R. E. 1970. Capacity, overtime and empirical production functions, *American Economic Review,* vol. 60, March.

Malinvaud, E. 1982. Wages and unemployment. *Economic Journal,* March.

Marglin, S.A. 1984. *Growth, Distribution and Prices,* Cambridge, Mass., Harvard University Press.

Marglin, S. A. and Bhaduri, A. 1986. *Distribution, Capacity Utilisation and Growth*, WIDER/ Harvard (mimeo)

Marglin, S. A. and Bhaduri, A. 1990. *Profit squeeze and keynesian theory,* in Marglin, S. A. (ed.), *The Golden Age of Capitalism : Reinterpreting the Postwar Experience,* Oxford, Clarendon Press.

Marris, R. 1964. *The Economics of Capital Utilization,* Cambridge : Cambridge University Press.

Nicolis, G. and Prigogine, I. 1977. *Self Organization in Nonequilibrium Systems,* New York, John Wiley

Pasinetti, L. L. 1981. *Structural Change and Economic Growth,* Cambridge : Cambridge University Press.

Robinson, J. 1962. *Essays in the Theory of Economic Growth,* London, Macmillan

Rowthorn, R. 1981. Demand, real wages and economic growth, *Thames Papers in Political Economy,* Autumn.

Schor, J. B. 1985. Changes in the cyclical pattern of real wages : evidence from nine countries, 1955-80, *Economic journal,* vol. 95, no. 2, June.

Solow, R. M. 1987. Unemployment : getting the questions right, *Economica,* Vol 53 (supplement special issue on unemployment).

Taylor, L. 1985. A stagnationist model of economic growth, *Cambridge Journal of Economics,* vol.9, no. 4.

Thompson, E. P. 1963. *The Making of the English Working Class,* New York, Vintage Books.

APPENDIX A

The definition of the average rate of profit r in (7) permits investment function (8) to be rewritten as,

$$I = I\ (z,h) = I\ (z,r/za)$$

Its total differentiation at a constant rate of profit $r = r$ yields,

$$(dI/dz)|_{r=r} = I_z - (h/z)I_h \qquad (A1)$$

Note that the left hand side of (A1) is simply the partial derivative of investment with respect to capacity utilisation at a constant rate of profit. Therefore, when the investment function (8) of the text is replaced by an investment furnction with specifications,

$$I = F(r,z),\ F_r > 0 \text{ and } F_z > 0 \qquad (A2)$$

it implies from (A1) and (A2),

$$F_z = dI/dz|_{r=r} = I_z - (h/z)\ I_h > 0 \qquad (A3)$$

or,

$$zI_Z > hI_h$$

which is exactly inequality (13) in the text, characterising the cooperative zone in he stagnationist regime. Therefore, assuming investment function (A2) is tantamount to assuming a cooperative stagnationist regime.

APPENDIX B

In defence of the investment function (8) in the text, it was pointed out that the rate of profit, r, is a problematic concept as an argument entering the investment function, because, by definition (7), the two constituents of r – h and z– can move in opposite directions to maintain the *same* profit rate. (This results in restrictions on the investment function, already examined in Appendix A.) Since the same rate of profit can be associated with either a low profit margin/share *(h)* coupled with a high degree of capacity utilisation *(z)* and *vice versa,* it neglects the important economic possibility that the response of investment to profit margin/share, captured by the magnitude of the coeffiecient I_h, may be influenced significantly by the *existing* degree of capacity utilisation. For instance, if existing capacities are heavily underutilised, it is probable that the lure of a higher profit margin would fail to induce much fresh investment in creating additional capacity, implying a low value of I_h. This could make

$$sz > I_h \text{ at 'low' initial values of } z \qquad \text{(B1)}$$

resulting in the stagnationist regime (see 6 or 10).

Contaiwise, at high rates of utilisation of existing capacities, investors may respond enthusiastically to a higher profit margin to make feasible the emergence of the exhilarationist regime, i.e.

$$I_h > sz \text{ at 'high' initial values of } z \qquad \text{(B2)}$$

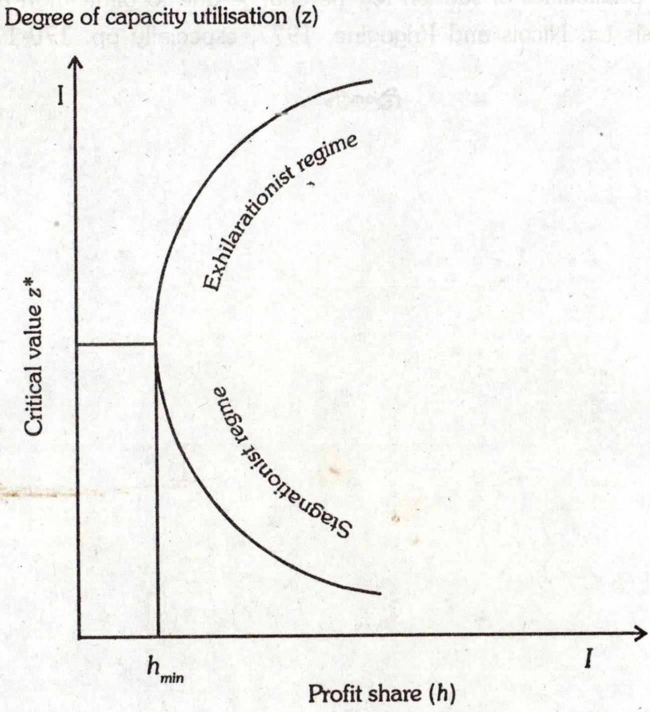

Fig. B1. *Non-linear, IS-schedule with both stagnationist and exhilarationist regimes.*

Condition (B1) suggests that the stagnationist regime is more likely when the prevalent economic situation is recessionary with low capacity utilisation; whereas condition (B2) suggests the possibility of an exhilarationist regime being ushereed in by an economic boom.

The combination of these two conditions result in a *non-liner IS*-schedule which is downword-sloping (stagnationist) at relatively low values of z, but upward-sloping (exhilarationist) at relatively high values of z. This could be represented by the C-shaped *IS*-curve in Fig. B1 (various other shapes are plausible though; see Marglin and Bhaduri, 1986 and 1990). It may not be altogether premature to conjecture that non-liner *IS*-curves traversing both the regimes have complex and interesting possibilities of sudden regime change due to bifurcation and/or hysteresis (cf. Nicois and Prigogine, 1977, especially pp. 170-178).

JOBLESSNESS

Historical Background

It is somewhat paradoxical that market economies, even under the system of representative political democracy, can live with high unemployment, and place relatively little emphasis on this problem, except perhaps at times of elections. Various plausible explanations can be offered, and perhaps they all contain some elements of truth. After all, the deep change in the climate of economic management, in sharp contrast to the post-WWII years of policies in pursuit of full employment in advanced market economies, is unlikely to be the consequence of any single cause. As historical narratives often remind us, changes in history are seldom mono-causal; instead, they are usually the result of several factors and processes coinciding at a particular juncture of time.

The climate of opinion against the Keynesian style of demand management in pursuit of high employment advanced gradually for at least three inter-related reasons. **First**, the Keynesian argument was almost self-consciously set in the context of an economy closed to international trade and capital flows. The intention may well have been to emphasize the importance of domestically oriented economic policies for fighting unemployment. After all, the disastrous consequences of "beggar-thy-neighbor" policies of trying to export unemployment through competitive devaluation of the national currencies during the inter-war period was still fresh in memory, while the prestige of the 'City of London' in propounding the virtues of 'sound finance' was in ruins (Bhaduri and Steindl, 1985). It was rather natural in that context to look inward for a domestic solution to the problem of unemployment.

Secondly, although the contest between the competing systems of capitalism and socialism was most visible in the Cold War arms race, its ideological dimension was essentially economic. The socialist system appeared capable of providing full employment through deliberate state policies, although much of that employment was neither satisfactory to the employees nor socially gainful. (A common joke of the time in these countries was, "they pretend to pay, we pretend to work".) In the capitalist market economies the level of employment depended largely on the decision of private business, posing an opposite problem : although the jobs it provided had to be gainful to the private employer, even if private and social gain differed, the level of economic activity was prone to cyclical fluctuations, at times resulting in severe and persistent unemployment. Given this known difference in the performance of the two systems, even initiatives like Marshall Plan tended to be influenced at least partly by the economic competition between the two systems (Hobsbawm, 1994). It was also around this time that the welfare state found wider political acceptance, with its theoretical rationale in Keynesian demand management policies. The rising real wage with near-full employment, leading to rapidly improving standard of living for the working population under this new style of economic governance in most western democracies could be posed as a counter-challenge to the socialist ideology.

Thirdly, the very success of demand management, high employment, and rising mass consumption, which had ushered in a 'golden age' of welfare capitalism through rapidly expanding domestic markets for nearly a quarter century, came to be troubled by its own contradictions (Marglin and Schor, 1990). Years of high employment had reduced the fear of job-loss for the workers, and increased workers' wage claims. Against this background, the experiences of the two major oil price increases of the 1970s made it clear that the burden of such shocks could not be passed on easily to the workers. The model of co-operative capitalism of the welfare state was giving away to the model of conflictive capitalism, in which struggle over the distribution of income tended to manifest itself through inflationary or stagflationary price rise (Rowthorn, 1977). Even more problematically, the fiscal policy of the state itself got entangled in this distributive conflict, as both the workers and their employers tended to pass on the additional tax burden to one another (Bhaduri, 1986; ch. 6). Understandably, targeting inflation rather than enemployment became the new focus of policies. New economic doctrines, at times reviving old ideas that had been pushed aside by the success of Keynesian economic policies, returned in academic circles and policy discussions under the board heading of Monetarism. Ironically, monetarism revived the Marxian idea that a 'reserve army of labour' is needed to keep a check on the real wage. Kalecki (1943, reprinted in 1971) had already made use of a similar idea towards the end of the second world war to predict that 'political trade cycles' would be imposed deliberately, particularly in the name of sound finance (read : no deficit financing), to inflict unemployment from time to time in order to keep control over the workers. These ideas returned in the orthodox monetarist framework as the 'natural rate' of unemployment (Friedman, 1968), or as the non-accelerating inflation rate of unemployment, NAIRU (Layard, Nickell and Jackman, 1991). The common theme held that keeping inflation and inflationary expectations under control requires accepting a certain, even fairly high, rate of enemployment. In particular, it requires giving up demand management policies intended to keep the rate of unemployment lower than that 'natural' or NAIRU rate. Since deficit financing by the government had been the most potent instrument used for demand management, unsurprisingly it came under specal attack. The doctrine of 'public choice' theory proclaimed the virtues of a balanced budget and the evils of a fiscal deficit by a self-seeking government, and held these as general truths, applicable to almost all countries under all circumstances.

These theories and policy perspectives directed against the welfare state and Keynesian policies were embedded in the wider process of globalization that had been going on mostly through gradual expansion in post-war international trade. However, they gathered irresistible momentum with the deregulation of the national capital markets, beginning in the mid-1970s in the OECD countries. The greater economic opening in the trade of goods and services meant an increase in the reative importance of the foreign or external market compared to the domestic or internal market. It encouraged countries to stimulate demand through export surplus, rather than through demand management by government fiscal policies. As a result, each country will try to be more price competitive than its neighbours by cutting unit cost through wage restraint and labour market flexibility, on the one hand, and by rising labour productivity, on the other. Yet there is an obvious 'fallacy of composition' in this strategy : all countries cannot achieve export surplus at the same time, as the export surplus of some must be matched by the import surplus of others. Moreover, even for any particular country that *does* manage to achieve an export surplus in this international zero sum game, such policies may turn out to be counter-productive if the contraction in the size of its internal market more than outweighs the expansion of its external market.

The danger of contraction of domestic demand from such policies is serious. Wage restraint depresses consumption by working people, while labour productivity growth brought about by corporations through downsizing of the labour force reinforces this depressive effect. The overall consequence might be a decrease in the size of the domestic market despite an increase in the external market through export surplus. Analytically, this may be identified as the wage-or-consumption-led regime, in which wage restraint and downsizing have depressive effects that outweigh their possible stimulating effect on investment and export (Bhaduri and Marglin, 1990). Nevertheless, this danger of a sharp decline in domestic demand tends to be overlooked for reasons that have become almost the defining characteristic of the current phase of globalization.

It is well known that the deregulation and liberalization of capital markets since the mid-1970s has phenomenally increased the volume of private trade in foreign exchange. With a daily volume of some 1.2 trillion dollars, such trade far exceeds the total foreign exchange reserves of all the central banks put together. Foreign trade and investment combined account for less than four per cent of private trade in foreign exchange. Thus, in formulating their economic policies, national governments feel obliged to abide by the sentiment of the extremely powerful financial markets, particularly because finance can move across borders at a moment's notice. Expansionary fiscal policies for fighting unemployment through either a) deficit spending or b) imposing higher taxes on the rich to expand government programs, are generally not favoured by the financial markets. In this context, tax cuts remain almost the only option for stimulating demand, which might, of course, cause larger budget deficits. Similarly, so-called 'easy money' policies, in which low interest rates aim to boost economic activity, are often seen as suspect, as signals of the government's intention to embark on expansionary policies which might, in turn, lead to trade deficits or capital outflows.

The typical consequences of abiding by the sentiments of the financial market have been, over-sensitivity to inflation, insistence on the independence of the central bank, and a near-paralysis of fiscal and monetary policies. Variations on this policy package are found not only in some developing countries, but also in developed countries. They tend to deliberately keep the domestic interest rate high for attracting short-term capital inflows, even if it discourages investment at home.

Note the general point that all such policies have the same economic consequence of reducing the relative importance of the domestic compared to the external market.

Multinationals tend to erode further the space left for national economic policies. Governments in developed economies tread softly in so far as taxing corporate profits are concerned. Not only are footloose corporations capable of shifting to low-tax locations, but they can also make use of transfer pricing : out-sourcing through various practices of intra-firm trade to show profit at more convenient points. And, although intra-firm trade, estimated conservatively at 40 per cent of all manufacturing trade, appears as international trade, national governments have little control over it. Governments in developed countries try to deal with multinationals by forming supra-national arrangements about uniform taxes, competition policies, etc. However, among the developing countries, typically a 'race to the bottom' takes place. As countries hope to improve their trade balance by becoming part of intra-firm trading networks, the link to such networks may indeed be the most tangible benefit of FDI, though the level of technology or skills transfer varies across country and sector, and remains a topic of great controversy.

Theories And Counter-Theories On Unemployment

This alternative perspective, marked by its neglect of domestic demand and the domestic market, and which aspires to replace the Keynesian consensus, is neo-liberal in essence. Contrary to the Keynesian view that markets fail seriously — as when insufficient domestic demand inflicts serious unemployment — and thus need to be managed through public action, neo-liberalism emphasizes the opposite point of view. It wants to roll back government, on the assumption that the market by and large performs better than the state. The extreme view is to claim that markets never fail. Put differently, it is claimed that market outcomes with available information cannot be improved upon by government intervention, a view associated with the so-called 'new classical' school of economic theory. A more moderate view is to suggest that the markets fail only because the price mechanism does not function properly at times, mainly due to incomplete information, e.g., inormation being asymmetrically distributed. This view, associated with various versions of 'neo-Keynesianism', leaves some room for government action through correcting the price mechanism. Nevertheless, in so far as unemployment is concerned, both schools share a common economic philosophy that, in shorthand, may be described as the 'neo-classical' view of unemployment. This view more or less rules the current academic and policy orthodoxy, and has three distinguishing characteristics contracy to the original Keynesian paradigm.

First, unlike Keynes and Kalecki, who identified the lack of effective demand in the market for goods and services as the *central* cause of unemployment, these theories look directly at the labour market to explain unemployment. Thus the causation runs directly from the labour market, and not indirectly from the product market, to unemployment. In terms of policy, this means demand management in the product market becomes less important that correcting the bad-functioning of the labour market.

Secondly, even the branch of neo-classical theory sympathetic to the Keynesian view (e.g. the neo-Keynesians), tends to make a distinction between the 'short run', when there may be insufficiency of demand in the product market, and the 'long run', when somehow the demand problem is resolved. This kind of dichotomy between the short and the long run is most starkly visible in nearly all versions of neo-classical long run growth theory.

Thirdly, and perhaps most basic to this neo-classical way of thinking, is the philosophy of 'methodological individualsm'. It uses some procedure of optimization by the individual agent as the central organizing principle of macroeconomic theory. Approaching macroeconomic problems exclusively in this way has many serious ramifications, and with regard to the unemployment problem, perhaps its most serious consequence is to blur the distinction between 'voluntary' and 'involuntary' unemployment. All unemployment, even mass unemployment, begins to look voluntary in this framework, because it has to be explained through some optimizing decision by the individual worker. The problem then becomes attributable to the imperfect functioning of the price mechanism for giving wrong signals to the unemployed worker. In some theories, government interventions, mostly related to the welfare state, are supposed to distort the signals carried by wages in the labour market. In this framework either the jobless worker becomes responsible for his or her own situation or the blame is put on government intervention. Needless to add, this serves well the neo-liberal case.

A basic attraction of this neo-liberal theory stems from the idea that the market has a very different kind of an advantage over the government. It is not mentioned explicitly, but follows from the present body of theoretical knowledge on the subject :

Even under the most idealized circumstances of perfect competition—when the competitive equilibrium has all the desirable properties of Pareto optimality by the so-called "fundamental theorem" of welfare economics—nothing in economic theory specifies *how long it might take to reach that equilibrium*. This ambiguity helps in sustaining the market ideology. In democracies, the government and the politicians in power remain accountable to their people at regular time intervals through elections, but the market mechanism has no such definite time horizon for showing results. It can always be claimed that, given 'sufficient' time and 'sufficiently' wide ranging pro-market reforms, the desired results would materialize, without having to specify how long is sufficiently long. In this respect, the market mechanism, like a dictator, can always promise without actually delivering!

The enormous power wielded by the electronic media and television images in shaping public opionion was noticed even in the very early stage of globalization by perceptive commentators (e.g. McLuhan, 1960). In particular it helps in spreading a sort of a popular culture of economic policy, which is the lowest common denominator of economic theory, and can be easily comprehended by men and women of 'practical affairs'. In this respect, easiest to comprehend, is the analogy of the individual. Since spending beyond one's means is bad, a government budget deficit is considered bad; since the demand for apples can be raised by lowering their price, the demand for labour can also be raised by lowering the wage rate; since hard work helps one to get ahead, so a corporate manager helps the economy to get ahead by downsizing its labour force. Underlying all of these popular pronouncements in the media is the neo-liberal foundation of 'methodological individualism'. Unfortunately, even politicians who know better often feel helpless, because political expediency demands that they do not swim against the popular current.

This popular culture of viewing macroeconomic policies exclusively through the lens of methodological individualism goes against the very logic of Keynesianstyle demand management, which followed from a demonstration of the misleading nature of the analogy of the individual.

The macro-economy is characterized by a circular flow of expenditure and income where, unlike in the case of the individual, expenditure, i.e. demand, may determine income and output in situations of serious unemployment.

THE BASICS OF POLICIES FOR HIGH EMPLOYMENT

It is against this intellectual background that we need reconsider policies for attaining and sustaining higher employment in developing countries. At the outset it is worth pointing out that many different types of projects may be devised for generating employment. By and large, these projects would be country-specific, dependent on geography, stage of development, degree of openness, etc. The purpose of macro-economic theory in this context is not to list a set of such projects irrespective of their country-specificity, but to indicate how to devise a programme for generating and sustaining high employment in developing countries.

The preceding discussion already pointed that the responsibility of maintaining high employment has gradually passed from the government to the market. This view is reinforcfed further in developing countries in two ways. **First,** the 'less-government-more-market' economic philosophy propounded generally by the Bretton Woods institutions operates with full force through 'conditionalities' imposed on developing countries experiencing balance-of-payments difficulties. **Second,** it is further reinforced by the governments in developing countries themselves, in so far as they often find it politically expedient to escape accountability by attributing the problem to the market and to the Bretton Woods institutions. The result is a set of 'market-friendly' policies for employment generation which may or may not produce the desired results in any given time horizon. In either case, the market cannot be held responsible for delivering within a given time period.

In the context of the unemployment problem, the most important feature of market-friendly policies has been to look upon wage simply as the major element of production cost for private employers, and not as an important factor in determining the size of the total domestic market. The result is to focus exclusively on the labour market, instead of paying sufficient attention to the fact that no cost-cutting measure can succeed in isolation without sufficient demand. The various measures that are undertaken—wage restraint, downsizing of the labour force, change in labour laws that makes it easier to hire and fire employees, revision of pension fund, laws in favour of the employer, curbing workers' rights to strike, etc.—are like designing a more and more efficient privately owned boat without enough water or demand in the public river for it to float!

The dependence on the private sector to solve the employment problem is also a slippery path, especially in the context of globalization. The more a developing economy tries to integrate with the world market, the stronger the pressure becomes for reducing unit cost through the labour market for achieving international competitiveness, or for attracting foreign direct investment and other forms of capital flows. This dependence impacts employment policies adversely in two different ways.

First, labour productivity growth that makes more goods and services available for domestic use is not pursued as a desirable objective in and of itself; instead, its desirability is judged in terms of enhancing international competitiveness. Note also that more goods and services would be available in the aggregate from higher productivity *only* if higher productivity does not quantitatively outweigh a decrease in employment; whereas unit cost would decrease and enhance competitiveness so long as productivity per worker rises, irrespective of the level of employment. Thus, the exclusive focus on competitiveness separates the employment objective from the productivity objective, making, for example, the downsizing of the labour force attractive in terms of unit cost, but not necessarily in terms of either aggregate supply or demand. Moreover, if demand fails to expand sufficiently fast to absorb both productivity and labour force growth, the result would be growing unemployment, and various scenarios of jobless growth.

Second, the preoccupation with cost reduction leads to a focus on micro-efficiency at the level of the enterprise. but downplays macro-inefficiencies that result such as serious unemployment due to insufficient demand. This has led to a blurring of the distinction between good management of an enterprise or household, and sensible management of the economy as a whole. The former usually takes the market size for a product as broadly given (with some product differentiation, related new products, etc.) by the income of the actual and potential customers. The typical objective of any particuular enterprise is to increase market share rather than the total market size through competitive micro-efficiency; whereas it is precisely the purpose of macro-management to ensure that the overall market size expands at a sufficient pace to absorb both the growth in the labour force and its productivity. There are, however, two rather special circumstances in which this enterprise management view might succeed : either by stimulating exports, or by raising private investment sufficiently through these micro-incentives of cutting costs.

In the former case, the micro-efficiency paradigm could increase the international market share of the country concerned in a successful scenario of export-led growth. But, it must be remembered that this is an international zero sum game, and there must be winners as well as losers in this game. It cannot help all developing countries, especially the most disadvantaged among them that suffer from acute technological backwardness, limited diversification of exports, etc. In the latter case, the micro-efficiency paradigm might stimulate sufficiently the profitability of private investment to expand demand, and therefore the size of the market, through the multiplier in a scenario of investment-led growth (Bhaduri and Marglin, 1990). Nore, however, that in both these cases the central point is that micro-efficiency in cost reduction has to result in sufficient expansion of macro-demand. The frequently made policy mistake is to think that this is an automatic outcome.

The pitfalls in this process are indeed many. For instance, exports not only need to expand, but must exceed imports sufficiently to produce the necessary export surplus; otherwise demand would not expand sufficiently. Therefore, this strategy can work only for those countries that can achieve a sufficient export surplus, while other countries with corresponding import surplus depressing their demand would face a serious problem. For this reason, trying to promote exports with very high levels of imported content typically fails in many developing countries.

There is no certainty either that private investment on a macro scale would be sufficiently stimulated through micro efficiency at the enterprise level. Private investment in fixed capital needs to take a long view of the prospects for profit. Therefore, it tends to respond sluggishly in general to an increase in current profitability. More important, however, is an inherent coordination problem. Unless many firms become simultaneously convinced that their profit prospect has increased over a relatively long time horizon, aggregate demand will not increase in sufficiently through private investments. On the other hand, each individual firm will hesitate to move first, so long as other firms remain passive in their investment demands. Thus, relying exclusively on micro-efficiency at the enterprise level to solve the unemployment problem becomes fraught with many difficulties. In general, the more severe the problem of unemployment is, the more difficult becomes the problem of coordination, and of convincing the private investors that the climate for investment has indeed improved.

Given these difficulties, perhaps the most obvious starting point for breaking the inertia of low employment is through the budgetary policy of the government. Current orthodoxy in economic theory, greatly helped by the Bretton Woods institutions in the developing countries, takes the view that budget deficits are undesirable in general, and insists that the fiscal deficit of the government, estimated with or without interest payments on outstanding public debt, must not exceed a certain percentage of the GDP. There are two common objections against running large deficits. The first stems from the burden of servicing this debt; the second from repeated recourse to large deficit as a 'soft option' by an irresponsible government with dangers of inflation.

The first objection has greater force if the debt is external, and needs to be serviced in foreign exchange by a developing country. A high level of external debt squeezes import capacity, and carries in addition the danger of precipitating a financial crisis, if for some reason foreign lenders try to withdraw their credit in a panic. However, with internal debt these objections are less serious, and often invalid. When an economy is growing and the government remains credible, there is no obvious limit to the extent a government can borrow further to service its debt. It is rather one-sided to suggest that only the level of borrowing, and no other indicator, like growth or employment level, affects the credibility of the government. Thus, in the face of serious unemployment the central issue should not be whether the government should run a large deficit to finance its employment generating strategies, but whether such a strategy would be effective and sustainable. Three conclusions regarding the government's budgetary policy follow : (a) More caution should be applied in contracting foreign debt, and premature capital account convertibility; (b) a bureaucratic limit on the extent of the permitted budget deficit is no solution; and (c) close examination is needed not of the deficit, but of whether the deficit can be effective in fighting unemployment and sustaining a high level of employment with growth.

The second objection, about government budget deficit as a dangerous soft option, is mostly ideological. It follows from a general mistrust of the government, which is often, but not always justified. The government, like the market, often fails, and fails miserably. The way to approach this issue is to consider whether some correction mechanism would be in place in case of serious and continuous failures by either institution. As already pointed out the market mechanism is not self-correcting in the sense of being 'close' to equilibrium within any given time horizon; nor does it have any in-built mechanism to correct income distribution or promote development and high employment. Thus, it might be rational to accept a solution that improves upon what the market might attain within some given time frame.

However, it must also be remembered that the experiences of bureaucratic central planning showed how disastrously things could go wrong with no self correcting mechanism in place. This is especially true without the economic accountability of the government in the absence of political democracy. In the light of experience, a pragmatic compromise between these two most essential institutions, the state and the market, seems unavoidable.

A more balanced approach that adopts a less ideologically colored position would be to let both these eeessential institutions develop in a historical 'double movement' (Polyani, 1944). In this process, each would have to restrain the other from becoming over-dominating. By and large, this seems to have happened in most cases of successful development of the market economies. Employment policies, like any others, need to be devised without upsetting this dynamic balance. Thus, when the market fails visibly to cope, as in the case of serious unemployment, the state has to initiate actions, and not leave matters to market incentives. Conversely, when the state over-reaches and tries to create socially unproductive employment in an unsustainable manner, the market has to reassert its ability to restore the balance. There is clearly no once-and-for-all answer in this complex game of balancing that is valid under all circumstances. It is more correct to view this process as a 'challenge and response' situation between these two major and equally essential institutions.

Both for employment creation and for longer run growth, it must be remembered that the notion of a resource constraint for the economy as a whole is different from that of the financial budget constraint facing an individual unit. With serious unemployment, excess capacity and inventories, the economy is not constrained by finance, but by how well it can make use of these underutilized resources. In these situations, it makes little sense to restrain the government from deficit financing by some inflexible rule in the name of 'sound finance'. It also seems rather beside the point to talk of the "independence" of the central bank to follow a tight money policy. It would be far better instead to start from the real economy and arrive at more flexible monetary and financial policies and rules. The mistake of monetarism has typically been to start the other way round.

In particular, if excess capacity exists in the relevant domestic capital goods industries with unemployment, useful economic and social infra-structural investments can be undertaken through budgetary or financial support from the government. It is not wise to wait for domestic or foreign private investment to solve the problem of growing unemployment or deepening recession, because the more persistent and serious the problem, the more difficult it becomes to turn around private expectations. As a matter of fact, in many developing countries public investment would act as a catalyst to 'crowd in' rather than 'crowd out' private investment, first by increasing the size of the domestic market and second, by providing better infra-structural facilities to raise profitability. Needless to add, the impact of these investments on employment would be positive, and stronger if some of its construction components can be made labour-intensive.

Nevertheless, the fundamental Keynesian insight that higher expenditure by the government would activate underutilized recourses to generate more income and saving to finance the higher level of government spending has to be applied with some caution to suit the conditions of particular countries. So long as basic wage-goods are not in cripplingly sort supply or, as a second best option, can be imported, identifying the broad direction for starting a public investment programme is easier. Widespread poverty, or at least concentrated pockets of poverty, presents an opportunity for policy-makers to devise useful public works through guaranteed employment schemes at some minimum wage for a certain number of days per year. The minimum wage would have a degree of self-selection to attract mostly the poor and needy.

However, despite some self-selection, these schemes tend to be wasteful in different ways. Policy packages that are often chosen by a remote, non-accountable bureaucracy often turn out to be useless, because they fail to be sensitive to local needs. Very often, they also suffer from 'giantism', i.e., unnecessarily big and technologically complicated projects which a centralized bureaucracy can handle more easily, but in which the unutilized and relatively unskilled labour cannot contribute effectively. A large percentage of the funds also tends to leak out in administering these public works, with the result that only a small fraction usually reaches the needy poor for whom it is intended in the first place. On the other hand, a large machinery for supervision increases the leakage by raising administrative cost, but without it, there is the danger of non-performance, inefficiencies and corruption.

The only way out of this dilemma is to take recourse to decentralization as far as possible with two added provisions. **First,** while the decentralized local bodies would have control over the use of the funds, there must be transparency of their budget through a legally recognised right to information which has to cover both the central bureaucracy *and* also the decentralized local bodies choosing and implementing the projects. The free availability of information naturally must apply both to the available funds and their disbursements. **Second,** to sustain such programmes over time, attempts should be made to more increasingly towards the principle of "(s)he who benefits should (partially) pay". This has to be based on two different pillars. The first is the pro-private sector policy. It would extend the schemes to specified types of capital formation on private property, chosen on the basis of their desirability by the local community, and having some social benefits or positive externalities—e.g. small irrigation, land improvement, linked pathways through private land, etc. These would benefit directly one or more private owners, but also indirectly the larger community. They should also have the potental for sustaining employment at the local level, even when undertaken on private land or property.

The second pillar of this policy would be to ensure that the private owners who belong to the local community, and voluntarily participate to benefit directly, have to bear a part of the cost—e.g. in terms of paying part of the minimum wage bill, or in paying a lump-sum to the local body as capital gains on completion of the projects. Additionally, which such payments would be to the local entities for their own use, they must be based on transparent rules. This would reduce both the cost to the local bodies and the need for supervision as the beneficiary himself or herself would be interested in the quality of the work done. In other words, it would be a way of subsidising socially useful capital formation through private cooperation at the local level without losing sight of the employment objective. Within limits, the above argument may also be extended to the use of some social infra-structural facilities like secondary schools and vocational training centers, where the beneficiaries should bear part of the cost, which could be on a progressive scale decided by the local bodies.

It has often been suggested that better training schemes raise the aggregate level of employment. Experiments with various 'voucher schemes' to determine the type of training demanded by the voucher-holders have been tried on a limited scale to make these schemes more responsive to individual needs and preferences by creating miniature local markets, in which the vouchers act as 'votes' for choosing the particular training schemes. The schemes devised to mimic the market mechanism often turn out to be flawed, in so far as the schemes with maximum votes do not always turn out to be either very useful for the community or for getting jobs (Lepenies, 2004). The reason for the latter is that training facilities by themselves usually cannot generate more employment on the macro-scale, because they are pure supply side policies. There must either be latent demand in the market for those skills, or conscious demand-side policies must complement them. Training either raises the bar on entry to the labour market, or it becomes like shuffling the long queue for jobs, where the better trained are placed in the front without shortening the queue.

The connecting thread in this argument so far has been to point out the importance of domestic demand-led growth with adequate policy space for government action as the essential pre-requisite for high employment policies in developing countries. Although larger-sized countries have the advantage of a larger domestic market, this perspective on policy is also useful for the smaller countries. However, large and small are rather relative terms in this context, especialy because the size of the market depends both on population and on per capita income. Therefore, regional co-operation, based on the guiding principle that the domestic policy space should not suffer, is to the advantage of all, irrespective of size. This would be a feasible proposition only if democratic rights are observed. And, in the international context, the defining characteristic of any civilized democracy is the protection of minority rights, i.e. the right of the smaller or poorer nations, rather than the brute force of majority rule by the larger nations. The current process of globalization has generated discontent and disenchantment precisely because it has failed in this respect.

Concluding Observations

The basic elements of a policy for generating and sustaining high employment may now be summed up briefly.

a) *A minimum-wage employment guarantee scheme* : This will kick-start the program in face of serious unemployment, especially in rural areas.

b) *Decentralization of activities and administration* : This should take place through local bodies with gradual extension to private properties based on the principle of "(s)he who benefits should (partially) pay".

c) *Transparency regarding the allocation and use of funds* : Ensuring this requires recognizing the right to information at all levels with respect to funds.

d) *Domestic demand-led expansion* : This is the corner stone of this strategy, which means placing due emphasis on the domestic market, rather than being preoccupied with the external market. In this sense, it is not an export-led growth strategy, because most developing countries cannot achieve an export surplus in an international zero-sum game. Nor is it an import substitution policy, because that too is motivated largely by considerations of the external maket and foreign exchange. Our emphasis instead is on changing the composition of investment to promote and sustain employment.

e) *Ensuring that the objective of productivity growth is not separated from employment growth* : This separation typically happens if productivity growth is considered only as an instrument for enhancing competition or generating surplus. But it is forgotten that higher productivity along with higher employment makes more goods and services available for the domestic market.

f) *An environment of sufficient growth* : Only a sufficiently expanding market can accommodate both labour productivity and labour force growth. While government policies can influence to some extent the rate of expansion of the market through its monetary and fiscal policies, it is important not to follow policies exclusively in search of productivity growth, since the latter maks sense only if productivity is considered a weapon for international competition. It is more important to recognize that, specially in poor countries with various types of technological backwardness and handicaps regarding international marketing, increased productivity is desirable to augment the availability of total output from the supply side, to be matched by an increased level of demand through higher employment.

g) *Increase the social content of wages* : Decentralized public works leading to more economic and social overhead and infra-structural facilities helps in increasing the social content of wage and earnings from self-employment, especially of the poor people. Local bodies should try to ensure that this becomes a reality. Ths would help in reducing the need for an increase in private wages and make such employment generating schemes more self-sustaining.

The Role Of The Informal Sector In Employment Generation Some Observations

Many developing countries are facing the serious problem of rapidly expanding cities and mega-cities with deteriorating infrastructure due to the massive influx of jobseekers in the urban sector. This has meant, on the one hand, more and more resources going into the cities in desperate attempt to cope with the problems of urban infrastructure, with an attendant lack of resources being used to improve rural infrastructure. The result has been a steadily growing urban-rural divide, and a phenomenal growth of the so-called informal sector. Thus, it is not only the direct pull of higher expected earning in urban employment that leads to in-migration into cities (Harris and Todaro, 1970), but also the indirect pull that operates because the urban centres are generally far better enquipped with economic and social overheads. This can be looked upon as the 'social content' of wage or earning, and an objective of decentralized public works would be to reduce the gap in the social wage and earning.

Employment in the informal service sector has grown very rapidly in many developing countries. A high percentage of this employment is not wage employment but self-employment, and for these workers the separation of total earning between wage and profit income is rather meaningless. The entire self-employed category consists of a relatively small percentage of high-level professionals, and, often, a very large percentage of the poor who take refuge in it part or full-time both in the urban and in the rural sector, because they have no other opportunity for livelihood. In any employment policy, it is essential to consider this segment, typically with massive disguised underemployed. By and large, the productivity of these workers, at least in the short run, depends not so much on the capital equipment or skill they possess, but on the level and composition of demand, and on the infra-structural facilities that they can use (Reddaway, 1962; ILO, 1972). One of the advantages of domestic demand - led policies, which would usually involve also improving local infra-structural facilities, especially in non-urban areas, is to be able to reach out to these people who are often among the very poor.

For generating and sustaining employment in the informal, less-skilled services at a higher level of earning, several interrelated aspects need to be considered. First, and in a way most obvious, is the emphasis on better irrigation and water management, as well as communication. Apart from increasing the productivity and intensity of land use, better water management allows crop diversification to absorb considerably more labour per hectare of land, and better communication is a prerequisite for the commercialization of agriculture, without which crop diversification can not succeed. In countries that are not predominantly agricultural, or have natural limitations, conscious attempts have to be made to develop a symbiotic relationship between the organized and the unorganized sector through sub-contracting, out-soursing, etc. For this relationship not to be exploitative, the government might have to use both regulations and incentives (e..g tax breaks for such sub-contracting to informal units). At the same time, independent artisan producers need design and marketing support, channeled as much as possible through decentralized local bodies receiving performance-related funds for this specific purpose from the government.

The way to visualize the strategic link between the general macro-economic policies for domestic demand led expansion and the informal sector is to develop the notion of 'nodal points' of economic activities for employment generation. They would mostly have to work backwards from demand, somewhat like the 'accelerator principle' in economic theory. In the past, policies in this respect often failed in many countries, because more emphasis was laid on the supply side, without creating the necessary demand links, either from the local markers in the rural areas or from the organized industries or urban centers. The concept of a 'node' might be a helpful starting point, in so far as various types of demand from these different sources would have to converge for the transformation of the informal sector from mostly a 'refuse sector' of the poor and desperate job-seekers into a genuinely dynamic sector of the economy.

References :

Bhaduri, A. and J. Steindl (1985) "The rise of monetarism as a social doctrine", *In* P. Arestis and T. Skouras (eds.) *Post-Keynesian Economic Theory.* Sussex : Wheatsheaf : 24-56.

Bhaduri, A. and S. Marglin (1990) "Unemployment and the real wage : the economic basis of contesting political ideologies". *Cambridge Journal of Economics* (14) : 375-93.

Bhaduri, A. (1986) *Macroeconomics : The Dynamics of Commodity Production.* London : Macmillan.

Friedman, M. (1968) "The role of monetary policy". *American Economic Review (58) 1-17.*

Harris, J.R. and M.P. Todaro (1970) "Migration, unemployment and development : a two-sector analysis". *American Economic Review,* (60) : 126-142.

Hobsbawm, E. (1994) *The Age of Extremes : A History of the World, 1914-1991,* New York : Pantheon Books.

Ilo—International Labor Organization (1972) *Employment, Income and Equality,* Geneva : ILO.

Kalecki, M. (1971) "Political aspects of full employment" in his *Selected Essays in the Dynamics of the Capitalist Economy.* Cambridge : Cambridge University Press.

Lepenies, P. (2004) "Exit, voice and vouchers : using vouchers to train entrepreneurs — observatins from the Paraguayan voucher scheme". *World Development* (32) : 713-724.

Marglin, S. and J. Schor (1990) *The Golden Age of Capitalism*. Oxford : Clarendon Press.

McLuhan, M. (1960) *Explorations in Communications.* Ontario : University of Toronto Press.

Polyani, K. (1944) *The Great Transformation*. New York : Holt, Rinehart and Winston.

Reddaway, W.B. (1962) *The Development of the Indian Economy.* London : Allen and Unwin.

Rowthorn, R. (1977) 'Conflict, Inflation and Money'. *Cambridge Journal of Economics,* (I) : 215-239.

LABOUR-MARKET FLEXIBILITY AND ECONOMIC EXPANSION

INTRODUCTION

The major economies of Western Europe have been facing almost chronic unemployment, often hovering around double digits, for nearly two decades now. This is especially true of Germany, which acted as the economic powerhouse in the consolidation of the European Union. It is all the more paradoxical that advanced market democracies can live with high unemployment placing relatively little emphasis on this problem, except perhaps at times of elections. A deep change in the climate of opinion has occurred in striking contrast to the postsecond world war years, when the pursuit of full employment was the agreed policy objective of almost all shades of political opinion. History is seldom mono-causal; several causal factors and processes usually coincide at a particular juncture of time to bring about such a dramatic change in the climate of opinion.

To a significant extent, this change of opinion began as a reaction against the Keynesian style of demand management in pursuit of high employment, which gradually lost ground for several interrelated reasons. **Firstly,** the Keynesian argument was almost self-consciously set in the context of an economy closed to international trade and capital flows. The intention might have been to emphasize the importance of domestically oriented economic policies for fighting unemployment. The disastrous consequences of 'beggar-my-neighbour' policies of trying to export unemployment through competitive devaluation of the national currencies during the interwar period (until the stand-still agreement of 1936) was still fresh in memory. At the same time, the prestige of the City as the financial centre of the world was in jeopardy, and its views propounding the virtues of 'sound finance' was in ruins. It was rather natural in that context to look inward for a solution to the problem of unemployment which relied more on domestic industries, and less on 'high finance' (Bhaduri and Steindl 1985).

Secondly, although the contest between the competing systems of capitalism and socialism was most visible in the arms race during the cold war, its ideological dimension was essentialy economic. The socialist system appeared capable of providing full employment through deliberate state policies, although much of it was neither satisfactory to the employees nor socially useful. (A common joke of the time in these countries was, "they pretend to pay, we pretend to work".) The capitalist market economies where the level of employment depended largely on the decision of private business, had the opposite problem. The employment it provided had to be necessarily gainful, that is profitable for the private employer, even if private and social gain differed. But, the level of economic activity was prone to cyclical fluctuations, at times resulting in severe unemployment. Given this visible difference between the two systems, even initiatives like the Marshall Plan tended to be influenced, at least partly, by the economic competition between the two systems (Hobsbawm 1994). It was around this time that the welfare state also found wider political acceptance. Its theoretical rationale derived from Keynesian demand-management policies, whereas the rising real wage with near-full employment, leading to rapidly improving standards of living for the working population under this new sytle of economic governance in most Western democracies, posed a counter-challenge to the socialist ideology.

Thirdly, the very success of demand management, high employment and rising mass consumption, which had ushered in a 'golden age' of welfare capitalism through rapidly expanding domestic markets for nearly a quarter century, came to be troubled by its own contradictions (Marglin and Schor 1990). Years of high employment had reduced the fear of job-loss for the workers leading to higher wage claims. It was in this context that the experiences of the two major oil price shocks of the 1970s served as almost the watershed years. They made it clear that the burden of such shocks could no longer be passed on easily to the workers. The model of cooperative capitalism of the welfare state was giving away to the model of conflictive capitalism, in which conflict over the distribution of income tended to manifest itself through inflationary or stagflationary price rise (Rowthorn 1977). Even more problematically, the fiscal policy of the state itself got entangled in this distributive conflict, as both workers and their employers tended to pass on the additional tax burden to one another (Bhaduri 1986 : ch. 6). Understandably, targeting inflation rather than unemployment became the new focus of policies under these changed circumstances, and new economic doctrines, at time reviving old ideas that had been pushed aside by the success of Keynesian economic policies, returned in academic circles and policy discussions under the broad heading of Monetarism. Ironically, Monetarism reinvented the Marxian idea that a 'reserve army' of labour is needed to keep a check on the real wage (Kalecki 1943, reprinted in 1971) had already foreseen towards the end of the Second World War that 'political trade cycles' would be imposed deliberately, particularly in the name of sound finance (read, no deficit financing) to inflict unemployment from time to time on the workers, in order to keep control over the workers. These ideas returned in the orthodox monetarist framework of economic theory as the 'natural rate' of unemployment (Friedman 1968), or as the non-accelerating inflation rate of unemployment, NAIRU (Layard, Nickell and Jackman 1991). They all had a common theme insofar as they propounded the view that, keeping inflation and inflationary expectations under control requires accepting a certain, it may even be a fairly high, rate of unemployment. In particular, it requires giving up demand management policies intended at keeping the rate of unemployment lower than that 'natural' or NAIRU rate. Since deficit financing by the government had been the most potent instrument used for demand management, unsurprisingly it came under special attack. The doctrine of the virtues of a balanced budget, and the evils of a fiscal deficit by a self-seeking government in the name of 'public choice theory' were propounded as general truths, applicable to almost all countries under all circumstances.

The wider process of globalization that gathered almost irresistible momentum with the deregulation of national capital markets since the mid-1970s in OECD countries also contributed to this change in the climate of opionion to a significant extent. The greater economic opening-up in goods and services trade has meant an increase in the relative importance of the foreign or external market compared to the domestic or internal market. It encourages countries to stimulate demand through export surplus, rather than through demand management by the fiscal policies of the government. As a result, each country tries to be more price competitive compared to its rivals, by cutting unit cost through wage 'flexibility' on the one hand, and raising labour productivity on the other. Yet there is an obvious 'fallacy of composition' in this strategy; because all countries cannot achieve export surplus at the same time as the export surplus of some must be matched by the import surplus of others. But, even for any particular country, which does manage to achieve an export surplus in this zero-sum game, such policies may turn out to be counter-productive if the contraction in the size of its internal market more than outweighs the expansion of its external market.

The danger of over-contraction of domestic demand from such policies is serious in many countries. Wage restraint depresses consumption by the working people, while labour productivity growth brought about by the corporations through the downsizing of the domestic labour force reinforces this depressive effect. Analytically, this may be identified as the wage or consumption-led regime in which the depressive effect on consumption of wage restraint and downsizing outweigh its possible stimulating effect on investment and export (Bhaduri and Marglin 1990). And yet, this danger of a sharp decline in domestic demand tends to be overlooked in policy discussions, not due to ignorance, but for reasons that have become intrinsic to the current phase of globalization.

Successive waves of deregulation and liberalization of capital markets since the mid-1970s has unleashed private trade in foreign exchange on an historically unprecedented level. In comparison to its daily volume of some 1.2 trillion dollars (BIS 2001-2002), the total foreign exchange reserve of all the central banks is insignificantly small, while foreign trade and investment together do not account for even 4 per cent of it. The economic policies of national governments seem overwhelmed by the power of the financial markets. In particular, this has generally meant that expansionary fiscal policies for fighting serious unemployment through budget deficits are generally not favoured options by financial markets; and therefore by national governments. Similarly, easy money policies with lower interest rates are not favoured either, insofar as they stimulate consumption and investment expenditure (for example hire-purchase, inventory accumulation, housing and so on), and tend to strain the current account of the balance of payments through lower borrowing cost. Moreover, financial markets often read the lowering of the interest rate as signalling the government's intention of embarking on expansionary fiscal policies. The fear that private capital would vote with its feet in the foreign exchange market by crossing borders on a massive scale has crippled fiscal and monetary policies required to fight growing unemployment.

However, there has been a significant difference in this respect between the United States and Europe. Due to the reserve currency status of the dollar, the United States manages to run growing current account deficits and a relatively free national demand-management policy, while the rest of the world, especially Japan and Germany as important export surplus countries, continues to finance the US import surplus in the form of capital inflow into the USA. This is no longer because of the international 'store of value' property of the US dollar; these export surplus countries are almost locked into this arrangement, because economically they have come to depend too heavily for their export surplus on the US market for maintaining demand, while politically they perceive their national defence capability as being dependent on the USA.

The consequence has been a peculiar paradox about national employment policies which is seldom commented upon. The current strength of the euro has been bought at the cost of restrictive fiscal policies imposed by the Maastricht 'stability pact', and even more restrictive monetary policies pursued by an independent European Central Bank. But if the euro becomes an international 'store of value' through its strength replacing largely the dollar, capital inflows to the USA would be sharply reduced, reducing in turn the export market, particularly for the large export surplus nations like Germany or Japan. As a result, they would face an even more serious unemployment problem. Thus, with the present international financial arrangements and policies, the paradox is that the euro and the yen seem doomed to remain 'strong' currencies without becoming alternative international stores of wealth. Consequently, the privilege to run large trade deficits continuously by issuing paper liabilities accepted by the rest of the world—the privilege based on the international store of value status of a currency — which England had before the first world war, and the USA has enjoyed since the second world war, needs to be denied to these countries. The wisdom of following restrictive monetary and fiscal policies that inflict high unemployment also needs to be examined in the light of this paradoxical international financial arangement.

THEORIES AND COUNTER-THEORIES FOR ECONOMIC POLICIES

The macroeconomic perspective justifying restrictive monetary and fiscal policies is neoliberal in its essence. since its general philosophy is to roll back the economic role of the state, it is natural that it would view adequate employment creation as the job of the private sector, and not of the state. At best, the role of the state is seen as creating the 'right' climate for the private sector by increasing its profitability, so that it offers sufficient employment. In this respect it has three distinguishing characteristics contrary to the Keynesian theory.

First, unlike Keynes and Kelecki, who identified the lack of effective demand in the product market as the central cause of unemployment, these theories locate the central cause of unemployment in the labour market. In terms of policy, this means demand management in the product market becomes less important than correcting the malfunctioning of the labour market. This deemphasizes the role of demand management on the one hand, and brings to the forefront the importance of labour-market 'flexibility' on the other.

Secondly, even the branch of theory relatively sympathetic to the Keynesian view (for example the neo-Keynesians), tends to make a distinction between the 'short run' and the 'long run'. It is claimed that there may be insufficiency of demand in the product market in the short run, but somehow the demand problem is resolved in the long run by the market. This is starkly visible in almost all versions of neo-classical long-run growth theory which assumes away the demand problem as a short-run phenomenon.

Thirdly, and perhaps most basic to this neo-liberal way of thinking, is its foundation of 'methodological individualism'. It uses some procedure of optimization by the individual agent as the central organizing principle of macroeconomic theory. Approaching macroeconomic problems exclusively in this way has many serious ramifications, and insofar as the unemployment problem is concerned perhaps its most serious consequence is to blur the distinction between 'voluntary' and 'involuntary' unemployment. Thus, all unemployment, even mass unemployment, begins to look voluntary in this framework, because it has to be explained through some optimizing decision by the individual worker, but not by a failure of the system which requires intervention.

This then becomes attributable to the imperfect functioning of the price mechanism for giving wrong signals to the worker. In some cases government interventions, mostly related to the welfare state, are supposed to distort the signals carried by wages. An important case in point is the criticism levelled against social safety nets like unemployment benefits provided by the government. A widely prevalent view, propagated by the media as well as some academic economists, is that it raises the 'reservation wage' so much that the worker chooses voluntarily to be unemployed. Another version with a similar thrust is to claim that the worker refuses to take up employment at the prevailing wage, either because (s)he is misinformed and spends all his or her time in search of a better job, or waits until the wage rate becomes higher. For a non-economist with some common sense these theories lie only a little distance away from the view that some are unemployed because they are lazy or unreasonably ambitious who do not know their 'market worth'. In this framework either the jobless worker becomes responsible for his or her own situation; or the blame is put on government intervention.

Neo-liberalism relying on the market rather than the government to deal with problems like unemployment has a different kind of advantage which is seldom recognized. Nothing in economic theory specifies how long it might take to reach 'equilibrium', through the market mechanism, even under the most idealized circumstances of perfect competition, when the competitive equilibrium has all the desirable properties of so-called Pareto-optimality by the 'fundamental theorem' of welfare economics. In democracies, the government and the politicians in power remain accountable to their people at regular time intervals through the elections, but the market mechanism has no such definite time horizon for showing results. And, this ambiguity helps in sustaining the market ideology insofar as it can always be claimed that, given 'sufficient' time and 'sufficiently' wide-ranging pro-market reforms, the desired results would materialize without having to specify how long is sufficiently long. The market mechanism, like a dictator, can always promise without actually delivering!

The virtues of sticking adamantly to pro-market policies as the solution to the unemployment problem get further strengthened by the role of the media. The enormous power wielded by electronic media and television images in shaping public opinion was noticed by perceptive commentators even in the very early stage of current globalization (see for example McLuhan 1960). It helps in spreading a sort of a popular culture in economic policy, policies that can be easily comprehended by 'practical' men and women. In this respect, most appealing is the analogy with the individual. Since spending beyond means is considered bad for the individual, a budget deficit of the government is also considered bad; because the demand for apples can be raised by lowering its price, the demand for labour can also be raised by lowering the wage rate; hard work helps, so a corporate manager helps the economy by downsizing its labour force. Underlying these pronouncements, popularized by the media, is the foundation of 'methodological individualism'. Unfortunately, politicians become victims of it, even if some of them understand better, because political expendiency often demands that they do not swim against the current of popular 'understanding'.

Nevertheless, this popular culture of viewing macroeconomic policies exclusively through the neo-liberal glass of methodological individualism goes against the very logic of having macroeconomics as a distinct branch of enquiry. The later is justified, precisely in those situations when the analogy with the individual is misleading. And, serious unemployment is perhaps the most important example of such a situation, as the Keynesian theory demonstrated. The common mistake in all arguments based on methodological individualism is to fall into the fallacy of composition. Thus, cutting wages may improve the profit margin for one firm, but the total volume of sales in the economy is likely to suffer. Downsizing the labour force may reduce unit cost for one firm, but when followed by many firms it may reduce total employment and the volume of sales in the économy. Even export surplus for one country must be balanced by the import surplus of another; so the strategy of export-led expansion cannot work for all. These familiar examples show why the argument that holds for the individual part may fail to hold for the whole system. Keynesian macroeconomic theory is based precisely on this premise, and the fundamental insight that, unlike in the case of the individual, the macroeconomy is characterized by a circular flow from expenditure to income. Expenditure by creating demand may determine output and employment in situations of serious unemployment and excess capacity.

Policies For High Employment

It is against this intellectual background that we need to reconsider policies for attaining and sustaining higher employment. However, at the very outset of this policy discussion it is worth pointing out that many different types of projects may be devised for generating employment. By and large these projects would be country-specific, dependent on geography, stage of development, degree of openness, and so on. The purpose of economic theory in this context is not to list a set of such projects irrespective of the country-specificity, but to indicate the direction in which an employment-generating and employment-sustaining programme can become feasible.

The problem of servicing debt exists, but it is far from clear why a government cannot take recourse to further borrowing to service its debt, so long as its higher spending is effective in raising the employment level and the rate of growth. The well-known result that so long as the growth rate exceeds the interest rate in real terms, the debt to income ratio tends to stabilize, might be invoked in this context to serve as a guide. On the whole it seems misplaced to argue that a growing debt-servicing burden necessarily strains the credibility of a government under all circumstances. A government's economic credibility might indeed suffer more due to persisting high unemployment and low growth. Therefore, the real issue to be faced is whether government spending can be effective in raising productive employment opportunities and growth prospects.

This is indeed the crux of the problem, and needs to be decomposed in two parts. First, to the extent the economy faces insufficiency of demand with excess capacity, the traditional Keynesian remedy should be reasonably effective provided the composition of demand, governed mostly by income elasticities, is broadly in line with the pattern of excess capacities in various industries. In that case, until it really begins to overheat the labour market, even the financial markets might not react unfavourably. Anyway, with considerable excess capacity, inaction is no solution in the face of growing unemployment.

The second part of the problem is to devise suitable programmes for government spending. Going against received wisdom, it needs to be pointed out that extensive labour training schemes of various sort can not be of much help. Because, although it might improve labour productivity, without strong demand-side policies such training would only raise the bar for entering the labour market. Thus, while the better trained persons would probably have a higher chance of getting a job, macroeconomically it would not be a very effective policy for the entire labour force. It would be rather like changing the positions of the candidates in a long queue for a fixed number of jobs, without being able to shorten the length of the queue.

A better policy with respect to training might be to have a government and private sector forum to agree on the types of training needed in view of both the composition of demand and cost-effectiveness. The training programmes would be partly financed by the government on the understanding that the private firms would simultaneously provide on-the-job training as the rest of the financing.

Second, instead of large centralized projects, it might be better to decentralize them. This would at least have the advantage of identifying the regions in which government spending has been relatively more effective in fighting unemployment, and would thus introduce an element of competition into the allocation of public funds.

Finally, in the post-industrial societies with aging populations, there might be considerable scope for creating innovative services for the aged. Note that better care of the aged is a demand that cannot be easily saturated, and therefore provides a longer-term perspective on the directions of training and public spending. For financially sustaining these programmes, the government and beneficiaries might share the costs through voluntary schemes of using part of pension and insurance funds. It is the increased quality and productivity of labour in these so-called non-tradable areas of services, directed at the domestic rather than the external market, in which the future for a better quality of life with higher employment in post-industrial societies may well lie.

Beyond this suggested long-term path of development of the service industry, the problem of labour-market flexibility also has another long-run aspect which is overlooked in current policy discussions. Higher labour productivity tends to reduce prices by reducing unit costs in the more competitive industries. For given money wages, this raised the product wage rates in these industries, normally implying an increase in the overall real wage rate. therefore, unless labour productivity rises more or less in line with increasing real wage, the share of wages in income would tend to increase over time. However, the observed relative stability of the wage share over the longer run suggests that productivity growth itself adjusts to rising real wages, just as the wage claims of workers have to adjust to the growth in labour productivity. In the long run, therefore, a two-way relationship seems exist between the growth rate in wage and in productivity which might be a central driving force of 'endogenous' growth, making technology appear as 'neutral' to distribution in successful market economies (Bhaduri 2006) . In this virtuous circle of positive feedbacks or cumulative causation, growth in productivity tends to raise the real wage rate by lowering unit costs and prices due to competition among firms, while rising real wages induces firms to increase productivity for maintaining their profit margins. Viewed from this longer-run perspective, artificially imposed wage restraints might well weaken this complex positive feedback mechanism between productivity and real-wage, generating economywide increasing returns. This process has been recognized as a potent dynamic force in the successful development of capitalism, at least since Adam Smith identified division of labour as a main source of the wealth of nations. To ignore this dynamic force propelling long-term growth in the name of labour-market flexibility might turn out to be counter-productive, and not a sign of wisdom for the successful management of capitalism.

REFERENCES :

Bank for International Settlements (2001) *Central Bank Survey of Foreign Exchange and Derivatives Market Activity in April 2001,* preliminary global data, press release (9 October).

Bank for international Settlements (2002) 'Quarterly Review of International Banking and Financial Markets Development', *Statistical Annex* (March 2002).

Bhaduri, A. (1986) *Macroeconomics : The Dynamics of Commodity Production* (London : Palgrave Macmillan).

Bhaduri, A (2006) 'Endogenous Economic Growth : A New Approach', *Cambridge journal of Economics* 30 : 69-83.

Bhaduri, A. and Marglin, S. (1990) 'Unemployment and the Real Wage. The Economic Basis of Contesting Political Ideologies', *Cambridge Journal of Economics,* 14 : 375-95.

Bhaduri, A and Steindl. J. (1985) 'The Rise of Monetarism as a Social Doctrine', in P. Arestis and T. Skouras (eds) *Post-Keynesian Economic Theory* (Sussex : Weatsheaf).

Friedman, M. (1968) 'The Role of Monetary Policy', *American Economic Review,* 58 : 1-17.

Hobsbawm, E. (1994) *The Age of Extremes. A History of the World, 1914-1991* (New York : Pantheon Books).

Kalecki, M. (1971) 'Political Aspects of Full Employment' [1943], in M. Kalecki, *Selected Essays in the Dynamics of the Capitalist Economy* (Cambridge : Cambridge University Press).

Layard, R., Nickell, S. and Jackman, R. (1991) *Unemployment Macroeconomic Performance and the Labour Market* (Oxford : Oxford University Press).

Marglin, S. and Schor, J. (eds) (1990) *The Golden Age of Capitalism* (Oxford : Oxford University Press).

McLuhan, M. (1960) *Explorations in Communications* (Ontario : University of Toronto Press).

Rowthorn, R. (1977) 'Conflict, Inflation and Money', *Cambridge Journal of Economics,* 1 : 215-39.

ON THE DYNAMICS OF PROFIT-LED AND WAGE-LED GROWTH

The Problem

In the traditional multiplier analysis saving as an endogenous variable adjusts to investment as an exogenous variable in two different ways. The adjustment takes place either through changes in the level of income (Kahn, 1972; Kalecki, 1971; Keynes, 1936, 1937) or in its distribution, the latter brought about by disparate movements between the price level and the money wage rate leading to 'profit inflation' and forced saving by the workers (Hicks, 1967; Kaldor, 1956; Keynes, 1930; Pasinetti, 1962). Consequently, the same multiplier mechanism has the dual task of determining both the level of output and its distribution through the single equation of saving investment equality in equilibrium.

The problem of how to determine endogenously both the level and the distribution of income can be dealt with from different-angles. It is simplest to assume that output adjusts below full employment, while at full employment prices rises faster than money wages to close the inflationary gap. The same problem can also be dealt with through larger models within a Keynesian demand-determined framework, providing additional equations for the labour market, the money market, inventory adjustment etc.[1] However, following the original lead of Keynes (1930, 1936), this paper examines the multiplier mechanism by focusing exclusively on the product market. By removing the assumption that a precise level of full employment or full capacity output separates quantity from price adjustment, our approach permits both the level and the distribution of income to adjust simultaneously at different speeds during the working of the multiplier process. It results in a characterisation of this process in a dynamic 'partial' equilibrium framework involving two adjustment equations for the product market relating to the level and distribution of income. Thus, the paper extends the multiplier analysis to situations characterised by the two-way feedback between changes in investment and saving on the one hand, and variations in capacity utilisation and distribution on the other. The dynamic interaction among the variables gives rise to a range of possibilities, which are classified with a view of exploring their ability to restore saving investment equilibrium, while the accompanying changes in output and distribution also link them analytically with profit-led or wage-led expansion in both in and out-of-equilibrium situations.

Profit-led And Wage-led Equilibrium Locus

In a closed economy, any redistribution of income between profits and wages affects aggregate demand through two different channels. If the propensity to consume out of wage income is higher than that to consume out of profit income, redistributing income against the wage earners would depress total consumption expenditure, but at the same time it might stimulate investment expenditure through higher profit-share to counteract the depressing effect of lower consumption on aggregate demand. Depending on which of these two effects dominates quantitatively, two alternative possibilities emerge for demand-led expansion. The case dominated by greater consumption expenditure due to higher real wages and lower profit-share is called wage-led, whereas the case dominated by greater investment expenditure due to higher profit-share and lower real wages is termed as profit-led.[2]

The essential formalism of these two regimes is easy to capture by normalising the relevant variables with respect to full capacity output (Y*). Thus, under the simplifying Classical assumption that no fraction of wage and a constant fraction, s, $(1 \geq s > 0)$ of profit is saved, the (normalised) saving, S, of the economy is written as,

$$S = s.h.z, \;\; 1 \geq z, h \geq 0, \tag{1}$$

where h = share of profit in output; and $z = (Y/Y^*)$ degree of capacity utilisation, with $z = 1$, i.e. the normalised level of full capacity output.

To examine the interaction between investment and saving in response to variable levels of output and income distribution, we assume that (normalised) investment (I) depends positively also on the same two variables, z and h. Expectations are assumed to be formed in a climate of business as usual', so that 'conventions' rule (Keynes, 1937), and the ruling expectations formed by extrapolating the current state of affairs into the future, are static. On these assumptions, the investment function is written as[3],

$$I = I(z,h),\ I_z>0,\ I_h>0. \tag{2}$$

Total differentiation of equations (1) and (2) yields the slope of the equilibrium locus of saving-investment equality, or the IS curve in the h.z space as,

$$dz/dh = (I_h\text{-}sz)/(sh\text{-}I_z). \tag{3}$$

Along the equilibrium IS locus, a positive slope of the IS curve in equation (3) means that a higher profit share *(h)* is associated in equilibrium with higher capacity utilisation (*z*), characterising a regime of profit-led equilibrium positions. Alternately, a negative slope in equation (3), associating a lower profit share with higher capacity utilisation corresponds to the wage-led equilibrium positions.

It is well known that the convergence of the one-variable output adjustment through the multiplier process requires saving to be more responsive than investment to changes in income, implying the Keynesian stability condition,

$$(sh\text{-}Iz)>0. \tag{4}$$

When equation (4) is satisfied, the denominator on the right hand side of expression (3) is positive, while a positive numerator of equation (3) implies,

$$(I_h - sz)>0 \tag{5}$$

Conditions (4) and (5) together yield a positively sloped IS curve depicting a continuum of profit-led equilibrium positions. Since inequality (5) also means that the stimulating effect of a higher profit share on investment outweighs its depressing effect on consumption expenditure, it is natural at least provisionally to interpret condition (5) as the requirement for profit-led regimes. And, with inequality (5) reversed, i.e.

$$(I_h\text{-}sz)<0, \tag{6}$$

The economy satisfies, for the opposite reason, the requirement of wage-led regimes (Bhaduri and Marglin, 1990). Note, however, that this equilibrium interpretation of profit-led and wage-led regimes in terms of the responses of investment and saving to profit share (equations 5 or 6) depends crucially on the stabilising leakage from saving being greater than the stimulating injection of investment due to changes in income (equation 4), while profit share is treated as exogenous.

Stability

Since the equality between investment and saving holds, all points on the IS curve are equilibrium rest points for both z and h. Comparisons of different points on the IS curve could be interpreted as 'movement' along the IS curve by treating one of the variables, z or h, as a policy parameter whose value can be exogenously fixed. In effect, this reduces the underlying dynamical system to a single variable, with the other variable treated as exogenous. In the above analysis h is treated as exogenous, reducing the system to the usual Keynesian income determination process, with capacity utilisation (z) as the only variable adjusting to excess demand in the product market. In this case the quantity-adjustment equation is written explicitly from equations (1) and (2) as,

$$dz/dt = \alpha\,[I(h,z)\text{-}shz],\quad \alpha > 0, \tag{7}$$

where α is some arbitrary positive speed of adjustment, h is exogenously given by assumption, and condition (4) holds for the stability of the adjustment process.

However, the adjustment process in equation (7), although stable under condition (4), might not remain stable if income distribution h is also allowed to adjust endogenously.[1] The endogenous adjustment in h takes place if both the price level and the money wage rate rise at disparate rates in response to the product market disequilibrium.[5] In general the price-money wage dynamics would be influenced by the state of demand in the product market, the inventory positions of the firms, and in particular, by the extent of unemployment, and the bargaining power of the contending parties in the labour market (cf. Chiarella and Flaschel, 2000). However, these complications are avoided in the present analysis to focus exclusively on the flow equilibrium (I=S) in the product market.[6]

If both z and h adjust in response to investment saving disequilibrium, in addition to equation (7) we have,

$$dh/dt = \beta[I(h,z)\text{-}shz],\quad \beta > 0 \text{ or } \beta < 0 \tag{8}$$

Equation (8) generalises the usual Keynesian argument. In the neoclassical interpretations of Keynesian theory, it is argued that an excess demand in the product market is closed through a higher level of output produced by profit-maximising firms at a lower real wage rate. Thus, profit-maximising equilibrium is reached through forced saving by the workers, either owing to 'money illusion' (Keynes, 1936; Trevithick, 1975), to unanticipated inflation (Friedman, 1968) or to some other form of information failure (Blachand, 1990).[7] In our formalism, forced saving by the workers corresponds to the case of $\beta > 0$ in equation (8), because it ensures a falling real wage rate and rising profit share in response to excess demand in the product market ($I > S$). However, the present formulation is more general, in so far as it allows also for the opposite case of profit squeeze imposed on the firms by the workers. It is captured by $\beta < 0$ in equation (8), as in this case the money wage rate rises faster than the price-level with the result that the real wage rises and the profit share falls in response to excess demand in the product market. Between forced saving and profit squeeze lies the borderline case in which the real wage rate remains constant, i.e. $\beta = 0$ (Kalecki, 1971; also Keynes, 1939). However, this particular case will not be considered further, as it leaves us formally with only the case of pure quantity-adjustment in equation (7).[8]

Equations (7) and (8) are identical except for the multiplicative factors of the speeds of adjustment α and β, respectively. Consequently, the dynamical system defined by them is under-determined. Thus, in equilibrium the adjustment speeds play no role, and the investment saving equality provides only one equation for determining endogenously both h and z. However, in the out-of-equilibrium dynamics the speeds of adjustment play their role in guiding the trajectories. The slope of the integral curve obtained from dividing equation (7) by equation (8) at non-zero (i.e. out-of-equilibrium) values indicate how the adjustment speeds influence the out-of equilibrium behaviour of the system on the $h.z$ plane, i.e.

$$dz/dh = \alpha/\beta, \text{ where } \alpha>0, \text{ and } \beta>0 \text{ or } \beta<0. \qquad (9)$$

When $\alpha > 0$ and $\beta > 0$, in view of equations (7) and (8) both z and h rise endogenously in response to excess demand in the product market, and the out-of-equilibrium dynamics appear profit-led with forced saving by the workers. On the other hand, if $\alpha > 0$, but $\beta < 0$, an excess of investment over saving would drive h and z in opposite directions, and the out-of-equilibrium dynamics would become wage-led with profit squeeze (Goodwin, 1967). Therefore, we are able to ascertain the equilibrium and the out-of-equilibrium slope on the *h.z* plane by using equations (3) and (9) respectively.

The local stability of the dynamical system (7) and (8) is examined through routine calculation of the trace and the determinant of the relevant partial derivatives evaluated at an equilibrium point on the IS curve. The condition of a negative trace for stability is,

$$\alpha(I_z\text{-}sh) + \beta(I_h\text{-}sz) < 0. \tag{10}$$

However, the determinant is zero because the two linearised equations (7) and (8) around the equilibrium value are linearly dependent, i.e. $\begin{pmatrix} \alpha(I_z-sh) & \alpha(I_h-sz) \\ \beta(I_z-sh) & \beta(I_h-sz) \end{pmatrix} = 0$ showing a continuum of equilibria along the IS curve.

With the determinant zero and the trace negative, one characteristic root is negative and the other zero, implying local stability.

The local stability analysis might be extended to a larger neighbourhood domain of the equilibrium by considering the function,

$$V = (1/2)[I(z,h) - shz]^2, \tag{11}$$

Since in that domain all the partial derivatives are assumed to exist and are continuous, and *V* is positive definite, stability within the domain is guaranteed by the second method of Liapunov so long as dV/dt < 0 (Arrowsmith and Place, 1982, p. 198; Gandolfo, 1995).[9] Differentiating equations (1) and (2) with respect to time, and substituting from equations (7) and (8), we obtain,

$$dV/dt = (I - S)^2.\ [\alpha(I_z - sh) + \beta(I_h - sz)] < 0, \tag{12}$$

yielding the same trace stability as in condition (10).

Interpreted economically, elimination of excess demand in the commodity market requires that (dI/dt) < (dS/dt) for (I–S) > 0, and (dI/dt) > (dS/dt) for (I–S) < 0. Differentiating equations (1) and (2) with respect to time, and substituting from equations (7) and (8), inequality (10) can be derived as a product term covering both situations (I–S) > 0, and (I–S) < 0. Therefore, with stability condition (10) satisfied, the generalised multiplier converges within the given domain, as the net 'leakage' from the income generation process through saving from changes in both *z* and *h* exceeds the net 'injection' to the same income generation process through investment.

Stability condition (10) involves four terms, and if each were allowed to take either a positive or a negative value, there would be $2^4 = 16$ possible combinations. However, with α restricted by assumption to positive values, the number of possibilities gets reduced to $2^3 = 8$, which can be classified into two equal groups of four each in terms of their stability properties. In the former group, the stability property is unambiguous, irrespective of the magnitudes of the speeds of adjustment, whereas in the latter group, the relative magnitudes of the adjustment speeds matter.

When both the product terms, $\alpha(I_z — sh)$ and $\beta(I_h — sz)$, have the same sign, expression (10) is unambiguously either positive (i.e. unstable) or negative (i.e. stable). Thus, the system is unambiguously unstable in 2 cases, i.e. if, either $\alpha > 0$, $(I_z — sh) > 0$, $\beta > 0$, and $(I_h — sz) > 0$, or $\alpha > 0$, $(I_z — sh) > 0$, $\beta < 0$ and $(I_h - sz) < 0$. In the former case, according to equation (3) the combination of parameter values implies wage-led equilibrium along the IS curve but its out-of-equilibrium unstable dynamics is profit-led according to equation (9). In the latter case, the opposite holds, namely that the system is profit-led in equilibrium along the IS curve, but when out-of-equilibrium it is wage-led and unambiguously unstable.

The system is unambiguously stable in the opposite case when both the product terms involved in the stability condition (10) are negative, i.e. $\alpha>0$, $(I_z — sh)<0$, $\beta>0$, $(I_h — sz) < 0$, implying wage-led equilibrium along the IS curve according to equation (3), but profit-led stable out-of-equilibrium dynamics by equation (9) (Figure 1). Or, alternatively, $\alpha > 0$, $(I_z — sh) < 0$, $\beta < 0$, $(I_h — sz) > 0$, implying equilibrium along the IS curve is profit-led by equation (3), but stable out-of-equilibrium dynamics is wage-led by equation (9) (Figure 2).[10]

Closer geometric inspection of the phase diagrams reveals the pattern that in cases of unambiguous stability (or instability), equilibrium movement along the IS curve according to equation (3), and out-of-equilibrium movement according to equation (9) are characterized by contradictory properties of the two regimes. Thus, in the unambiguously stable cases, if the equilibrium movement is wage-led because h and z are negatively related along the IS curve, the out-of-equilibrium stable dynamics is profit-led as h and z move together along the trajectory of the resultant arrow (see Figure 1), and vice versa (see Figure 2).[11]

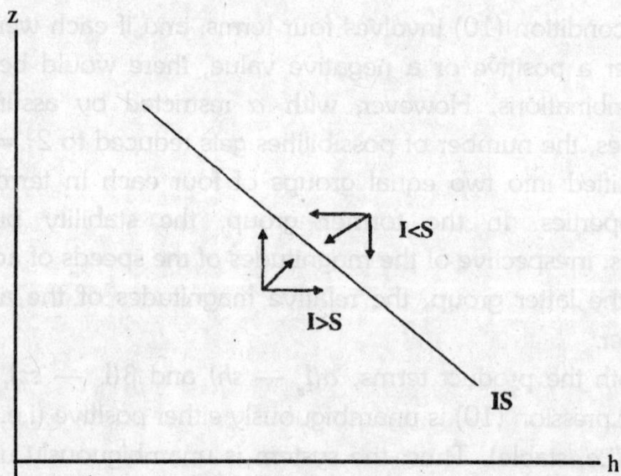

Fig. 1. *Wage-led in equilibrium;profit-led out-of-equilibrium. Below the line, I> S at low output:* $(I_z - sh) < 0$; *or low profile share:* $(I_h - sz) < 0$. *Output rises (stabilising) with forced saving (stabilising):* $\alpha > 0$, $\beta > 0$.[12]

The relative magnitudes of the speeds of adjustment enter the stability condition (10) in an essential way in the remaining group of four cases yielding ambiguous stability property (Figures 3-6). In these cases, the stability condition (10) involving the two product terms, $\alpha(I_z - sh)$ and $\beta(I_h - sz)$, have opposite signs, so that the relative magnitudes of α and β become critical in determining the sign of their algebraic sum. Since the negative term implies leakage from, and the positive term entails injection into aggregate demand, leakage has to dominate injection quantitatively to satisfy stability condition (10). From this point of view, the relation between in and out-of-equilibrium movement also needs to be understood in terms of the behaviour of excess demand (I > S) or supply (I< S) in the product market. The IS curve divides in all cases the phase plane into regimes of excess (I > S) or deficit (I < S) of investment over saving.[13] From an economic point of view, in situations of excess demand (I > S), stability requires that the leakage of demand from increases in saving outweighs the injection from increases in investment, while the quantitative strengths of leakage and injection depend also on the magnitudes of the speeds of adjustment. Thus, when Keynesian stability condition (4) is violated but condition (6) holds, the equilibrium IS regime is profit-led according to the slope of the IS curve (Figure 4). In this case, net leakage increases at a higher profit share owing to inequality condition (6), which has to be fortified by the further assumption that the speed of adjustment in profit share $\beta > 0$ is sufficiently large to close the excess investment gap, as saving increases faster than investment with increasing profit share (Figure 4, upper right corner). This implies an apparently paradoxical situation in which saving increases more than investment with higher profit share in a regime which is profit-led, according to not only the equilibrium slope condition in equation (3), but also the disequilibrium slope condition (9) (Figure 4). Similarly, if falling profit share due to profit squeeze reduces investment more rapidly than saving, the excess demand gap decreases at a lower profit share in an otherwise wage-led regime and stabilises the system, provided the speed of adjustment, $\beta < 0$ is sufficiently large in absolute value (Figure 6). Therefore, our previous classification of regimes needs to be qualified by the understanding that

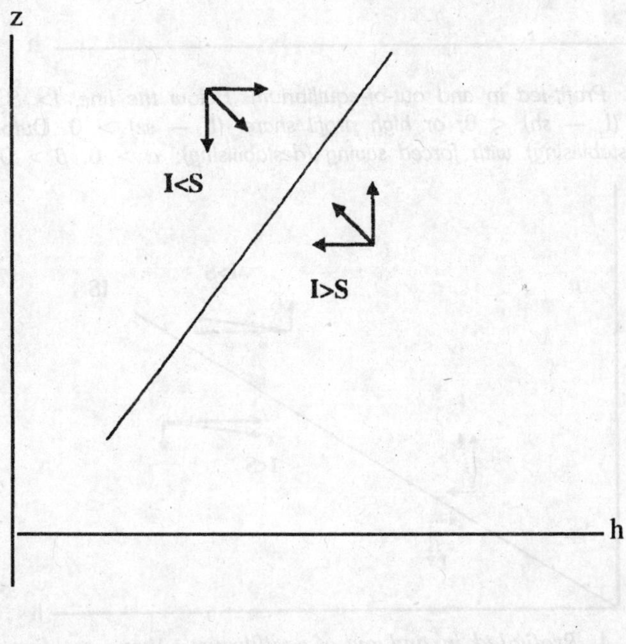

Fig. 2. *Profit-led in equilibrium; wage-led out-of-equilibrium. Below the line, I> S at low output:* $(I_z - sh) < 0$; *or high profit share: (If, — sz)* > 0. *Output rises (stabilising) while profits are squeezed (stabilising):* $\alpha > 0$, $\beta < 0$.

investment does not necessarily rise more (less) than saving with increasing (decreasing) profit share in a regime that appears profit-led (wage-led) by the signs of the slopes in equations (3) and (9), which is positive (negative) for profit-led (wage-led) regimes.

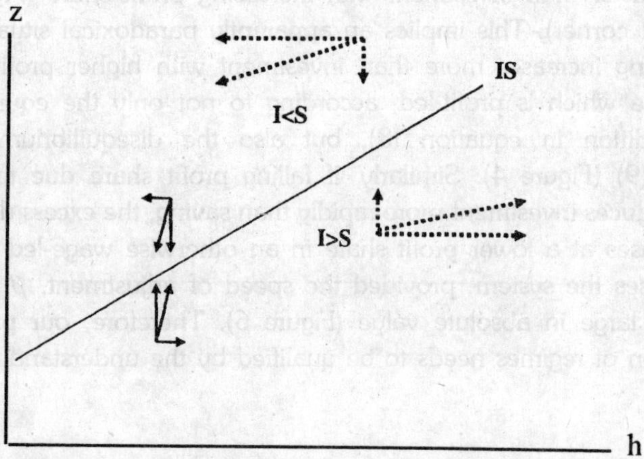

Fig. 3. *Profit-led in and out-of-equilibrium. Below the line, $I > S$ at low output: $(I_z - sh) < 0$; or high profit share: $(I_h - sz) > 0$. Output rises (stabilising) with forced saving (destabilising): $\alpha > 0$, $\beta > 0$.*

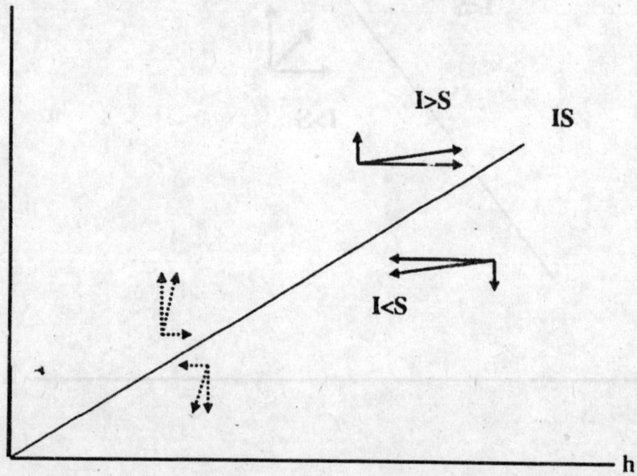

Fig. 4. *Profit led in and out-of-equilibrium. Above the line $I > S$ at high output : $(I_z - Sh) > 0$, or low profit share : $(I_h - sz) < 0$. Output rises (destabilising) with forced saving (stabilising) : $\alpha > 0$, $\beta > 0$.*

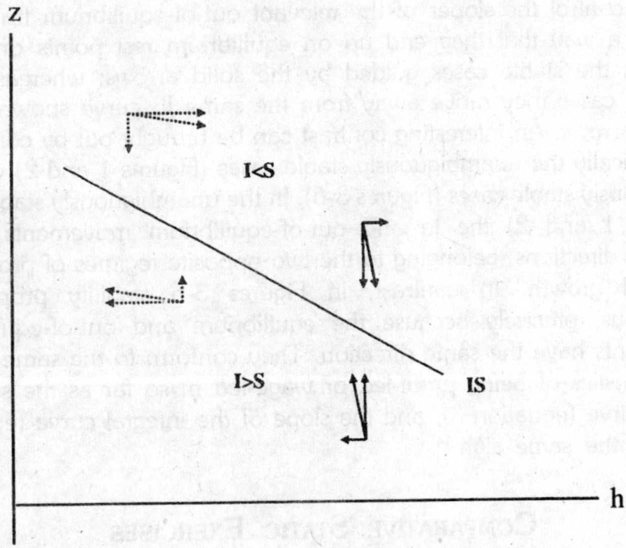

Fig. 5. *Wage-led in and out-of-equilibrium. Below the line,* $I > S$ *at low output:* $(I_z - sh) < 0$; *or low profit share:* $(I_h - sz) < 0$. *Output rises (stabilising) with profit squeeze (destabilising):* $\alpha > 0$, $\beta < 0$.

All the four phase diagrams of ambiguous stability in Figures 3-6 reveal a general pattern. The relative magnitudes of the speeds of adjustment, shown by the relative lengths of the vertical and horizontal

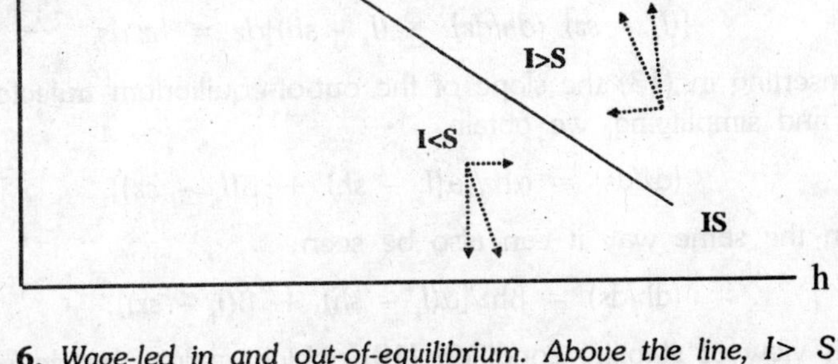

Fig. 6. *Wage-led in and out-of-equilibrium. Above the line,* $I > S$ *at high output:* $(I_z - sh) > 0$; *or high profit share:* $(I_h - sz) > 0$. *Output rises (destabilising) with profit squeeze (stabilising):* $\alpha > 0$, $\beta < 0$.

arrows, control the slopes of the relevant out-of-equilibrium trajectories in such a way that they end up on equilibrium rest points on the IS curve in the stable cases guided by the solid arrows; whereas in the unstable cases they move away from the same IS curve shown by the broken arrows. An interesting contrast can be brought out by comparing geometrically the unambiguously stable cases (Figures 1 and 2) with the ambiguously stable cases (Figures 3-6). In the unambiguously stable cases (Figures 1 and 2) the in and out-of-equilibrium movements are in opposite directions, belonging to the two opposite regimes of profit- and wage-led growth. In contrast, in Figures 3-6 stability property is ambiguous, precisely because the equilibrium and out-of-equilibrium movements have the same direction. They conform to the same regime characteristics of being profit-led or wage-led in so far as the slope of the IS curve (equation 3), and the slope of the integral curve (equation 9) have the same sign.[14]

Comparative Static Exercises

Our interest in comparative static exercises in the present context arises from the fact that they relate not to particular equilibrium positions, but to a continuum of equilibria along the IS curve. The equilibrium slope of the IS curve from equation (3), and the out-of-equilibrium slope from equation (9) are linked by the stability condition (10) to ensure that the relevant trajectories end up on the equilibrium IS curve. The comparative static exercise uses this property to examine how displacement through some parameter from the IS locus sets up trajectories in the stable cases for a return to the IS curve.

Consider first a parametric variation of the saving propensity.[15] Totally differentiating equations (1) and (2) with a variable saving propensity, and collecting terms, we obtain,

$$[(I_h - sz)\ (dh/dz) + (I_s - sh)]dz = hz.ds. \tag{13}$$

Inserting in (13) the slope of the out-of-equilibrium trajectory from (9), and simplifying, we obtain,

$$(dz/ds) = \alpha hz/[\alpha(I_z - sh) + \beta(I_h - sz)]. \tag{14}$$

In the same way it can also be seen,

$$(dh/ds) = \beta hz/[\alpha(I_z - sh) + \beta(I_h - sz)]. \tag{15}$$

In view of stability condition (10), which makes the denominator negative in equations (14) and (15), the comparative static result follows, i.e.$(dz/ds) < 0$, while $(dh/ds) < 0$ if $\beta > 0$, and $(dh/ds) > 0$ if $\beta < 0$.

A slightly different type of comparative static exercise can be carried out when a parameter, say the rate of interest *i*, affects investment and saving, i.e.

$I(h,z,i) = s(i)hz$, with the usual specifications $I_i < 0$ and $s'(i)>0$. (16)

Proceeding in the same way it can be seen that

$$(dz/di) = \alpha[hzs'(i) - I_i]/[\alpha(I_h - sz) + \beta(I_z - sh)] \quad (17)$$

$$(dh/di) = \beta[hzs'(i) - I_i]/[\alpha(I_h - sz) + \beta(I_z - sh)] \quad (18)$$

In view of equation (10), the above implies that in stable cases, $(dz/di) < 0$; $(dh/di) < 0$ if $\beta > 0$ and $(dh/di) > 0$ if $\beta < 0$. Note that the comparative static results about capacity utilisation involving α are unambiguous in sign irrespective of whether the regime is profit-led or wage-led. However, results about profit share involve the sign of β, and therefore depend on, whether the out-of-equilibrium regime is profit-led or wage-led according to equation (9).

Summary And Observations

With its focus exclusively on the product market in a partial equilibrium framework, this paper examines the convergence of the multiplier process in a setting of variable output (z) and income distribution (*h*) interacting with changes in investment (I) and saving (*S*). The approach is formalised on the assumption that both S and I depend on *h* and *z* (equations 1 and 2), while the gap between I and S affects both *h* and *z*, giving rise to a pair of identical differential equations, which differ only with respect to their speeds of adjustment (equations 7 and 8). This leads in turn to different characterisations of profit-led and wage-led regimes, both in and out-of-equilibrium, according to the signs of the slopes of the IS-locus (equation 3) and the out-of-equilibrium trajectories (equation 9) on the *h.z* plane. The framework is also able to accommodate a wide range of possibilities for adjustment in the distribution of income through downward as well as upward variation in the real wage rate. While forced saving on the part of the workers owing to money illusion, unanticipated inflation or some other form of information failure is analysed ($\beta > 0$), the less discussed opposite case of profit squeeze is also considered ($\beta < 0$). Depending on the values of the various parameters, the formal analysis establishes that both forced saving and profit squeeze can lead to stability (condition 10), and restore the equilibrium between investment and saving. In some cases the system can even be unambiguously stable under profit squeeze irrespective of the speeds of adjustment of capacity utilisation and income distribution (Figure 2). Therefore the neoclassical postulate is unwarranted that some version of money illusion is critical for output expansion through the stimulation of demand.[16]

Our analysis classifies the (eight) cases considered into two analytically distinct groups of equal size. Two unambiguously stable and two unambiguously unstable cases form the first group. The other group of the remaining four cases have ambiguous stability properties because stability in these cases depends on the relative magnitudes of the speed of adjustment of capacity utilisation *(z)* and distribution *(h)*. A comparison of equilibrium and out-of-equilibrium dynamics traced by the two groups revealed a contrast. In the unambiguously stable (or unstable) cases equilibrium movement indicated by the sign of the slope along the IS curve (equation 3) and the out-of-equilibrium movements given by the sign of the integral curve (equation 9) belong to opposite regimes, i.e. if the equilibrium movement along the IS curve is wage-led, the out-of-equilibrium movement is profit-led, and vice versa (Figures 1 and 2, respectively). In contrast, in the latter group of cases of ambiguous stability, both the equilibrium and the out-of-equilibrium movements belong to the same regime, as the slope of the IS in equation (3) and, of the integral curve in equation (9) have the same sign. This implies that movements both in and out-of-equilibrium are either profit- or wage-led (Figures 3-6), subject to the qualification already pointed out that profit-led (wage-led) does not necessarily imply that investment rises more than saving at higher (lower) profit share in all circumstances.

The significance of the analytical framework developed in this paper may be appreciated better in the context of a wider theoretical debate concerning the link between production and distribution. The link is established at the aggregate level of neoclassical macroeco-nomic theory (see also Keynes, 1936) through the postulate of a production function with standard properties coupled with the behavioural assumption of profit maximisation leading to the marginal productivity theory of distribution. However, it is now beyond dispute that the aggregate production function has insurmountable problems, and its use with capital as a factor of production cannot be justified logically outside a one-commodity world (Samuelson, 1966; Sraffa, 1960). Therefore, the neoclassical link between production and distribution through an aggregate production function is unacceptably restricted. The analysis presented here suggests an alternative route to linking production with distribution by attempting to integrate the views of the Classical economists with the Keynesian theory of effective demand, especially in the short-period context. The Classical approach was based on uncoupling long-period distribution from production. This paper suggests a different way in which the uncoupling of production and distribution might be achieved in the demand-determined framework. At the same time, it suggests how some supply-side problems might be incorporated in the Keynesian framework through explicit considerations of the speeds of adjustment in capacity utilisation and distribution. For instance, we might plausibly postulate that the speed of adjustment in capacity utilisation and its level, *z*, are usually inversely related. As the level of capacity utilisation increases, various bottlenecks or rigidities appear on the supply side, which tend to delay and slow down the speed of adjustment in capacity utilisation. As a matter of fact, this was presumed in drawing the phase diagrams in Figures 3-6 through suitable variations in the lengths of the vertical arrows (representing the magnitude of a) at relatively high and low levels of *z*. Similarly, it might be worth pondering whether the degree of tightness of the labour market and rising pressure on wages could be reflected in some ways through suitable modifications in the speed of adjustment of distribution.[17]

The dependence of the speeds of adjustment and on the variables *h* and *z* might result in non-linear trajectories with complex properties that need further exploration. However, consider a simple case in which β remains constant, but although always positive is inversely proportional to *z* according to the relation:[18]

$$\alpha = (k/z), z>0. \tag{19}$$

This implies that the constant, $k = \alpha_{min}$, which is denned at the maximum value of z = 1. Inserting equation (19) into stability condition (10) reduces to

$$[(I_z - sh)\alpha_{min}] + [z(I_h - sz)\beta]<0. \tag{20}$$

Moreover, *z* reaches a critical value z_c when the left hand side of equation (20) vanishes to yield,

$$z_c = [(I_z - sh)\alpha_{min}]/[(sz - I_h)\beta]. \tag{21}$$

Thus z_c, the point of bifurcation, separates stable from unstable cases.

In the light of equation (20), consider the four cases corresponding to the phase diagrams in Figures 3-6. In Figures 3 and 5, the first square bracketed term is negative, and the second positive. In Figures 4 and 6 the opposite sign pattern holds. For instance, as the gap *(I - S)* > 0 increases to raise *z*, the positive second term in equation (20), corresponding to phase diagrams in Figures 3 and 5, increases tending to destabilise the system, whereas in the phase diagrams in Figures 4 and 6 it tends to stabilise the system for the opposite reason. However, whether the system actually attains stability depends in each case on whether the relevant negative term increases sufficiently in absolute value to cross the bifurcation value z_c in equation (21). For instance, stability cannot be achieved in the cases of the phase diagrams in Figures 4 and 6 if even at the maximum value of $z = 1$, the left-hand side of the expression remains positive, implying that $(I — s)/(sh — I) > (\alpha_{min}/\beta)$, where the relevant partial derivatives are evaluated at $z = 1$.

We might also conjecture that with the trace (i.e. local stability) condition changing sign at the critical value, $1 > z_c > 0$, only a necessary condition for sustained endogenous fluctuations (e.g. limit cycles) is satisfied. However, since the determinant is strictly zero in the degenerate system of this model, it rules out possibilities of sustained fluctuations until richer dynamical systems are considered.

NOTES :

1. Recent important examples of research along these lines are Taylor (2004), Chiarella and Flaschel, (2000) and Skott (1989) among several others. Both Taylor and Chiarella also provide critical surveys of the literature and reformulations, constructing sophisticated higher dimension models involving various markets.
2. Bhaduri and Marglin (1990), Marglin and Bhaduri (1990) in their original formulation called the wage-led regime stagnationist, and the profit-led regime exhilarationist. See also Taylor (2004, p. 128); Foley and Mitchl (1999).
3. With money wage *(w)* as the only variable cost, x = labour productivity, and m = proportional mark-up on cost, price, p = $(1 + m)(w/x)$, so that $(1 - h) = (w/px)$, from which h is related positively to profit margin (m) by the expression, $h — m/(1 + m)$, implying $I_m > 0$ in equation (2).Thus, higher profit share might stimulate higher investment through higher profit margin, and also probably from higher retained profit.
4. Intuitively speaking, adjustment in z may be counteracted sufficiently by adjustment in h through its impact on I or 5.
5. It should also be mentioned here that the profit share may vary for other reasons, e.g. contra-cyclically due to fixed administrative wage cost and labour hoarding over the cycle (Kalecki, 1971; Okun, 1981).
6. Ignoring complications due to inventories restricts even the product market analysis to flow equilibrium without adjustment in the stock of inventories (Hicks, 1974).

7. In this way the theory of effective demand was reconciled with profit-maximising equilibrium under the assumption of diminishing return to labour in *The General Theory* (Keynes, 1936). However, Keynes (1939) soon realised that this way of dealing with the supply side, instead of strengthening damages the theory of effective demand. Nevertheless, this profit-maximising assumption is the distinguishing mark of mainstream textbooks interpreting Keynesian theory. The real wage rate, determined endogenously in the Keynesian system through the link between the money wage rate and the price-level cannot be treated as a policy variable, unlike in some neo-classical discussions; also see Taylor (2004, pp. 132-6) on this point.
8. When the nominal money wage rate chases the rising price level at the same rate, but with a constant time lag, the real wage rate is depressed by a constant fraction once for all with perpetual inflation at a constant rate (Keynes, 1940; Trevithick, 1975). Kalecki (1976) develops similar ideas to explain stagflation in a developing economy.
9. If (dV/dt) is negative definite, the equilibrium is asymptotically stable. A weaker Liapunov function would also guarantee stability if (dV/dt) is negative semi-definite.
10. Note that the unambiguously unstable cases violate the Keynesian stability condition (4), while the unambiguously stable cases satisfy the same stability condition.
11. The phase diagrams for the two unambiguously unstable cases are not included for reasons of space. They can be easily drawn to check that their unstable out-of-equilibrium trajectories have exactly the opposite direction to those indicated in the phase diagrams in Figures 1 and 2.
12. Note that in all the phase diagrams, Figures 1-6, classification of profit-led and wage-led regimes are done according to the signs of the slopes of the IS curve (equation 3), and of the integral curve (equation 9) to represent in and out-of-equilibrium directions of movement on the phase plane. However, unlike in the case of adjustment only in capacity utilization, discussed in relation to inequalities (5) and (6), the classification does not consider whether investment increases more or less than saving as profit share increases.
13. The division of the phase plane into $I > S$ and $I < S$ is done by considering the direction of the vertical arrow. By equation 7 if it directs upwards (downwards) $I > S$ ($I < S$).

14. Subject to the qualification discussed above that profit-led (wage-led) regime does not necessarily mean that / will rise more (less) than 5 with rising *h*. See also p. 7, fn. 2.
15. A decrease in the saving propensity due to the wealth effect of a boom in the stock market (Bhaduri, Laski and Riese, 2006; Maki and Palumbo, 2001) or in the housing market (Baker, 2006; Campbell and Cocco, 2006), as has been reported widely in recent years, could be analysed in this framework. See also Bhaduri (2005) for a similar exercise in the context of growth theory.
16. The assumption of profit-maximising equilibrium might be essential for neo-classical micro foundation, but it is not needed for the theory of demand-determined output (Kalecki, 1971; Keynes, 1939). See also p.4, fn. 4.
17. While a negative relation between *a* and *z* is presumed in the phase diagrams of Figures 3-6, variation in (3 in relation to a is assumed arbitrarily to facilitate geometric exposition of stability or instability property.
18. I owe to a referee the observation that the speed of adjustment can be negative in a long-run context when the two sided role of investment in capacity utilisation as well as in capacity creation comes into play. If capacity creation (Y^*) proceeds at a faster pace than capacity utilisation (Y) in certain boom conditions, the ratio (Y/Y^*), i.e. *z* might be falling, implying negative. Complication belonging to the longer run is avoided in the Keynesian short run analysis of the paper.

References :

Arrowsmith, D. K. and Place, C. M. 1982. *Ordinary Differential Equations,* ch. 5, London, Clapham and Hall

Baker, D. 2006. The menace of an unchecked housing bubble, *Economists' Voice,* Berkeley

Electronic Press, www. bepress.com/eu, March 1-5 Bhaduri, A. 2005. On different regimes of accumulation, pp. 195-203 in Gibson, W. (ed.), *Joan*

Robinson's Economics, Cheltenham, Edward Elgar Bhaduri, A. and Marglin, S. 1990. Unemployment and the real wage: the economic basis for

contesting political ideologies, *Cambridge Journal of Economics,* vol. 14, 375-93

Bhaduri, A., Laski, K. and Riese, M. 2006. A model of interaction between the virtual and the

real economy, *Metroeconomica,* vol. 57, 412-27 Blachand, O. J. 1990. Why does money affect output, in Friedman, B. M. and Hahn, F. H. (eds),

Handbook of Monetary Economics, Amsterdam, Elsevier Campbell, J. and Cocco, J. 2006. 'How Do House Prices Affect Consumption? Evidence from

Microdata' NBER Working Paper No. 11534, February Chiarella, C. and Flaschel, P. 2000. *The Dynamics of Keynesian Monetary Growth: Macro-foundation,* Cambridge, Cambridge University Press Foley, D. and Mitchl, T. 1999. *Distribution and Growth,* Harvard, Harvard University Press Friedman, M. 1968. The role of monetary policy, *American Economic Review,* vol. 58, 1-17 Gandolfo, G. 1996. *Economic Dynamics* 3rd edn, ch. 23, Berlin, Springer Goodwin, R. 1967. A growth cycle, in Feinstein, C. H. (ed.), *Socialism, Capitalism and Growth,*

Cambridge, Cambridge University Press Hicks, J. R. 1967. The Fundamental equation of the Treatise, in Hicks, J. R. (ed.), *Critical Essays in Monetary Theory,* London, Oxford University Press Hicks, J. R. 1974. *The Crisis of Keynesian Economics,* Oxford, Clarendon Press Kahn, R. F. 1972. *Selected Essays in Employment and Growth,* Cambridge, Cambridge University Press

Kaldor, N. 1956. Alternative theories of distribution, *Review of Economic Studies,* vol. 23, 83-100 Kalecki, M. 1971. *Selected Essays in the Dynamics of the Capitalist Economy, 1933-1970,*

Cambridge, Cambridge University Press Kalecki, M. 1976. The problem of financing economic development in a mixed economy, in

Kalecki, M. (ed.), *Essays on Developing Economies,* Hassocks, Harvester Press Keynes, J. M. 1930. *A Treatise on Money,* Volume I, London, Macmillan

Keynes, J. M. 1936. *The General Theory of Employment, Interest and Money,* London, Macmillan Keynes, J. M. 1937. The General Theory: fundamental concepts and ideas. *Quarterly Journal of*

Economics, vol. 51, 1-19 Keynes, J. M. 1939. Relative movements of real wages and output. *Economic Journal,* vol. 49, 34-51

Keynes, J. M. 1940. *How to Pay for the War,* London, Macmillan

Maki, D. M. and Palumbo, M. G. 2001. 'Disentangling the wealth effect: a cohort analysis of household saving in the 1990s' Mimeo, Board of Governors of the Federal Reserve System Marglin, S.

and Bhaduri, A. 1990. Profit squeeze and the Keynesian theory in Marglin, S. and

Schor, J. (eds), *The Golden Age of Capitalism,* Oxford, Clarendon Press; Cambridge, MA,

Harvard University Press Okun, A. M. 1981. *Prices and Quantities. A Macroeconomic Analysis,* Washington, The Brookings Institute

Pasinetti, L. L. 1962. The rate of profit and income distribution in relation to the rate of economic growth, *Review of Economic Studies,* vol. 29, 267-79

Samuelson, P. 1966. A summing up, *Quartely Journal of Economics,* vol. 80, 568-3 Skott, P. 1989. *Conflict and Effective Demand in Economic Growth,* Cambridge, Cambridge

University Press

Sraffa, P. 1960. *Production of Commodities by means of Commodities, Prelude to a Critique of Economic Theory,* Cambridge, Cambridege University Press Taylor, L. 2004. *Reconstructing Macroeconomics,* Cambridge, MA, Harvard University Press Trevithick, J. A. 1975. Keynes, inflation and money illusion, *Economic Journal,* vol. 85, 71-82

THE POLITICAL ECONOMY OF SOCIAL DEMOCRACY

The interplay of continuity and change in history is echoed in political movements that are part of that broader historical process. Tensions invariably arise in an attempt to combine the longer term radical objective of changing the society with the short term goal of maintaining continuity in day to day politics. Thus, the short term practicality of politics requires accepting, at least partly, the continuing circumstances which the movement purports to change in the longer run. This tension, and the dilemma that it generates, has been especially acute in the history of the social democratic movement.

Universal Suffrage And The Socialist Movement

The dilemma surfaced historically as universal suffrage became increasingly a possibility in many parts of Europe. The Reform Act of 1867 in Britain—the very year of the publication of the first volume of Marx's 'Capital'—accepted an electoral system that recognized partly the right of the working class to vote. Although it did not mean 'parliamentary democracy' in the modern sense of the term, it did indicate an emerging trend. That trend gathered momentum through successive electoral reforms in 1884-5,1918 and 1928. As a matter of fact, already in 1868, about half of the adult male population in Britain enjoyed voting rights. And, by the end of the decade of the 1880s, both in France and in Bismark's Reichstag (though not in the more important Prussian Parliament) universal male suffrage had been achieved.[1] The growing tendency towards greater political democracy was becoming the 'ground reality' in western Europe. And, socialists of all description came increasingly under the pressure of evaluating its political consequences for the socialist movement, especially in relation to their strategy for capturing state power. Social democracy, it might be said, was born at that historical juncture.

However, this apparent tendency towards greater political democracy was too close to the time to be interpreted unambiguously. Both the socialist Left and the conservative Right interpreted it with almost equal scepticism. Marx's own understanding of the process of capitalist development had inclined him to argue that universal suffrage which empowers the working class to vote, must turn out to be incompatible with private ownership of property. In his account of the 1848-50 working class upheavals in France, he argued that the logic of universal suffrage would lead from 'political to social emancipation' (Marx, 1952: p. 62) of the workers ultimately through the social ownership of all the means of production. The scepticism of Marx, and of the revolutionary Left in general, about the ability of capitalism to accommodate political democracy was matched by the scepticism displayed by the conservative Right. In the House of Commons debates of 1866-67 conservative politicians like Cecil argued passionately against the impending electoral reforms that would empower (male) workers to vote. In their eyes, democracy would inevitably lead to socialism.[2]

Ironically, at a time when both the revolutionary Left and the conservative Right agreed in effect on their assessment of the irreconcilability of capitalism with universal suffrage, the political climate seemed to be changing precisely in that direction. For instance, unlike in earlier times when the propertied upper classes in Britain mobilized every force in their command to oppose successfully successive electoral reform and Chartism in 1839, 1842 and 1848, they failed to stall the reform of 1867 which empowered electorally a significant section of the British working class.

Nevertheless, so long as universal suffrage remained only a partially attained goal, the broad socialist movement of the time had no compelling ideological reason to get divided between a 'parliamentary' and a 'revolutionary' Left. The reason was simple: the revolutionary Left could view political mobilization for universal suffrage as a way of 'unchaining class struggle,'[3] while the parliamentary Left could pin their hope on achieving a commanding economic position for the working class through universal suffrage. This latter more moderate view was being articulated within the socialist movement by political thinkers like Bernstein and Kautsky. Bernstein characterized socialism as the economic system in which political democracy reaches its 'logical, conclusion', while Kautsky emphasized the tactical importance of taking electoral advantage of the 'growing proletarization' of the capitalist society. The contest between revolution and reform in the socialist movement was clearly coming to a head.

Political And Economic Democracy

With the advantage of historical hindsight, we can identify the errors of oversimplification in the understanding of both the revolutionary and the reformist Left. The unfolding of events turned out to be more complex in two crucial respects. **First,** both sides turned out to have exaggerated the quantitative importance of the working class in the process of capitalist development, based on the Marxian Schema of the growing proletarization of the population. As a matter of fact, even at its peak, workers as a proportion of the total electorate hardly ever exceeded 40 percent under industrial capitalism. For instance, it reached a peak 37 percent in Germany in 1903 and 40.6 percent in Sweden in 1952. And, only in Belgium, the first country in continental Europe to industrialize, it peaked at 50.1 percent in 1912.[4] Since the numerical strength of the working class turned out to be insufficient even in the heartland of industrial capitalism, it was unclear how political democracy would place the working class in a position of command. To some, it appeared that the narrower economic interests of the working class had to be 'compromised', i.e. diluted through alliance with other classes (e.g. self-employed or small proprietors in agriculture and services). This was an ideological anathema to the revolutionary Left. Alternatively, the role of political democracy and majority rule had to be underplayed in the economic interest of the working class, as Lenin had done. Whichever way one looked at it, the ideological distance between the reformists and the revolutionaries in the socialist movement could only increase in these circumstances.

Secondly, the Marxian model of capitalist development had not merely been over-optimistic about the numerical dominance of the industrial proletariat. At the same time, in its prediction about the immiserization of the working class through falling real wage, it had been over-pessimistic. And this was another obvious source of ideological confusion, particularly for the revolutionary Left. It was hardly convincing to argue that the working class would maintain its revolutionary zeal, while the standard of living was rising in a secular manner over time.

However, the case was not much easier to argue for the revisionist Left either. Although workers' strikes aimed at the extension of suffrage had been quite successful, e.g. in Belgium and in Sweden, even more widely supported mass strikes directed at economic demands of the workers failed almost invariably all over Europe—in Belgium in 1902, in Sweden in 1909, in France in 1920, in Norway in 1921, and in Great Britain in 1926.[5] It was becoming apparent that despite the move towards universal suffrage, capitalism was less accommodative towards the economic compared to the political demands of the workers.

From The United Front To The Welfare State

The elasticity of capitalist democracies in meeting the political demands of the workers coupled with the fact that the working class could not dominate numerically the electoral politics in these countries, created a new political dilemma which was made even more acute by the apparent inability or unwillingness of these democracies in meeting the economic demands of the workers. The way out of the political dilemma, at least for the section of socialists who accepted parliamentary democracy as their framework for mobilization, was to broaden their electoral base. This meant that 'class politics' based on the narrower interests of the industrial proletariat had to be transformed into some sort of 'coalition politics' based on the broader interest of a united front. This shift, often debunked by the revolutionary Left as a 'historical compromise' of working class interests, was an outcome of the accommodative capacity of capitalist political democracy. However, social democrats like Kautsky saw that the workers alone would not constitute the dominant majority of the electorate to take advantage of this accommodative political system. This caused a shift in the paradigm of socialist political thinking. Although earlier revolutionary socialists like Engels had also suggested on occasion the need to form united fronts, this was viewed entirely as a matter of political expediency. In contrast, the coalition politics of the united front proposed by the social democrats accepted the impossibility of capturing state power through the numerical dominance of the working class. As a result, they had to give up the idea of'proletarian dictatorship' in favour of more lasting political coalition between the industrial workers, and some other classes as electorally desirable. United front politics, from being a mere short-term tactics became an integral strategy not only for the capture of state power, but for its exercise over the longer run. The ideological break between the revolutionary and the reformist Left was now almost complete.

This rather pragmatic turn towards the strategy of coalition politics raised, however, an awkward economic question. Experiences, particularly during the first three decades of the twentieth century had shown that the political accommodation permitted by the capitalist democracies was not matched by its elasticity in terms of meeting the economic demands of the workers.[6] Therefore, coming to political power through coalition politics had to be justified also in economic terms. Although the revolutionary and the revisionist socialists differed openly about the method of capturing state power, they continued to agree on the basic socialist proposition that private ownership of property made capitalist democracies incapable of responding sufficiently to workers' economic demands. The way out was to commit socialist-led united fronts to economic programmes of'socialization of the means of production', involving large-scale nationalization and public ownership of industries. However, this was happening around the time, when evidence was also filtering in regarding the discouraging performance of nationalized industries in the Soviet Union, as well as other economic and political malaise afflicting the Soviet system in general. It contributed to strengthening the belief in democratic politics on the one hand, but dampened the doctrinaire enthusiasm for nationalizing industries on the other.

More important however, were the rules of the game set by the property-owning democracies. While the rules of political democracy allowed the socialists to share or even control power, the rules of private property permitted the capitalists as well as small property-owners, e.g. peasants or the self-employed who could be partners in a political coalition, to react against socialistic economic measures which they found unacceptable. Thus, private industrialists could strike back against nationalization or pro-labour laws by reducing private investment sharply which, in turn, would reduce demand and employment in the short run as well as slow down the expansion of job opportunities in the longer run. Moreover, it could even create panic or upheaval in financial circles, and in the stock exchange. This ability of industrial capital to hit back through precipitating an 'investment strike' acted as an impending threat to socialist policies. If trade unions and labour movements of an earlier era had provided a countervailing power to capital, such an 'investment strike' now provided capital's countervailing power against a socialist government's policies.

The limit of coalition politics was reinforced by the threat of an 'investment strike' against the background of the often disappointing experiences with the performance of nationalized industries. Together, they discouraged doctrinaire nationalization policies. Another pragmatic turn in social democratic ideology came gradually; in their economic programmes, 'socialization of the means of production' began receiving lower priorities compared to improving the immediate standard of living of the working class, and of other poorer sections who might support the politics of coalition. This meant a change of economic focus which, in the context of Sweden, Ohlin described perceptively as a shift of emphasis from 'nationalization of the means of production' to 'nationalization of consumption'.[7] It also meant reassuring the captains of industry and avoiding possible investment strikes by them. From this emerged ideas of 'social partnership' between the contending classes which, for example, Bruno Kriesky visualized in the case of Austria even before the second world war. A cooperative 'welfare state' began to become an integral part of the social democratic ideology.

In search of its economic rationale, this nascent ideology of the welfare state turned often to an old under-consumptionist argument.[8] In essence, it claimed, that redistribution of income in favour of the poorer classes with a higher propensity to consume, would increase the purchasing power of the whole economy, and provide incentives to industry to expand employment and output. This was an appealing argument for socialists, especially in the context of the depressive economic conditions of the 1930s. Not surprisingly, in 1936 when the Popular Front in France came to power, it made much use of such arguments for justifying its pro-labour economic policies.[9]

In a way, this under-consumptionist argument which identifies the principal problem of capitalism as over-production in relation to its consumption expenditure, carries the justification for coalition politics, and social partnership among the classes, almost to its logical extreme: it claims that higher income for the poorer classes, even through redistributive taxes, is beneficial also for the capitalists in so far as it expands the size of the market by raising the aggregate level of consumption expenditure. And, in a parallel vein, it could also be argued that, an increase in the 'social component' of wages, e.g. better education, housing, health and communication facilities provided by the state, would raise consumption expenditure on other goods and services provided by the private industries, through reducing the proportion of their earning spent on these necessities by the poor.[10] Moreover, this would also carve out a special economic role for the state as the provider of these services. Thus, the rationale for the 'welfare state' could be found without much difficulty in terms of the under-consumptionist logic. And yet, these under-consumptionist arguments turned out to have been built on shaky foundations in the Great Depression of the early 1930s.

Full Employment Keynesianism

Whatever political gains the social democrats might have made through redistribution of income and extension of public services, came to be haunted by the experiences of the Great Depression. The labour unions had witnessed helplessly at that time the collapse of the welfare state under the weight of mass unemployment. So long as the fear that such a crisis could easily recur again haunted historical memory, the gains of the welfare state, and of social democratic policies could not but seem extremely fragile.[11] The policies for demand management, derived from the theory of aggregate demand formulated independently by Keynes and Kalecki around the same time, showed a way of overcoming this fragility. At the same time, it provided the social democratic project for establishing the welfare state with an almost compelling intellectual coherence.

Keynes distanced himself from the narrow under-consumptionist position by pointing out that either consumption or investment could be raised to increase aggregate demand, to avoid disastrous economic depressions with mass unemployment. Contrasting his views from those of early under-consumptionists like Malthus and Sismondi, he writes, 'Practically I only differ from these schools of thought in thinking that they may lay a little too much emphasis on increased consumption at a time when there is still much social advantage to be obtained from increased investment. Theoretically, however, they are open to the criticism of neglecting the fact that there are *two* ways to expand output'.[12]

Kalecki pointed out more precisely the entire range of possibilities for managing demand.[13] Each of the three major components of aggregate demand—private consumption, private investment or government expenditure—could be manipulated through a different set of policies to influence the level of aggregate demand. To these 'three ways to full employment', must be added also the possibility of generating demand through a larger export surplus in an economy open to foreign trade.

Of all these different routes to demand management, by far the speediest and the most convenient way is to increase the level of government expenditure through deficit financing. Understandably, governments of very different political persuasion took repeated recourse to this method for averting serious unemployment. Thus, the share of government spending in GDP in major OECD countries rose from 18 percent before the second World War to 27 percent in 1950, and to 37 percent in 1973.[14] However, more important than the actual method of demand management was the confidence that governments acquired to fight economic depression. Keynesianism brought about this dramatic change in the climate of opinion with more or less continuous full employment set as an achievable goal under capitalism. Thus, following the publication of the Beveridge Report in 1942, the maintenance of 'a high level of employment' was recognized by 1944 as a primary objective of the British government.

Opinions differ as to the contribution actually made by the Keynesian style demand management in the maintenance of high employment (Matthews, 1968). Nevertheless, no matter how one explains it, unprecedented prosperity with near full employment followed for roughly quarter of a century with a remarkable consensus of opinions about the conduct of economic policy. That consensus was centred on Keynesian demand management, covering a wide political spectrum across governments, economists and opinion-makers.

The advantage of this consensus for social democracy was tremendous. The economic role of the state in maintaining high employment through high state expenditure became the accepted norm for the conduct of economic policy across a wide political spectrum. It also meant an expanding role for the welfare state. This was rooted in the consensus view that cooperative capitalism among the contending classes is practicable, because both sides gain through the action of the state in maintaining high demand. More than two decades of sustained near full employment with high growth seemed to reinforce this view. It was the golden age of capitalism. Perhaps, it was also the golden age for social democracy.

From Welfare Keynesianism To Monetarism And Conservatism

Economic policy that deals successfully with the immediate problems of the economic environment is likely to change the environment in that process. In this respect, it is somewhat like the grand algorithm of evolutionary selection, where successful adaptation at each round of evolution might call for a different type of adaptation at the next round. In other words, it was not that the Keynesian theory of demand management was wrong: rather, its success in dealing with the problem of unemployment created new problems, requiring different solutions and institutions.

It is not even that these problems were altogether unforeseen. Already in 1943, Kalecki expressed his scepticism about the political sustainability of long periods of full employment.[15] As he saw it, a shift of power in favour of the workers generated through long periods of sustained full employment would create new problems of workers' 'indiscipline', as the fear of job-loss as a disciplining device in the labour market begins to erode. This problem would arise despite the fact that high employment and capacity utilization might be good for both profit and wage-earners, as maintained by the basic postulate of cooperative capitalism. Kalecki pointed out that workers' indiscipline threatens the very authority structure of economic decision-making under capitalism. As a consequence, the government supported by captains of industry would retreat from time to time from demand management, perhaps in the name of 'sound' public finance and balancing the budget, to precipitate 'political trade cycles' and impose discipline on the workers.

The idea of 'political trade cycles' is an astute variation on the classical Marxian theme of the maintenance of the reserve army of labour as an integral feature of capitalist development. However, it needs some crucial modifications to suit the circumstances of modern capitalism. To start with, it should be recognized that the authority structure of economic decision making under capitalism is threatened not merely by the indiscipline of the workers. The growing presence of the state itself in economic activity— in several OECD countries, government expenditure exceeds 40 percent of GDP—shifts the balance in favour of the government bureaucracy in decision making. The demand for 'rolling back the state' through economic liberalization, deregulation or privatization, finds wide support from the captains of industry in these circumstances, especially because, a democratic government seeks legitimacy through maintaining some degree of neutrality between the contending classes. Viewed from this angle, the discontent with the 'welfare state' in business circles is not simply due to its perception that it strengthens the bargaining power of the workers, and encourages workers' indiscipline by reducing their fear of job-loss (due to unemployment benefit, social security etc.) perhaps even more fundamentally, it is an expression of dissatisfaction by the captains of industry with the neutrality of the state itself as an arbiter between the contending classes.[16] And yet, this very neutrality of the state is the central, unstated assumption underlying traditional Keynesian policies of demand management.

The precise economic consequences of workers' indiscipline in the political trade cycle was left somewhat ambiguous. Marx had postulated that the presence of a 'reserve army' of labour would prevent real wages from rising. That prediction, literally interpreted, had turned out to be false. Nevertheless its obverse implication that cooperative capitalism has a marked tendency to degenerate into conflictive capitalism over the distribution of income under conditions of low unemployment and increased bargaining power of the worker, cannot be so readily dismissed.

Thus, workers' indiscipline can take the economic form of demand for higher money wages, out of line with labour productivity growth to threaten the economy with inflation, and a squeeze on profits.[17]

Some of these ideas got a sharper quantitative focus in Phillips' statistical analysis which showed that money wages generally tend to rise faster at lower levels of unemployment.[18] From this, one could also infer an awkward choice between the two economic objectives of maintaining higher level employment and a reasonable degree of price stability—the 'employment-inflation trade-off' as it came to be known in policy debates. The first cracks in the traditional Keynesian-style demand management seemed to have appeared.

A way out of this dilemma, especially attractive to the social democrats, was to press for a 'wage policy', or more generally an 'income policy' which included both wage and profit income. It is often lamented that this polity was not usually successful in the major OECD countries. However, the political reason for its failure is not difficult to identify. Like demand management policies, it is premised on the role of the state as a neutral arbiter between the classes. And yet, unlike demand management which allows for cooperation between the classes through increasing the level of national income, any income policy would necessarily involve the state directly in the distributive conflict between the classes. And, the premise of the neutrality of the state is almost bound to be challenged by either or both the classes in these circumstances.

At a time when traditional Keynesianism was grappling rather unsuccessfully with the problem of employment-inflation trade-off, the Monetarist attack led by Friedman[19] changed the terms of the debate. Based on more recent statistical evidence, Friedman denied the possibility of any such trade-off in the longer run. His theoretical argument gave particular twist to an obvious fact. Everyone knows that workers are interested in their standard of living. Therefore, the increase in money wages under collective bargaining takes into account not only the unemployment rate, but also the rate of inflation.[20] While normally this might lead to some sort of official or unofficial indexation of money wage increase to the rate of inflation, Friedman's twist postulated that the increase in money wage compensates exactly the *anticipated* rate of inflation. As a result, so long as the inflation rate is correctly anticipated, the real wage does not change. Using conventional (neo-classical) theory, it can then be argued that the profit incentives to the firms also remain unchanged, because real wages remain unaltered, and firms have no incentive to change the level of employment or output.[21] Therefore, unless inflation is *unanticipated,* it does not affect the level of employment. Moreover, because, workers come to anticipate correctly the going rate of inflation, in the longer run, dent on unemployment can be made only by raising continuously the inflation rate, so that part of the rising inflation rate remains unanticipated. In other words, expansionary fiscal and monetary policy on which the Keynesian demand management relies for fighting unemployment, can work only by raising the inflation rate continuously.[22] Thus, Keynesian demand management policies tend to get trapped into higher and higher rates of inflation without any trade-off against unemployment in longer run.

Playing on the fear of inflation that may be caused by higher wage claims at sustained full employment, theoretical constructs such as the 'natural rate' of unemployment or the 'non-accelerating-inflation rate of unemployment' (NAIRU) justified, in essence, the need for maintaining a 'reserve army' of labour under capitalism. The old idea, was recycled in new theoretical terms. It has been reinforced further by the monetarist view that, expansionary fiscal policies financed through budget deficit, necessarily magnifies manifold the total money supply in the economy to cause inflation,[23] quite apart from being ineffective in reducing unemployment in the longer run. Monetarists were clearly taking no chances, by attacking the earlier Keynesian consensus on full-employment policies, and the welfare state on all possible fronts.

The heart of the matter—at least in so far as the theoretical debate on the unemployment problem between the Keynesians and the Monetarists is concerned—revolves around the relative importance of the cost factors on the supply-side proxied by real wage versus the demand-side captured by aggregate demand analysis, in determining the level of employment. However, the resilience of Keynesianism stems from the fact that the analysis of aggregate demand pioneered by Kalecki and Keynes has a much wider political range than the conventional Keynesian policies of demand-management suggest. This fact is seldom recognized even by the Keynesians themselves. Thus, although the theoretical schemes are different, many of the typical conservative monetarist policies could be derived also from simple extensions of the Keynes' theoretical framework.[24] Its theoretical generality becomes in a way the source of its political ambiguity.

Since the stimulation of private investment is a distinct route to demand-management in a closed economy, measures aimed at achieving this become logically justifiable within the Keynesian framework. For instance, reduced taxes on corporate profits or restraint on wages has been considered helpful for improving the climate for private investment. Such measures constitute the case for a politically conservative style of demand-management based on profit-led and private investment driven economic expansion within the Keynesian intellectual tradition. Moreover, in so far as such private investment-led economic expansion also creates sufficient jobs with a relatively slow rise in real wages in relation to the growth in labour productivity, private profitability is increased, but, at the same time, the working class also gains in terms of higher real wages and expanding employment opportunities.

The original under-consumptionist thesis of wage-led and consumption driven economic expansion, which argued essentially that 'high wage' is beneficial to both the classes, finds its antithesis in this case of profit and private investment driven economic expansion. Ironically, both can be interpreted as models of cooperative capitalism. And, both are based on the Keynesian theory which assigns centrality to aggregate demand in determining output and employment[25] However, their policy consequences are almost diametrically opposite. While the under-consumptionist view, supplemented later by the need for higher public investment in case of serious short-fall in aggregate demand makes the case for the welfare state, the view of economic expansion driven by profit and private investment makes a case decisively in favour of private business.[26] And, Keynesianism in this wider sense, leaves ambiguous the economic basis of social democratic politics by accommodating different forms of cooperative capitalism. Helmut Schmidt, as the social democratic chancellor of the-then west Germany articulated this conservative alternative by pointing out: 'The profits of the enterprises today are the investment of tomorrow, and the investments of tomorrow are the employment of day after'.[27] It symbolized complete reliance on private industry and investment to solve the problem on unemployment, rather than creating jobs through direct expansion of public investment. In a way, this view was also an intellectual watershed in social democratic thinking. It marks the beginning of a new conservative era, when it becomes increasingly difficult to distinguish social democratic from conservative economic policies.

Internationalization Of The Nation State

Theoretical ideas supporting 'conservative' and 'progressive' policies contest against one another in the larger democratic polity; and within each political movement that is alive. The long evolution of the socialist movement, from the time when universal suffrage became a distinct possibility, has been no exception to this. The interesting question, therefore, is not why these different political tendencies coexist in the social democratic movement, but why a particular tendency dominates at a particular historical juncture. In short, what made conservatism so widely acceptable in recent times?

At the level of the relevance of theory, there can be little doubt that the Kalecki-Keynes model of the closed economy which had emphasized the critical role of the home market, had become increasingly obsolete as world-trade, particularly among the industrialized countries, began to grow rapidly in the post-war years. In an economy increasingly open to foreign-trade, the under-consumptionist argument of mass consumption-led growth through a 'high wage' policy becomes less compelling. Because, in so far as higher wages through higher prices at home also leads to lower international price competitiveness, aggregate demand may actually decline, if the resulting deterioration in trade-balance outweighs the increased demand for consumption at higher wages. As a result, the increased relative importance of the 'foreign' compared to the 'home' market would dampen enthusiasm for promoting aggregate demand through 'high wage' policies. In that case, a basic tenet of welfare capitalism has to be given up. In contrast, both conservative Keynesianism and Monetarism, which for different theoretical reasons agree on the virtues of a 'low wage' policy for propelling economic expansion led by profit and private investment, would find that policy compatible with increasing openness in trade.[28]

Growth in international trade under contemporary capitalism has been linked intimately with the internationalization of production by the multinational corporations. Some claim, as high as 40 percent of the trade in manufacturing is accounted for by intra-firm trade among the subsidiaries of these corporations.[29] As a result, attracting direct foreign investments of the corporations assume special significance for improving the trade performance of a nation and alleviating its balance of payments problems. Since foot-loose corporate investments would tend to choose the most profitable locations, a 'race to the bottom' follows among the nations by reducing competitively corporate tax rates and restraining wages. This only reinforces the conservative perspective of a growth process driven by profit and private investment on the one hand, and led by export promotion on the other.

Traditional Keynesianism which assigned to the national governments the specific economic role of demand management, and situated itself almost self-consciously in the context of the nation state, finds it naturally difficult to counter these powerful economic tendencies to internationalize the nation-state. However, even more than the multinationalization of production, the tendency towards the integration of the world capital markets can be singled out, perhaps, as the most important aspect which makes autonomous conduct of economic policies by the nation-state, not only difficult, but also exceptionally risky. On a very rough estimate, the daily transactions in the foreign-exchange markets exceeding at present one trillion dollars per day, outweigh the total foreign-exchange reserves of all the central banks put together. Only a very small fraction, of these daily transactions, is related directly either to foreign-trade or direct foreign investment. Most of the transactions remain purely 'financial' in nature; they are sales, purchases and recontracting of existing financial claims in the secondary markets by various private traders in the foreign- exchange market. They generate highly volatile short-term capital flows. Since this involves speculations about the strengths and weaknesses of various currencies almost on a moment-to-moment basis, each national government finds itself constrained to follow policies that would not 'disturb' the private traders and set off speculation against its currency. The most obvious victim of this, has been Keynesian expansionary policies to fight unemployment, which relies traditionally on government spending through deficit financing or taxation.[30] These policies are usually perceived as leading to a worsening of the climate for investment in financial assets. In addition, they usually create at least temporary difficulties for the balance of payments through partial spill-over of the higher aggregate demand into imports. Consequently, they run the risk of triggering off adverse speculation against the national currency.[31] Even financing government expenditure through 'borrowing from the market' may not be a viable option : persuading the market to hold more government securities would raise the rate of interest on government bonds, and create additional debt servicing burden for governments with large overhang of public debt.

The result of such financial integration has been visible in an almost total paralysis of social democratic policies in promoting the vision of 'welfare capitalism' and fighting unemployment through public expenditure. The fear of inflation at home has been reinforced by the apprehension of 'disturbing' the international capital and foreign-exchange markets. And, the captains of industry, multinational corporations and financial institutions in their common dislike of surrendering their authority-structure of economic decision-making to the government, have made out a strong case that the only viable option in these circumstances is a process of economic growth that is driven entirely by private investments, profits and export promotion.[32] In this way, the most conservative aspect of Keynes' theory has been combined with the political orthodoxy of Monetarism, to create a powerful counter-ideology against traditional social democracy.

The collapse of the former Soviet Union, and the end of competition between the two systems has removed almost the last traces of resistance to this ideology. The end of the cold war did not signify just a decisive victory for political democracy and the market-economy over the authoritarian political system of the command economy. It also encouraged the captains of industry to reject ideologically almost all forms of economic cooperation between the classes. Gramsci had pointed out that successful capitalism is based on cooperation and co-opting, in so far as the capitalists elicit consent of the workers by offering material concessions combined with implicit threats of coercion.[33] And, for the political legitimacy of the capitalist system eliciting such consent of the workers through material concessions had been strong so long as socialism posed a serious challenge as the alternative economic system. When this challenge collapsed finally, so did the need to legitimize capitalism through material concessions to the workers. This is reflected in the almost festive mood with which the 'rolling back' of the welfare state is greeted in business and academic circles these days. And this refusal even to legitimize the economic system throws up the most direct conservative challenge against all social democratic policies. While modern social democracy has been premised on the fundamental postulate that cooperative capitalism is the most legitimate system, this postulate is now under challenge. However, if the system really loses its legitimacy in the eyes of some of the major contending classes,[34] cooperation runs the danger of degenerating into conflict and disintegration of social cohesion. This danger of abandoning the social democratic ideal of cooperative capitalism should not be minimized, either by modern social democrats or by their political opponents. It is time that the debate turns towards the problem of how to restore cooperation, not how to destroy it.

Notes :

1. See Stone (1983), pp. 45-53 for further details.
2. Hobsbawm (1969), p. 125 provides more details.
3. Mare (1952), p. 47.
4. Przeworski (1985), p. 24.
5. Ibid., p. 12.
6. Przeworski (1985), in particular has emphasized the role of this factor in the development of social democratic politics.
7. Ohlin (1938), p. 5.
8. Thompson (1963, p. 206), quotes an interesting resolution of 1817 by the Leicester framework-knitters which puts quite succinctly the under-consumptionist argument: 'That if liberal wages were given to the mechanics in general throughout the Country, the Home Consumption of our Manufactures would be immediately more than doubled and consequently every hand would soon find full employment.'
9. Colton (1969) and Kalecki (1936).
10. An increase in the 'social component' of wages may be helpful in coalition politics in so far as it also raises the standard of living of some other partners in coalition politics who are not industrial wage-earners.
11. Glyn (1995).
12. Keynes (1936), p. 325: emphasis in original.
13. Kalecki (1944).
14. Maddison (1991).
15. Kalecki (1971).
16. The emphasis put on 'labour market flexibility' in almost all programmes of liberalization can be explained in these terms. It reduces workers' indiscipline and bargaining power through increasing the fear of job-loss on the one hand; and on the other, by cutting down the welfare measures for the unemployed, it also reduces the economic role of the state and gives back the initiative to the employers. Labour market flexibility is given such high priority, because it kills two birds with the same stone!
17. Wage in relation to labour productivity, i.e. the concept of 'efficiency wage' is particularly helpful for analysing how both the cost of production and the distribution of income are interrelated. A rise in the efficiency-wage, measured as the ratio of wage to labour-productivity, raises the cost of production, while raising the share of wages in manufacturing industries.
18. Phillips (1958).

19. Friedman (1968).
20. This was the 'augmented' Phillips curve which included the actual rate of inflation also as an explanatory variable. Many empirical works had introduced this modification prior to the work of Friedman, who later replaced the *actual* by the *anticipated* rate of inflation, to give the argument a twist.
21. In textbook terms, firms attain their profit-maximizing equilibrium level of output and employment when the real wage rate equals the marginal product of labour. Therefore, there is no incentive for the firms to change their output or employment level so long as the real wage remains the same. Whether employment is determined by aggregate demand or by profit-maximizing equilibrium is not merely a matter of theoretical debate (Benassy, 1986; Bhaduri. 1983, 1991; Malinvaud, 1977). It involves the important policy issue as to whether higher employment can be achieved only by expanding demand, without reducing the real wage. Keynes (1936) himself was ambiguous on this point.
22. In order to depress the real wage which is essential for higher employment according to both pre-Keynesian 'classical' and modern neo-classical theory; see also the preceding footnote.
23. Because budget-deficit creates high-powered money on which the money multiplier works. This view is better at explaining how *potential* money-supply increases, but not necessarily how an increase in *actual* money-supply takes place. The latter depends also on the demand for money, i.e. how a part or the whole of that potential money supply gets injected or transmitted into the economy. This debate revolves around the exogeneity versus the endogeneity of money-supply.
24. Bhaduri and Marglin (1990).
25. Ibid.
26. If the state has any economic role, it is only to support private business by improving the 'climate for investment', as conservative politicians often assert.
27. Le Monde, July 6, 1976.
28. See Bhaduri and Marglin (1990) for elaboration.
29. European Commission, (1995), p. 2.
30. Even in the case of government expenditure financed fully by taxes, there would be an expansionary impact through the 'balanced budget multiplier'. It arises because the government spends the entire tax revenue, part of which would have otherwise been saved, if it were left with the tax-payers.

31. A contrary scenario can be derived from the arguments of Flemming (1962) and Mundell (1961, 1963). Expansionary fiscal policies raise the interest rate, if domestic monetary policy is not sufficiently accommodative. The higher interest attracts capital inflow and strengthens the domestic currency in this first round. See also Bhaduri and Matzner (1990) for a related discussion.
32. There is an obvious 'fallacy of composition' in this strategy. Not all countries can achieve export surplus at the same time.
33. Gramsci (1971).
34. This could probably happen in countries which fail to achieve expansion led by private investment and export surplus, while giving up traditional Keynesianism of the welfare state, and suffering high unemployment.

REFERENCES :

Benassy, J. P. (1986), 'Theories of Unemployment.' In *Macroeconomics: An Introduction to the Non-Walrasian Approach.* London: Academic Press.

Bernstein, E. (1961), *Evolutionary Socialism.* New York: Schocken.

Bhaduri, A. (1983), 'Multimarket Classification of Unemployment: A Sceptical Note.' *Cambridge Journal of Economics,* vol. 7, pp. 235-41.

Bhaduri, A. and E. Matzner (1990), 'Relaxing the International Constraints on Full Employment.' *Banca Nazionale del Lavoro Quarterly Review,* no. 172, pp. 49-62.

Bhaduri, A. and S. A. Marglin (1990), 'Unemployment and the Real Wage: The Economic Basis for Contesting Political Ideologies.' *Cambridge Journal of Economics,* vol. 14, pp. 375-93.

Bhaduri, A. (1991), 'Keynesian and Classical Unemployment: A False Distinction.' *Economic Applique,* vol. 44, pp. 43-9.

Colton, J. (1969), 'Politics and Economics in the 1930s: The Balance Sheet of the Blum New Deal.' In Charles, K. Warner (ed.) *From the Ancient Regime to the Popular Front.* New York: Columbia University Press.

Flemming, J. M. (1962), 'Domestic Financial Policies under Fixed and under Floating Exchange Rates.' *IMF Staff Papers,* vol. 9, pp. 369-79.

European Commission (1995), *A 'Level-playing Field' for Direct Investment World-wide,*

COM (95) 42 (mimeo).

Friedman, M. (1968), 'The Role of Monetary Policy. *American Economic Review,* vol. 58, pp. 1-17. (1975), *Unemployment versus Inflation.* London: Institute of Economic Affairs.

Glyn. A. (1995), 'Social Democracy and Full Employment.' *New Left Review,* no. 211, May-June, pp. 33-55.

Gramsci, A. (1971), Q. Hoare and G. Nowell Smith (eds) *Prison Notebooks.* New York : International Publishers.

Hobsbawm, E. J. (1969), *Industry and Empire.* Pelican Economic History of Britain, vol. 3, p. 125, Pelican, Hammondswoth, Middlesex, England.

Kaldor, N. (1955-6), 'Alternative Theories of Distribution.' *Review of Economic Studies,* vol. 23, pp. 212-26.

Kalecki, M. (1936), 'The Lesson of the Blum Experiment.' *Economic Journal,* vol. 48, pp. 26^11.—(1944), 'Three Ways to Full Employment.' In Oxford Institute of Statistics (ed.) *Economics of Full Employment.* Oxford: Blackwell.—(1971), 'Political Aspects of Full Employment (Originally published in 1943).' In *Selected Essays on the Dynamics of the Capitalist Economy.* Cambridge: Cambridge University Press.

Kautsky, K. (1971), *The Class Struggle.* New York: W. W. Norton.

Keynes, J. M. (1936), *The General Theory of Employment, Interest and Money.* London : Macmillan.

Maddison, A. (1991), *Dynamic Forces in Capitalist Development.* Oxford: Oxford University Press.

Malinvaud, E. (1977), *The Theory of Unemployment Reconsidered.* New York: John Wiley and Sons.

Marglin. S. A. and A. Bhaduri (1990), 'Profit Squeeze and Keynesian Theory.' In S. A. Marglin and J. Schor (eds), *The Golden Age of Capitalism: Reinterpreting the Postwar Experience.* Oxford: Clarendon Press.

Marx, Karl (1952), *The Class Struggle in France, 1848 to 1850.* Moscow: Progress Publishers.

Mathews, R. C. 0.(1968), 'Why has Britain had Full Employment Since the War?' *Economic Journal,* vol. 78, pp. 411-19.

Mundell, R. A. (1961), 'Flexible Exchange Rates and Employment Policy.' *Canadian Journal of Economics and Political Science,* vol.

27, pp. 509-17. -(1963), 'Capital Mobility and Stabilization Policy under Fixed and Flexible Exchange Rates.' *Canadian Journal of Economics and Political Science,* vol. 29, pp. 475-85.

Ohlin, Bertil (1938), 'Economic Progress in Sweden.' *The Annals of the American Academy of Political and Social Science,* vol. 197, pp. 1-7. Phillips,

A. W. (1958), "The Relation between Unemployment and the Rate of Change of Money-Wage Rates in the United Kingdom; 1862-1957'. *Economica,* vol. 25, pp. 283-99.

Przeworski, Adam. (1985), *Capitalism and Social Democracy.* Cambridge: Cambridge University Press.

Sachs, J. and C. Wypolsz (1986), 'The Economic Consequences of President Mitterand.' *Economic Policy,* pp. 261-321.

Stone, N. (1983), *Europe Transformed, 1878-1919.* New York: Fontana.

Thompson, E. P. (1963), 'The Making of the English Working Class', New York: Vintage Books.

STRUCTURAL CHANGE AND ECONOMIC DEVELOPMENT

ON THE RELATIVE ROLES OF EFFECTIVE DEMAND AND THE PRICE MECHANISM IN A 'DUAL' ECONOMY

STRUCTURAL CHANGE AND DEVELOPMENT SOME STYLIZED FACTS

One of the most robust facts in development economics, exhibited by cross-section data among countries as well as time scries data of individual countries, is an inverse relationship between per capita GDP and the percentage of labour force engaged in agriculture. Richer countries have a smaller percentage of their labour force in agriculture, and in the primary sector.[1] This is reinforced by time series data; as countries become richer over time, the relative importance of the primary sector declines in terms of both its percentage contribution to GDP and the proportion of labour force employed. The numbers are indeed strikingly systematic in this respect: towards the end of the last century, in 1995, older industrialized countries like the UK and the USA had less than 3% of their total labour force engaged in agriculture, producing less than 2% of the GDP. Japan, which industrialized more recently, had less than 6% of the labour force, while (South) Korea still had 12.5% employed in agriculture, contributing 2% and 6% respectively to GDP. Brazil had nearly 20% of its workforce in agriculture, contributing 9% of the GDP, while Mexico had 24% in agricultural employment, contributing only 5% of the GDP. At the other end of the spectrum, poorer countries like China, India or Bangladesh, all had more than half of their labour force engaged in agriculture (China 54%, India 67% and Bangladesh 63%), while agriculture's contribution to GDP was 20% in China, 28% in India and 25% in Bangladesh.[2] Although these numbers are merely illustrative (and there are a few statistical 'outliers'), they reveal the pattern of structural changes that typically accompany economic development. Three propositions roughly sum up that pattern:

1. The relative importance of the agricultural (and the primary) sector declines in terms of both the percentage of labour force employed there, and its percentage contribution to GDP, as per capita GDP increases in the course of economic development.[3]
2. However, the percentage of labour engaged in agriculture is usually considerably higher than the percentage contribution made by the agricultural sector to the GDP, implying that labour productivity is lower in agriculture compared to the national average. This holds for both the developed and the developing countries. Thus, from the above figures, we may calculate that, in relation to their respective national averages, the labour productivity in agriculture was about 67% in the UK and in the USA, 33% in Japan, 48% in South Korea, 45% in Brazil, 21% in Mexico, 35% in China, 42% in India and 40% in Bangladesh.[4]
3. Available data (not presented here) also tend to show that intersectoral differences in labour productivity arc in the ratio of 1 to 2.5 for the developed economies, i.e. labour productivity in industry or in the service sector is about 2.5 times higher than that in agriculture. However, in developing countries, the same ratio tends to be much greater, perhaps as high as 8 to 10 times.[5]

The main thrust of these propositions, based on stylized facts, is to emphasize the pressure typically put on developing countries to industrialize at a rapid pace. Not only is agriculture marked by a considerably lower labour productivity than the national average, but the intersectoral productivity gap also tends to be especially large in developing countries. Therefore, transferring labour from the agricultural to the non-agricultural sectors entails large gains in overall labour productivity and in per capita income, propelling the process of economic development through structural change.[6] Nevertheless, this is merely an arithmetical truism. The real economic issues are to identify the nature of constraints and the processes that operate on the demand and on the supply side of a developing economy to regulate the process by which these structural changes occur. To this central problem we now turn.

Agriculture—Industry Interaction

Price and Quantity Adjustment In a Dual Economy

It has been an old idea in the history of economic thought to link the '*social division* of labour', that is to say the extent of diversification of the economy into different branches of activity with agriculture generating the *surplus* needed to support the consumption by workers in the non-agricultural activities. This link was seen as early as in the seventeenth century by Sir William Petty[7] and became a central tenet in later Physiocratic writings. Francois Quesnay's *Tableau Economique* exhibited how agricultural surplus supports through intersectoral exchanges other non-agricultural activities.[8] From the point of view of later theoretical developments in this area, at least two contributions of the Physiocrats seem to be of lasting value. **First,** they defined agricultural surplus as the 'gross produce' of agriculture *minus* 'productive consumption' by the farmers. 'Productive consumption' consists of agricultural raw materials required in its own production, and the subsistence, self-consumption by the farmers. The really fruitful Physiocratic idea was not the identification of agricultural surplus with rent and land revenue, which might have been valid in their particular socio-economic context, but their view that, rather the total agricultural product, only the surplus - a predetermined quantity, or an exogenous variable obtained by deducting the self-consumption of the peasants from agricultural value-added - enters the process of intersectoral exchange to support the consumption by workers and artisans engaged in the non-agricultural sectors for diversifying the economy.

Second, the Physiocratic notion of agricultural surplus as exogenous was justified insofar as both agricultural output and the self-consumption by the farmers are considered as given, the latter coinciding with subsistence consumption. In principle, however, this notion could be used for a more flexible formulation. Not only might higher agricultural price provide stronger incentive to increase agricultural output in the manner taught usually by textbooks (although empirical evidence on this point is ambiguous in developing countries) but more interestingly the availability of industrial goods, as well as their relative price in terms of agricultural goods, might also influence the amount the farmers decide to retain for self-consumption. And when these considerations are deemed to be important, the level of agricultural surplus becomes an endogenous variable, influenced by other factors within the system, for example the level of availability of industrially-produced consumer goods and their relative price in terms of agricultural goods.[9]

As reconstruction and decolonization became part of the international agenda after the Second World War, many of the Physiocratic and classical economists' concerns with economic development through structural change began receiving greater attention. Lewis' seminal paper on the dual economy[10] - a concept used earlier by Boeke[11] - was meant to capture the economic process through which the traditional, largely subsistence sector of a developing economy gets modernized. Lewis distinguished the 'modern' from the 'traditional' sector on the basis of the different methods by which production is organized in them. This corresponds only roughly to the division between agriculture as the traditional, and industry as the modern, sector of a 'dual' economy; but it echoes an old Physiocratic idea insofar as the Physiocrats were the first to recognize that production in agriculture is organized differently from that in industry, requiring an analytical division between the two sectors.[12]

Both in Lewis' own model, and in a whole series of models of the 'dual' economy that it subsequently inspired,[13] a pivotal role is played by the assumption that the *supply* of agricultural surplus is exogenously given, while the real wage rate in terms of agricultural goods (e.g. 'food') for which labour supply is unlimited remains constant. The consequence of this assumption is to determine the level of industrial employment sustainable from the supply-side simply as the ratio of agricultural surplus divided by the real wage rate. Any attempt to raise the level of industrial employment beyond that point would be thwarted, according to Lewis and his followers, by the price mechanism, namely the intersectoral terms of trade, or the price of industrial goods in terms of agricultural goods, because a faster pace of industrialization would raise further the demand for 'food' and therefore the price of agricultural goods. Real wages in terms of food, which is assumed to be constant, can remain constant only if the money wage rate also rises in the same proportion as the price of food. With industrial prices unaffected, this increase in money wages would squeeze profit in industry, while the terms of trade would move against industry. Using a version of 'Say's Law', in the form of the pre-Keynesian assumption that industrial profit as saving determines industrial investment, Lewis argued that the squeeze on industrial profit would slow down industrial investment and growth, until industrial employment returns to the level sustainable by the exogenously given agricultural surplus and the real wage rate.[14]

Using this Lewis-type dual economy framework as the benchmark, one can see how the argument could be developed further in two almost diametrically opposite directions. On the one hand, all the special structuralist assumptions of the dual economy model could be removed to make it look like the textbook competitive market economy. In that case, higher industrial growth, creating greater demand for 'food', would raise the relative price of agricultural goods, only to create stronger incentives to supply more agricultural surplus. With agricultural surplus no longer exogenously given, higher industrial growth through the working of the price incentives could become feasible. Moreover, the higher price of agricultural goods at any given rate of money wage would imply lower real wage. Thus, if labour supply is unlimited at a given money, rather than real wage, rate, a higher level of industrial employment could be sustained through agricultural price rise for any given amount of agricultural surplus. Thus, both through the price incentive to agricultural suppliers, and through a reduction in the real wage rate, the structural constraints on industrial growth in the economy may be relaxed considerably. It would not be too much of an exaggeration to claim that this sort of reasoning often underlies the emphasis that the 'Washington Consensus' of the IMF and the World Bank placed on 'getting prices right', particularly for the agricultural sector, and making the labour market 'flexible'.

The main problem with this view is that it makes the developing economy look almost like the perfectly competitive market economy of the text books. However, this is achieved only by assumptions, ignoring the peculiar structural characteristics that the dual economy model was meant to highlight. As a matter of fact, one could enrich the model by proceeding in the opposite direction, through incorporating additional, relevant structural features. Perhaps the most important feature, originally due to Kelecki,'[15] is to recognize that in agriculture, isolated peasants and farmers carry out production. Their supplies arrive in the market after harvest, prior to price formation. Given the level of supply, prices are formed subsequently in relation to the state of demand. In this sense, agricultural prices tend to be flexible in response to variations in demand, and can be claimed to be largely demand-determined. This flexibility of agricultural prices has been a well-documented fact in both developing and developed countries. For instance, 'with *the* exception of 1958, US wholesale prices of domestically produced food crops fell (absolutely) in every recession year since the World W'ar II'.[16]

In contrast to agricultural prices, industrial prices tend to be markedly less flexible in response to variations in demand. This is because, unlike in the case of agriculture, industrial prices are usually set prior to sales, while variations in demand are absorbed mostly through inventory changes. Since industrial prices are set prior to sales, i.e. without prior accurate knowledge of the state of demand, the standard procedure is to cover unit variable cost with some (usually fixed percentage) mark-up on that cost to allow for profit net of depreciation, interest payment on loans etc. In this sense, industrial prices tend to be largely *cost-determined*' on the assumption that the state of demand would be 'normal', while deviations from this normal state are usually met through inventory rather than price change in the short run.

This distinction between relatively flexible, demand-determined agricultural price, and relatively inflexible, cost-determined industrial price, when incorporated as a further structural feature of the dual economy model, has important economic consequences. Perhaps the most important consequence is the possibility of 'stagflation' in a dual economic structure.[17] With agricultural surplus assumed to be exogenously given, and a constant (subsistence) real wage rate in terms of 'food' as postulated in Lewis' original model, industrial growth at a pace faster than that sustainable by the available supply of agricultural surplus would lead to higher demand for 'food', and therefore higher demand-determined agricultural price, as had been argued by Lewis. The higher price of 'food' would raise the *money* wage rate proportionately in industry to keep the subsistence real wage rate constant. However, unlike the 'profit squeeze' in industry postulated in the Lewis model, the higher money wage will be transmitted to higher cost-determined industrial price. If markup is a fixed percentage on unit variable cost, assumed to be equal to wage cost per unit of output in a closed economy, the percentage rise in industrial price (as well as in agricultural price) will be equal to the rise in the money wage rate. Thus, the consequence would *not* be a squeeze on industrial profit, as Lewis had argued in the context of rising food prices, because industrial profits would be maintained by rising industrial price at that fixed mark-up, making the terms of trade between industrial and agricultural price inflexible in contrast to the Lewis model. The consequence would be stagflationary price rise in both sectors at a rate equal to the rise in the money wage rate.

A further interesting variation on this theme of stagflation in a dual economy occurs by combining it with another important fact of economic life, namely Engel's Law. This postulates that the demand for food tends to be inelastic with respect of variation in income. It can be argued plausibly that a rise in the price of food would typically result in a higher proportion of the money wage of the industrial worker being spent on food if the increase in money wage is proportionally less than that in food price. This would reduce the proportion of money wage left for spending on industrial goods. Consequently, higher food price could reduce overall effective demand for industrial goods, unless it is compensated by a correspondingly higher level of expenditure by the farmers from the higher income they earn from the higher price of food.[18]

The empirically-robust assumption that industrial prices tend to be highly sensitive to cost but not to demand also casts doubt on the efficacy of the terms of trade mechanism in maintaining balance between expansion in both the agricultural and industrial sectors. As we already saw, it can result in almost completely inflexible terms of trade and stagflation in a dual economy. Even more significantly, this opens the way for output rather than price adjustment in the industrial sector in response to excess demand, when that sector is operating under excess capacity. Note, however, that the existence of excess capacity in industry is usually assumed, and this tends to reinforce the rationale for the rule of mark-up pricing widely observed in industry.[19] In this context it becomes especially important to examine how the dual economy operates, when demand-determined price adjusts in the agricultural sector, but quantity adjusts in the industrial sector with excess capacity and cost-determined mark-up pricing. This indeed was the route pursued particularly by Kaldor to bring to the forefront Keynesian considerations for revising our understanding of the role of demand in a dual economy framework.[20]

Kaldor suggested that agricultural surplus plays a critical role in the process of industrialization, not so much by providing the supply of essential wage goods emphasized by Lewis and Kalecki, but by creating demand for industrial goods.[21] A larger volume of agricultural surplus entails a larger market for industry, bringing into operation the (trade) multiplier mechanism for the industrial sector. Thus, by treating agricultural surplus as largely autonomous, its role can be compared analytically to that of exogenous investment or export in the standard Keynesian model of income determination.

However, while this argument is suggestive, it has a serious lacuna.[22] Agricultural surplus creates demand for industrial goods by first being converted into monetary purchasing power. Thus, there is the problem of realizing monetary income from agricultural surplus. In a closed economy without government, it is industry which provides this market for the conversion through the industrial wage bill spent on 'food'. As a result, a greater degree of interdependence from the demand side exists between agriculture and industry in a closed economy than Kaldor's argument suggests. Note that this interdependence arises because all transactions have to be made in terms of money, and not through barter, i.e. as a result of money's being used as a universal medium of exchange.

The importance of this argument relating to monetary exchange becomes all the more apparent if we consider the role of the government in maintaining a minimum 'support price' for agricultural products. Since any amount of agricultural surplus can be sold at that price, there is no problem of realization of that surplus into monetary purchasing power. However, this resolves the problem of realization of surplus only insofar as the agricultural sector is concerned. Viewed from the perspective of industry, the problem of demand still remains unresolved. Unless this monetary purchasing power of agriculture is spent on industrial goods, industry would suffer from insufficient demand, although there is no problem of the realization of agricultural surplus. That this problem can be serious has become clear, for instance, by recent experiences in post-Green Revolution India. In 2001, India had a stock of some 60 million tonnes of foodgrains in government godowns, while 325 million people lived below the 'poverty line', and some 50 million people were on the brink of starvation.

The Indian experience in recent years has yielded a shameful paradox, in that 'too much' food is procured through the support price system, while too many people remain on the brink of starvation.[23] While this simply means that the poor have too little purchasing power, it assumes further significance in the context of a closed, dual economy model of agriculture-industry interaction. It shows why the realization of agricultural surplus into monetary purchasing power through government intervention is merely one facet of the more complex problem of managing effective demand in a sectorally-interdependent monetary economy. Because, unless this purchasing power is spent on domestic industrial goods, industry might suffer from insufficient demand and excess capacity, while the excess purchasing power is held by the agricultural sector in monetary assets. This may raise (agricultural) households' savings, without matching investment demand. In short, it is an illustration of the Keynesian 'paradox of thrift' in a dual economy: the use of money as a 'store of value' by the farmers leads to the failure of Say's law in a monetary economy.

Viewed from the opposite perspective, in the dual economy it is the slow-pace of expansion of the industrial sector which can be said to result in insufficient demand for agricultural goods or for 'food', through insufficient expansion of the industrial wage bill. While this provides the rationale of a support price system for agricultural goods, it could obversely be argued that a faster pace of expansion of the industrial sector (e.g. through public investment in infrastructure etc.) would have tended to alleviate the same problem. Thus, assuming the 'fiscal discipline' of a given government budget, the problem of the *composition* of public expenditure between the support price system for agricultural goods on the one hand, and the need for increased public investment for stimulating the demand for agricultural goods on the other, remains an important issue for the management of demand.

Outside the simplest dual economy model, at least two additional complications must be reckoned with in this context of managing demand. First, the incidence of (direct and indirect) tax tends to vary between the incomes of the two sectors; typically, the tax rate turns out to be higher for industry than for agriculture. Consequently, the support price system for agriculture tends to place a greater stain on the public finance position insofar as, through this policy, less money usually returns to the government as tax revenue, compared to an equivalent amount spent on industry to raise its capacity utilization. Second, in an open economy, with trade in goods and services largely liberalized, serious administrative and political problems might arise concerning the maintenance of the agricultural support price at a level different from the international price.[24] Moreover, there is a further problem, in that the monetized purchasing power of agricultural surplus through the support price policy may largely leak out into imported goods without creating the necessary demand for domestic goods. Expansion through public investment might also involve a similar problem, especially because demand may leak out through the import of capital goods. It is worth noting that the less developed the industrial sector of a country is, the more generally pressing is the problem of managing demand due to import leakage. An oft-presented counter argument is that agricultural surplus may be exported to alleviate simultaneously the problem of effective demand through the 'foreign trade multiplier' and the foreign exchange constraint. The plausibility of this argument depends on whether agricultural goods can be sold at all in the international market, and in particular without affecting too adversely the export price (i.e. the 'small country' assumption). Indeed, the very rationale for managing demand at home arises from the fact that most developing countries capable of exporting mostly primary agriculture-based products have grounds for 'export pessimism'.[20]

The Terms of Trade as Policy Instrument

So far, we have shown that the dual economy framework emphasizes how excess demand, arising from an imbalance between the different rates of expansion of 'traditional' agriculture and 'modern' industry, might typically lead to price adjustment in agriculture, but to quantity adjustment in industry. Although simple, this is a particularly useful framework of analysis insofar as several controversial policy issues in development economics hinge largely on whether excess demand affects mostly quantity, as is postulated in Keynesian economics, or price, as presumed in neoclassical economics. Consequently, the importance assigned to the 'terms of trade', i.e. the relative price of industrial goods in terms of agricultural goods, could be very different depending on how price and quantity adjustment are woven into the analysis. As we already saw, the Lewis-type analysis relies on price adjustment through *flexible* terms of trade to calibrate intersectoral imbalances in demand or supply. By contrast, the 'stagflation' phenomenon emphasized first by Kalecki, or the role of agricultural surplus in generating effective demand for industrial goods emphasised by Kaldor, have in common the idea of a 'structurally' determined terms of trade, which is relatively *inflexible* to the pressures of excess demand or supply. Insofar as the terms of trade shows any secular tendency to move, in this framework it is influenced mostly by structural factors like different rates of labour productivity growth in industry and agriculture, segmentation of the labour market along the sectors, and other factors that are not directly related to excess demand.

However, one could consider the same problem from the opposite angle insofar as the terms of trade might be considered not as an endogenous but as an exogenous variable. It could be treated as an instrument of policy, i.e. an exogenous policy parameter (especially in the context of planning), rather than an endogenous variable determined within the model.[26] This approach to the terms of trade has played a significantly important role in the past, for example in the Soviet Industrialization Debate of the 1920s.

Following the introduction of the New Economic Policy in the spring of 1921, Preobrazhensky[27] criticized it on the ground that it opened the Soviet economy to the risk of a relapse into a dominant private economy. The new state sector, he felt, would not be able to generate sufficient investible surplus to finance its growth at a decisively faster pace than the private sector. When 'taxing' a private sector consisting mostly of agriculture, Preobrazhensky suggested that the terms of trade should be made so unfavourable to agriculture that farmers would be forced to exchange an 'unequally' large amount of agricultural goods for a few essential industrial consumption items like salt, fuel or cloth. Thus, the amount of agricultural surplus made available for industrialization could be increased by changing the terms of trade *against* agriculture. This strategy of extracting agricultural surplus forcibly through the price mechanism would have the additional advantage that relatively few resources would need to be devoted to the production of only those few essential consumption goods, while the growth of heavy, capital goods industries could proceed faster with more resources devoted to them.

This strategy of forcibly extracting agricultural surplus by turning the terms of trade against agriculture runs contrary to the normal role of the price mechanism, because it adversely affects the price incentive to the agricultural suppliers. At the same time, however, it might also increase the demand for essential industrial goods through the operation of Engel's Law on those particular industries.

The strategy of extracting agricultural surplus by deliberately turning the terms of trade against agriculture did not go unopposed in the Soviet Debate on industrialization of that period. Bukharin, in particular, opposed it on the ground that the peasants might simply withdraw from such unfavourable exchange, if this policy were followed too rigorously. Instead, he advocated a more moderate policy of expanding light consumer goods industries, which would provide sufficient consumer goods as well as reasonable terms of trade in order that peasants could engage voluntarily in intersectoral exchange. Bukharin's strategy was also meant to strengthen the political alliance between the industrial workers and the peasants, while Preobrazhensky's policy would have put it under considerable strain.

It is now a matter for history that Soviet industrialization continued at a rapid pace while agriculture got collectivized, at least partly to overcome the problem of extracting agricultural surplus. In the process, an almost laboratory experiment of how the interaction between industry and agriculture may go wrong due to forced industrialization, took place. It is best summed up in the words of an experienced journalist-traveller to the Soviet Union in the 1950s:

> Hundreds of thousands of peasants partake steadily in what is a kind of passive revolt against the collective system. They concentrate on their private plots, at the expense of the work of the collective as a whole, sabotage procedures, and are careless of procedures and state property. They resent the rigidity of the system, taxes, and the prices they get for obligatory delivery quotas, and hence produce just enough to support themselves. Some say that they are worse off than their grandfathers who were serfs. Above all, they lack incentive. The peasant does not produce more, because even if he gets a substantial cash income as many do, he has no 'spending power'. Nothing worth buying is in the shops. This brings up one of the dramatic paradoxes of the Soviet economy. The government must, in order to improve the standard of living of the country as a whole get more out of the fanner, but at the same time is unwilling or unable to release more consumer goods to the farmer in order to stimulate him to more production.[28]

If the Soviet experience with forced industrialization highlighted the damaging consequences of treating agriculture merely as a passive sector-that would adjust easily to the needs of an unwarrantedly high rate of industrial growth, the post-Green Revolution experience in some developing countries like India warns, albeit less dramatically, against committing an error of the opposite type. This results in an overemphasis on generating surplus in agriculture without creating adequate conditions for the expansion of domestic industries at a sufficiently rapid pace to absorb that surplus. The Soviet example highlights the mistake of trying to extract agricultural surplus, without engaging the peasants voluntarily in intersectoral exchange through reasonable terms of trade, and availability of industrial consumers' goods. By not providing adequate incentives, it failed to generate a sufficiently high volume of agricultural surplus to cope with the rising demand from industry. In this sense it highlights the basic concern of the Lewis-type model, in which the supply of an adequate level of agricultural surplus plays the central role. Consequently forcible extraction, rather than voluntary generation of agricultural surplus, became an unfortunate feature of Soviet planning and collectivized agriculture.

By contrast, rapid growth in agricultural production was promoted by the technology of the Green Revolution, while the minimum support price system provided the necessary price incentive to agricultural producers. In some cases, agricultural surplus grew more rapidly than agricultural production, because the new technology was concentrated mostly in selected regions (in particular those with good access to water), and in the hands of relatively well-off, surplus farmers. In a situation of balanced intersectoral 'trade',[1] the rapidly growing volume of agricultural surplus would have translated into correspondingly rapid growth in the demand for industrial goods. In turn, this would have also led to a rapid expansion in industrial production by relaxing the demand-constraint. In contrast to Lewis, this was the type of scenario that was emphasized by Kaldor. It rightly underscores the equally important aspect of agricultural surplus as a generator of *demand* for industrial goods, in addition to its role as a supplier of 'food' to the industrial workers. Nevertheless, when industry does not expand at a sufficient pace to absorb the growing agricultural surplus, the support price system has to be relied on to provide price incentive for farmers, and to convert their surplus into monetary income. And yet, as observed in the Indian case, this incentive system for agriculture alone may not be sufficient, insofar as it lacks a complimentary policy instrument to ensure that the monetary purchasing power created through the support price system is actually spent on domestic industrial goods. If the farmers tend to hold too high a proportion of their money income either as a 'store of value', or spend it on imported goods - unlike the scenario painted by Kaldor, and in stark contrast to the Soviet case, the economy would run into a persistent problem of apparent 'over-production' of surplus foodgrains. In a dual economy, the Keynesian paradox of thrift' might manifest itself as the 'paradox of poverty amidst plenty'. This is a scene of widespread under-nutrition, even starvation, coexisting with rising inventories of foodgrains in government storage, while industry languishes due to insufficient demand. Unfortunately, this is a paradox not altogether unknown in some developing countries.

Notes :

1. 'Primary' sector includes agriculture, mining, fishing and animal husbandry. We use the term 'primary' sector and 'agriculture' interchangeably, implicitly referring to countries where agriculture is the predominant form of activity in the primary sector.
2. International Labour Office (ILO, 1999) is the source of the employment data, while the World Bank (WB, 2000) is the source of the value-added data.
3. Strictly speaking, this statement applies to the time series data of individual countries, rather than to the international cross section data. However, this proposition is consistent with both cross section and time series data. Limitation of space forces us only to mention this in passing, without going into the details of the historical time series of individual countries.
4. Let. Y=GDP, Z=Labour force, $^{y}/_{L}$ = X = national average labour productivity and, X_a = labour productivity in the agricultural sector. Then, for example, in the case of Brazil, we have $X_a = \left(\frac{0.09Y}{0.2I}\right)$ = 0.45 X etc, as the basis of the calculations given in the text.
5. Bhaduri 1993, p. 173, table 6 A.2; based on 1980 data.
6. See Johnson 1970 for a survey.
7. Petty 1963.
8. See Meek 1962.
9. As we shall discuss later, this point is particularly relevant in understanding certain aspects of the Soviet experience with the agricultural sector.

10. Lewis 1954.
11. Boeke 1942.
12. Bharadwaj 1987.
13. e.g. Fei and Ranis 1964: Jorgenson 1961; Zarembka 1970; Dixit 1973.
14. A slight variation on this argument is to use the assumption of profit maximization in industry. With given real wage in terms of agricultural goods, we have in self-evident notations, by assumption (W/P_a) = constant. As the terms of trade (P_i/P_a) moves in favour of agriculture, i.e. (P_aP_c) falls, the product wage in terms of industrial goods (W/P_i) has to rise to keep real wage (W/P_a) constant; because $(W/P_i) = (W/P_a) \times (P_aP_i)$. a relation which is satisfied if (W/P_i) and (P_a/P_i) rise proportionately. The higher product wage in industry which equals under profit maximization the marginal product of labour in industry is attained by reducing the level of industrial employment and output.
15. Kalcki 1971.
16. Okun 1981, p. 136.
17. Kalecki 1976; Kaldor 1976.
18. Taylor 1983; Krishnaji 1992; Storm 1993. See in particular Krishnaji (1992, p. 105), who argued empirically that, 'other things remaining the same, rising cereal prices depress the demand for manufactures' in the context of the widespread poverty in India.
19. cf. Bhaduri and Falkinger 1990.
20. Kaldor 1967, 1978, 1989; also Taylor 1983.
21. So long as the terms of trade are relatively inflexible (under conditions discussed earlier), the demand for industrial goods in real terms is provided for any given level of agricultural surplus.
22. Bhaduri and Skarstein 2001.
23. That this is not merely a problem of 'food security', or maintaining a buffer stock of essential food, is clear for two reasons. First, with so many people near starvation, it is not apparent what 'food security" is supposed to mean, unless it is defined exclusively in terms of protecting the interest of only that section of the urban population which is covered by the public distribution system. Second, reported estimates suggest that around 20% of the stock of procured foodgrains is lost every year through poor storage (a substantial quantity of which is said to be eaten by rats).

24. In a global system, developing countries face considerable international pressure to liberalize their agricultural markets. At the same time, however, the lower income and purchasing power of the average consumer in developing countries create political, even humanitarian, pressures at home to maintain lower food prices more in line with that lower, average income, while paying the. farmers a 'politically acceptable' price. The support price system with subsidy on food emerges as a compromise.
25. Despite lower wages, lower land and labour productivity in many developing countries result in their unit cost of production in agriculture being higher than that in many developed countries.
26. Important price-like, macroeconomic variables - e.g. the interest rate, the exchange rate or the wage rate - are often treated as instruments for policy formulation. The terms of trade between agriculture and industry could also be thought of as one such macroeconomic policy instrument.
27. Preobrazhensky 1965.
28. Gunther 1958, p. 394.

References :

Bhaduri, A and Falkinger,J, 1990, 'Optimal price adjustment under imperfect information', *European Economic Review,* 34 (4), pp. 941-52.

Bhaduri, A, 1993, 'Alternative development strategies and the rural sector' in A Singh and H Tabatabai, eds, *Economic Crisis and the Third World Agriculture,* Cambridge, Cambridge University Press, pp. 149-78.

Bhaduri, A and Skarstein, R, 2001, 'Effective demand and the terms of trade in a dual economy: a Kaldorian perspective', *Cambridge Journal of Economics* (forthcoming).

Bharadwaj, K, 1987, 'Analytics of agriculture-industry relation', *Economic and Political Weekly,* 17, pp. 19-21: AN 15-AN20.

Boeke, JH, 1942, *Economies and Economic Policy in Dual Societies,* Haarlem, Tjeenk Willnik.

Dixit, A, 1973, 'Models of dual economies' in JA Mirrlees and NH Stern, eds, *Models of Economic Growth,* London, Macmillan, pp. 325-52.

Fei,JCH and Ranis, G, 1964, *Development of the Labour Surplus Economy,* Homewood Illinois, Richard D Irwin.

Gunther, J, 1958, *Inside Russia Today,* London, Hamish Hamilton.

International Labour Office (ILO), 1999, '1999 Key Indicators and the Labour Market CD-Rom', Geneva, ILO.

Johnson, DF, 1970, 'Agriculture and structural transformation in developing countries: a survey of'research'', *Journal of 'Economic Literature,* 8 (2), pp. 369-404.

Jorgenson, DW, 1961, 'The development of a dual economy', *Economic Journal,* 71 (2), pp. 309-34.

Kaldor, N, 1967, *Strategic Factors in Economic Development,* Ithaca, Cornell University Press.___, 1976, 'Inflation and recession in the world economy', *Economic Journal,* 86 (4), pp. 703-14.

____, 1978, 'What is wrong with economic theory' in his *Further Essays on Economic Theory,* London, Duckworth, pp. 202-13.

____, 1989, 'Equilibrium theory and growth theory' in F Targetti and AP Thirlwall, eds, *The Essential Kaldor,* London, Duckworth, pp. 411-33.

Kalecki, M, 1971, 'Costs and Prices' in his *Selected Essays on the Dynamics of the Capitalist Economy,* Cambridge, Cambridge University Press, pp. 43-61.

———, 1976, 'The problem of financing economic development in a mixed economy', in his *Essays on Developing Economies,* Hassocks, Harvester Press.

Krishnaji, N, 1992, 'The demand constraint: a note on the role of foodgrain prices and income inequality' in his *Pauperising Agriculture: Studies in Agrarian Change and Demographic Structure,* Bombay, Sameeska Trust.

Lewis, WA, 1954, 'Economic development with unlimited supplies of labour'', *The Manchester School.* 22 (2), pp. 139-91.

Meek, RL, 1962, *Tie Economics of Physiocracy* (Essays and translations by Ronald Meek), London, George Allen and Unwin.

Okun, AM, 1981, *Prices and Quantities: A Macroeconomic Analysis,* Washington DC, Brookings Institution.

Petty, W, 1662, .A *Treatise on Taxes and Contributions* in CH Hull, ed.. *Tie Economic Writings of Sir William Petty.* Cambridge, Cambridge University Press, 1899; New York, revised Augustins M Kelly edition, 1963.

Preobrazhensky. E, 1965, *The New Economics,* London. Oxford University Press, (first published in Russian in 1926).

Storm, S, 1993, *Macroeconomic Considerations in the Choice of an Agricultural Policy:* a study into sectoral interdependence with reference to India, Hants, Avebury.

Taylor, L, 1983, *Structuralist Macroeconomics,* New York, Basic Books

World Bank, 2000. 'World Development Indicators, 2000 CD-Rom'', Washington DC, World Bank.

Zarembka, P, 1970. 'Marketable surplus and growth in a dual economy', *Journal of Economic Tieoy.* 2(2), pp.107-21.

SOME IMPLICATIONS OF ECONOMIC OPENNESS WITH SPECIAL REFERENCE TO INDIA

CORPORATE LOGIC FOR EFFICIENCY AND ECONOMIC OPENNESS

A high growth in GDP (around 7-8 per cent for India in recent years) but a low growth in employment (slightly over 1 per cent) necessarily implies that most of the GDP growth is accounted for by a growth in labour productivity (about 5-6 per cent), and not by expansion in employment. Jobless growth, both in China and India, is driven mostly by relatively high growth in labour productivity rather than in employment. It is arguable that this emphasis on raising labour productivity at the cost of the level of employment results to a significant extent from the thrust to integrate more rapidly with the world market. As globalization tends to increase the relative importance of the external vis-a-vis the internal market, the compulsions of globalization takes the form of exploiting successfully this greater dependence on the world market through greater international cost competitiveness, and pressure operates to reduce unit cost, not merely through wage restraint, but also through raising labour productivity.

However, since the size of the total world market is beyond the control of any individual country, especially India, the case is implicitly or explicitly made for focusing on increasing the share of India in the world export market. In so far as the main route for achieving this is greater international cost competitiveness, a host of measures that help in reducing unit production cost becomes justified. A general aim of all these measures is to achieve wage restraint in relation to labour productivity, and this justifies measures directed towards promoting productivity rather than employment growth while pressing for greater labour market flexibility. The route to higher productivity followed by the corporations are many, e.g. higher productivity through downsizing the labour force, longer hours of work without proportionate increase in pay, i.e. (efficiency wages) which helps to raise productivity in relation to wage rate per worker, voluntary retirements, privatisation, casualisation of labour contracts. It also involves through mechanisms of sub-contracting longer hours of work with no increase in pay in the informal sector (more than 90 per cent of Indian labour force), especially of the selfemployed workers (the largest category of workers in the informal sector). A common economic thrust of all these measures is to improve the international cost competitiveness as the economy becomes more open. The principle of applying the micro logic of corporate management for the reduction in labour cost to the economy as a whole, and viewing it in effect as a single corporation which is expected to increase its international market share by out-competing rival trading nations through cutting costs, appeals to economic nationalism as well as to untutored economic common sense. This sort of reasoning even underlies the Washington consensus, and many of the conditionalities set by the IMF (for stabilization), and by the World Bank for (structural adjustment) in developing countries. And yet, the reasoning often turns out to be seriously flawed because the micro logic applicable to a single corporation might involve some serious macro fallacies when applied to the system as a whole. This should be familiar from the wage cut controversy, because unit cost reduction through measures like wage restraint in relation to labour productivity raises the problem of having sufficient effective demand.

'Race To The Bottom' Strategy

This results in related problems associated with openness. It ignores the fact that all countries cannot be winners at the same time in the zero-sum game of competitive cost cutting for producing an export surplus needed to boost effective demand. Since the shares add up to unity, a larger share by some countries in the global market must mean smaller share by others, and the export surpluses of some countries must have their counterparts in the import surpluses for other countries. In this sense, the policy must fail for some countries, if it succeeds for some others. It causes in effect a race to the bottom, as each country tries in isolation to gain a larger share of the world market. In that process they might be forced to reduce competitively unit costs by cutting wages, lengthening the hours of work at the same wage, restrict workers' rights, refuse pensions and social security by casualising labour etc. In short, the increasing pressure to introduce greater flexibility in employment contracts becomes the name of the game. For developing countries such a «race to the bottom» also has a high political cost, as it leads to systematic undermining of solidarity and political cooperation among them in international negotiations. Most countries gain little from this race individually, while collectively they lose, as they weaken their international bargaining position through competition among themselves. Thus, the economic fallacy of composition that results from not taking into account the zero sum nature of the game of international competition manifests itself as a political weakness in their international negotiating position in trade, while at home the race to the bottom erodes the credibility of the governments with the poor sections of the working population. The same logic applies also to competitive concessions to direct foreign corporate investment involving competitive tax breaks, enforcing labour discipline through the law enforcing machinery of the state, granting special banking insurance and other financial facilities to potential corporate investors and other similar measures. Particularly telling in this respect is the recent proposal for giving unprecedented concessions in various ways to corporations that would operate from Special Economic Zones (SEZ) in India. In a parallel vein, concessions are being granted also for mining rights to various corporations mostly over tribal lands. While members of tribal communities were usually not allowed by their customary laws to sell land individually, the state governments, aided by federal government policies in India, are acquiring tribal and agricultural land, often forcibly at well below market price to hand that land over as concessions for attracting private corporate investments. A race to the bottom has started even among the various states in the Indian federal structure for acquiring land forcibly from the peasants on behalf of the corporations.

VALUE CHAIN IN PRODUCTION AND INTRA-FIRM TRADE

As a model for organizing production, corporatisation and international competitiveness usually involves creating or extending control over a long value chain in production. It can take different forms like vertical integration or various forms of outsourcing and sub-contracting to formal or informal subsidiaries. From the point of view of mainstream economic theory of endogenous institutional development (Coase, 1937), the size of the corporation would be determined by balancing the cost at the margin between producing within the firm (e.g. vertical integration) and procuring or transacting through the market (e.g. sub-contracting to another firm of entity). As the relative importance of the external market in relation to the internal market increases under globalization, entering the intra-firm value chain becomes an important reason for favouring MNC investments. In so far as developing countries are concerned, they are usually unable to penetrate foreign markets and the international distribution system without becoming a part of established intra-firm trade networks. This they try to achieve by lowering the transaction costs for the corporations in one way or another so that they are encouraged to set up subsidiaries in the country concerned. And, the race to the bottom re-appears again in the guise of lowering the transaction costs for the corporations, often by acquiring lands forcibly for extractive mining industry which would be a part of the international value chain. Apart from destroying many more livelihoods in rural areas than jobs ever expected to be created in this process, this way of becoming a part of the corporate value chain typically leads to lop-sided development of enclaves for exports without sufficient forward or backward linkages in domestic production. As a result, development fails to spread over a sufficiently wide range of domestic economic activities, leaving out especially the poorer sections of the population. A glittering urban centre or a high-tech exporting zone developing in isolation, and detached from the poverty and backwardness that surrounds it, often stand out as glaring symbols of this process both in India and China.

Global Finance

The defining characteristic of the current phase of globalization is financial capitalism. It has increasingly become its defining characteristic over the two decades, and had its origin in financial deregulation of capital markets in OECD countries since the mid-1970s. As is well known, over the years it has increased phenomenally the volume of private trade in foreign exchange denominated assets. In comparison to its daily volume of some 1.3 trillion dollars (BIS, 2001; 2002), the total foreign exchange reserve of all the central banks together barely amount to a couple of days of private trade in foreign exchange. In formulating their economic policies, national governments neither in developed nor in developing countries can ignore the sentiments of the private traders in the financial markets. Expansionary fiscal policies for fighting unemployment through budget deficit, or higher taxes on the rich to expand government programmes are generally not favoured by financial markets; instead regressive tax cuts favouring the rich, and stimulation of the stock and real estate market through monetary or tax policies are seen as preferred options for managing demand. Politically it makes a mockery of the original Keynesian and social democratic vision of co-operative capitalism, in which a neutral state is supposed to follow more even-handed policies benefiting both capital and labour. The typical consequences of abiding by the sentiments of the financial market have been over-sensitivity to inflation and a tight money policy to discourage capital outflows through insistence on greater independence of the central bank, and most importantly, a near paralysis of expansionary fiscal policies through higher government expenditure to fight unemployment. The result is controlling inflation rather than high unemployment has become the policy target.

Viewed from this angle, the Fiscal Responsibility and Budget Management (FRBM) Act of 2003 in India has implications that might have been less obvious at first sight. The Act was not crisis-driven, but strategy-driven, because it was enacted at a time when the Indian economy was not facing any particular international payments crisis; instead the foreign exchange position was comfortable and the stock market was booming. And yet, this Act, by crippling government spending even in the most needed areas of social welfare becomes in effect anti-poor. It is a cruel joke on the poor of India by academic economists to talk of inter-temporal optimal choice involving successive generations in the future, when about half of our children in the present generation remain undernourished, and in the twenty first century India heads as the country with the highest number of illiterates and homeless. The anti-poor face of financial prudence is shown up as it starves for fund the recent National Rural Employment Guarantee Act (with concessions being made as election time draws near). This is particularly unfortunate at a time when the excess demand from higher government spending can be met to a significant extent through utilization of existing excess capacity in many of the critical construction materials and wage goods sectors, and a comfortable reserve of foreign exchange has accumulated to smooth over particular supply side bottlenecks. The standard Keynesian argument has a good chance of succeeding in these circumstances in expanding productive employment without inflation.

The imprint of rising oligarchic financial interests on India's development strategy has been unmistakable in recent years. Things have been gradually developing in this direction in India over several years. The Dalal Street (Indian financial centre in Mumbai) nose-dived immediately after the 2004 general elections results, because a few large, mostly foreign institutional investors began to withdraw from the Indian capital market under the fear that a coalition government supported by the Left would be unfriendly towards private businesses. However, as soon as the United Progressive Alliance government named its top economic team, a trio of the prime minister, the finance minister and the deputy chairman of the planning commission, all known for their extreme pro-market, pro-finance and pro-corporation outlook, the stock markets began to stabilize in no time. Nothing had changed about ground realities of the Indian economy in those few weeks, except international finance capital needed assuring political signals. In the process, the future course of economic policies for the country got set. The confidence that this particular team of economic policy makers enjoy with the IMF and the World Bank is also a critical part of the story, because those two institutions are in a pivotal position to influence the perception of private foreign investors like multinational corporations, banks and other financial institutions.

Unlike China, India's comfortable foreign reserves position is mostly the result of accumulated portfolio investments and short term capital inflows from various financial institutions. To keep the show going in this way, the fiscal and the monetary policies of the government need to comply with the interests of the financial markets. That is the reason why successive Indian governments have willingly accepted the Financial Responsibility and Budget Management Act (2003) restricting deficit spending. Similarly, the idea has gained support that the government should raise resources through privatisation and so-called public private partnership, usually another name for various arrangements in which the risk is public and the profit is private. It is specially favoured these days by the World Bank in developing countries, which warns countries at the same time against raising fiscal deficit. The underlying logic on which both national governments and the Bretton Woods institutions agree is that, these measures rattle the sentiment of the financial markets, so governments must remain wary of them. The hidden agenda, vigorously pursued by governments of all colour has been to keep the large private players in the financial markets in a happy mood. Since the private banks and financial institutions usually take their lead from the IMF and the World Bank, this bestows on these multilateral agencies considerable power over the formulation of government policies without necessarily having to lend large amounts.

THE DYNAMICS OF GROWTH AND INEQUALITY UNDER GLOBALIZATION

The growth dynamics in operation is being fuelled continuously by growing inequality in the distribution of income both in China and in India. It results from a combination of policies like slow growth in regular employment, a largely inactive fiscal stance by the government, which hits particularly the poor through withdrawal of welfare measures, and the neglect of agriculture along with forced displacement of the rural population in the name of corporate-led industrialisation. On the other hand, with their income rapidly growing the richer group of Indians demand a set of goods, which lie outside the reach of the rest in the society (e.g. air conditioned malls, luxury hotels, restaurants and apartments, private cars, world class cities where the poor are to be made invisible). The market for these goods, both private and public, expands rapidly. For instance, recent official statistics point out that more than 3 out of 4 Indians have a daily expenditure of less than 2 US dollars in purchasing power parity (about 20 Indian rupees), and nearly 40 per cent has just about or below one dollar a day. They can hardly be a part of this growing market for relatively sophisticated goods. However, the logic of the market dictated by purchasing power still operates relentlessly as never before in India. Its logic is to produce those goods for which there is enough demand backed by money, so that high prices can be charged and handsome profits can be made mostly by corporations who are in a position to produce those goods. As the income of the privileged grows rapidly, the market for those luxury goods they demand grows even faster through the operation of the income elasticities of demand, which exceeds unity for these goods. Thus, the pattern of production is dictated by this process of growth through raising both the income of the rich faster than that of the rest of the society and, because the income elasticities drive even faster than that of the rest of society and, because the income elasticities drive even faster than income the demand for luxuries.

The production structure resulting from this market driven high growth is heavily biased against the poor. While demand expands rapidly for various up-market goods, demand for the basic necessities of life expands slowly under the same logic of the market. Not only there is little growth in the purchasing power of the poor, but the reduction in welfare expenditures by the state further stunts the growth in demand for necessities. Specific examples abound. India has state-of-the-art corporate run, computerised expensive hospitals, nursing homes and spas for the rich, but not enough money in rural health services to control malaria and TB, which require far less expensive treatment. So they continue to kill in large numbers. Lack of sanitation and clean drinking water transmit deadly diseases especially to small children which could be prevented at little cost, while bottled water of various brands multiply for those who can afford. Private schools for rich kids often have monthly fees that are higher than the annual income of an average unskilled Indian worker, while the poor often have to be satisfied with schools without teachers, black boards or even class rooms. The rapid shift in the output composition in favour of high-tech services which has been the engine of India's recent growth might be indicative of this process at the macro level (Rakshit, 2007) . Over time an increasingly irreversible production structure in favour of the rich is beginning to consolidate itself in India. Because the investments embodied in the specific capital goods created to produce luxuries cannot easily be converted to producing basic necessities. Capital that is accumulated over time is not malleable in this sense. And yet, it is the logic of the market to direct investments towards the most productive and profitable sectors for the efficient allocation of resources. The price mechanism sends signals to guide this allocation, but the prices that rule reflect largely the growing unequal distribution of income in the society. The market becomes an especially bad master for the poor when the distribution of income is bad.

The composition of output biased in favour of the rich that the more liberalised market system produces in India is highly intensive in terms of energy, water and other non-reproducible resources, and often does unacceptable violence to the environment. We only have to think of the energy and material content of air-conditioned malls, luxury hotels and apartments, air travels, or private cars as means of transport. These are no doubt symbols of becoming modern world class cities in a poor country, by diverting resources from the countryside where most live. It creates a black hole of urbanization with a giant appetite sucking in primary non-reproducible resources. Many are forced to migrate to cities as fertile land is diverted to non-agricultural use, water and electricity are taken away from farms in critical agricultural seasons to supply cities or multinational soft drink giants, and developmental projects displace thousands in villages to provide land and other resources to corporate industries. Hydroelectric power from the big dams is transmitted mostly to corporate industries, and a few posh urban localities, while the nearby villages are left in darkness. Peasants even close to the cities do not get electricity or water to irrigate their land as urban India increasingly gobbles up these resources.

The Composition Of Output

The content of growth is determined by the composition of output demanded by the rich. These goods are hardly producible by village artisans or the small producers who find no space either as producers or as consumers; instead, economic activities catering to the rich have to be handed over to large corporations who have the space increasingly vacated for them. The combination of accelerating growth and rising inequality begins to work in unison. The corporations are needed to produce goods for the rich, and in the process they make their high profits and provide well-paid employment for the rich in a poor country who provide a part of the growing market for luxuries. It becomes a different process of creative destruction: creation of corporate wealth through the destruction of the poor, helped by an emerging political consensus cutting across traditional Right and Left political division. The signboard of this road is progress through industrialisation. The middle class opinion makers and the media persons unite, and occasionally offer palliatives of fair compensation to the dispossessed. Yet, they are at a loss as to how to create alternative dignified livelihood caused by large scale displacement and destruction in the name of industrialisation. Talks of compensation tends to be one sided, as they focus usually on ownership and, at best use rights to those with land. However, the multitude of the poor who eke out a living without any ownership or use right to landed property, like agricultural labourers, fishermen, or cart-drivers in rural areas, or illegal squatters and small hawkers in cities, seldom figure in this discussion about compensation. And yet, they are usually the poorest of the poor, outnumbering by far, perhaps in the ratio of 3 to 1, those who have some title to landed property. Ignoring them altogether, the state acquires with single minded devotion land, water and resources for the private corporations for mining, industrialisation or Special Economic Zones in the name of public interest.

TOWARDS AN ALTERNATIVE

The vocal supporters of industrialisation never stop to ask, why the very poor who are least able, should bear the burden of economic progress meant for the rich. It has become imperative to face the issue of how economic openness and globalization of trade and finance have exacerbated that process. Facing the special problems of modern industrialisation in the largest democracy with innumerable poor people might require us to think differently about the issues involved. The alternative has to combine greater emphasis on the internal market which caters more to the poor with decentralised decision making by local bodies to generate employment in rural areas. The exact combination to be pursued will naturally evolve through experience and experimentation at the decentralised level, but the broad objective must be to think of the pace and pattern of GDP growth as a consequence, and not a cause of employment growth (Bhaduri, 2005). The main purpose of such intellectual work is to be able to formulate such an alternative going away from conventional wisdom that is imprisoned by the western model and experience of industrialization. This has to be done; because we would otherwise end up brutalising far too many of our fellow citizens in the name of development. Unless it is realised that India's economic success is heading for a political and human failure, and an alternative is found, economists and politicians would soon be judged as men and women who pretended to be wise, but did not have eyes to see or ears to hear the suffering of the majority of their fellow citizens.

REFERENCES :

Alternative Survey Group (2007), *Alternative Economic Survey, India 2006-2007*, New Delhi, Danish Books.

Bhaduri A. (2005), *Development with Dignity*, New Delhi, National Book Trust. — (2007), *Green Left Weekly*, issue no. 710, May.

Fisher S. (2003), Globalisation and its Challenges, *American Economic Review, Papers and Proceedings*, vol. 93, no. 2, pp. 1-30.

Jain A.K. - Gupta P. (2008), *Globalisation: the Indian Experience*, Mainstream, Delhi, Information from Forbes quoted in, February 8-14, 2008.

Mahendra Dev S. (2008), *Inclusive Growth in India*, New Delhi, Oxford University Press.

Ministry of Finance (2007), *Government of India, Economic Survey, 2006-2007*, New Delhi.

Radhakrishna R. (2008), *India Development Report*, Oxford, Oxford University Press.

Rakshit M (2007), Service-led Growth, *Money and Finance*, February.

Rangarajan C. - Kaul P. - Seema (2007), Revisiting Employment and Growth, *Money and Finance*, September.

SHORT-PERIOD MACROECONOMIC ASPECTS OF FOREIGN AID

INTRODUCTION

The traditional literature on the macroeconomic effects of foreign assistance concentrates mostly on the supply-side of the recipient economy. In the well-known Two Gap model (see, for example, Chenery and Bruno 1962; McKinnon 1964, Chenery and Strout 1966; Chenery and Adelman 1966), the binding constraints are associated with inadequate domestic savings to finance targeted investment or with inadequate imports for reaching a targeted or planned rate of growth of the economy. While discussing how foreign aid may remove these constraints, this literature pays hardly any attention to the influence that foreign assistance might exert on the level of effective demand in the economy.

Insofar as the more recent literature on the so-called Dutch Disease considers demand at all, it deals with changes in the composition rather than the level of output brought about by a change of the relative price between tradeable and non-tradeable goods, going back to the classification by Salter (1959). The disease is most clearly visible in a small open economy experiencing an exceptionally large but temporary inflow of foreign exchange, for example, through higher foreign aid. The consequent increase in income leads to higher expenditure which puts upward pressure on prices for non-tradeables,[1] while the prices of tradeables tend to be fixed in the small open economy as a price-taker in the international market. This movement of relative prices in favour of non-tradeables amounts to an appreciation of the real exchange rate, because in real terms more tradeables are needed in exchange for a unit on non tradeable good. Subsequently, this may also induce changes in the composition of (full employment) output against tradeables, which is the essence of the Dutch Disease. This is the purest neoclassical version of the Dutch Disease literature (Corden and Neavy 1982; Enders and Herberg 1983).

Under the assumption of (relative) price or real wage rigidity, Dutch Disease-like situations may be classified as disequilibria of the Malinvaud type, with 'Classical' or 'Keynesian' unemployment or 'Repressed inflation' as possible outcomes. In these disequilibrium models, there is no clear focus on how effective demand is formed, and all explanations of unemployment operate basically through some form of relative price misalignment (example, van Wijnbergen 1984, 1986). As a result, these models ignore the short-term impact of foreign aid through the multiplier mechanism on the level of effective demand, which is the main concern of this paper.

The reason why neither the Two Gap nor the Dutch Disease literature comes to grips with the problem of the influence of foreign assistance on the level of aggregate demand is not difficult to identify. Both have built into them a pre-Keynesian assumption of full employment of resources in the economy, where the full employment level of saving is automatically invested (Robinson 1978). Thus, for any target level of output growth, the Two Gap analysis works out the resource requirements in terms of domestic savings and imports through the familiar Harrod-Domar formula. This is done on the assumption that, once the required savings and imports are generated from domestic and foreign sources, they will be automatically invested. In other words, saving governs the level of investment to achieve the target rate of economic growth. Similarly, by focusing on the composition of domestic output through the influence of relative prices, the Dutch Disease literature follows the neoclassical Hecksher-Ohlin tradition, where resources are more or less fully employed along the production possibility frontier, in the sense that output levels are determined by supply conditions (including specific bottlenecks) but not by the level of aggregate demand.

This paper makes a departure from this pre-Keynesian tradition and analyses how the level of aggregate demand may be influenced also by the inflow of foreign aid through quantity adjustment rather than adjustment of relative prices. The analysis is set in the short-period context with given productive capacities, so that the longer-term impact of foreign aid on capital formation lies beyond the scope of our enquiry. Our purpose is to identify the short-run demand and supply constraints separately, and examine how they interact through the level of foreign aid in determining the level of economic activity in the recipient economy. However, in order to capture the demand and the supply implications of foreign aid, it is necessary to distinguish between the different forms in which aid may be used, for example, aid as free foreign exchange, aid tied to specific imports, aid as commodity import support for consumption, investment, or intermediate goods. These distinctions become relevant in the course of our argument in the next section, which also formulates the demand and supply side constraints operating on the economy in relation to the level of foreign aid received.

The section that follows examine the various patterns of interaction between demand and suply determining the level of econmic activity in the short period. We conclude by summarizing our main argument with comments on its policy implications, especially under conditions of economic liberalization.

The Model

Unnecessary accounting complications are avoided by assuming that all foreign inflows are in the form of pure grants and net international private transfers are negligible. On these assumptions, the trade deficit coincides with the deficit on the current account of the balance of payments. Moreover, we assume that the inflows of foreign finance—called foreign aid—are always used up within the short period for covering the trade deficit, so that aid used for the accumulation of foreign reserves is not considered further in the analysis.[2] Measuring the relevant variables in domestic currency at constant prices, we have

$$M - E = A \tag{1}$$

where M = imports of goods and services
E = exports of goods and services, and
A = net (equals gross, by assumption) inflow of foreign aid.

The extremely concessional nature of inflow of foreign finance as pure grant entails that it is not the recipient but the donors who decide the level of aid. Therefore, foreign aid may be treated as an exogenous variable from the point of view of the recipient country. Moreover, in many instances we may reasonably assme that the level of exports is given in the short period by the size of the foreign market. This means that the total import capacity of the economy ($E + A$) is exogenously given in the short period, and is being fully utilized within that period without affecting the foreign reserve position of the country.

The macroeconomic consequences of the full use of an exogenously given import capacity extend to the demand as well as to the supply side of the economy. Since the level of imports adjusts to the exogenous import capacity in accordance with equation 1, this forces the trade deficit to coincide with the exogenously given level of foreign aid. More simply put, the trade deficit becomes what the (exogenous) level of foreign aid would sustain during that peirod. Consequently, the aggregate level of demand y^d for domestically produced goods (=domestic income) in the recipient economy can be written in view of equation 1 as

$$Y^d = C + I - A \tag{2}$$

Alternatively, since domestic saving is domestic income less total expenditure on consumption,[3] it follows that

$$S = I - A \tag{3}$$

where C = total consumption
S = domestic savings, and
I = investment.

This familiar equation 3 from the Two gap models has a rather unconventional economic interpretation from the demand side, when an independent investment function is postulated. It shows the possibility of a contractionary role of foreign aid on aggregate demand under certain assumptions. For instance, given the level of investment, higher aid means a lower required level of saving in 3, which is generated through a correspondingly lower level of income by the usual multiplier mechanism.

Such downward adjustment of income to a higher inflow of foreign aid is most easy to visualize in situations where aid substitutes strictly for domestic 'savings' in the form of wage goods, which could otherwise have been produced at home. At any given level of investment and real wage rate, the demand for wage goods by the workers employed in the investment sector is also given. This could be met either from the surplus over the wage bill of the workers engaged in the domestic production of wage goods,[4] or it could be met through imported wage goods. A higher volume of imports of wage goods implies that less surplus of wage goods needs to the generated in the domestic economy as 'savings'. In turn, this would reduce the domestic production of wage goods by an amount which is greater than the volume of imports (through the multiplier mechanism), because the surplus or 'savings' of wage goods is only a fraction of domestic production. Thus, the multiplier operates in reverse, as aid takes the form of imports tied to wage goods, substituting domestic 'savings' of wage goods.

Obversely, if domestically produced investment or intermediate goods are replaced by imported investment or intermediate goods financed by foreign aid, then the demand for wage goods in the investment goods sector will fall; and as a consequence, output and employment in the consumer goods sector will fall as well, through the same multiplier process (Bhaduri 1986, ch. 2).

Such a situation may also arise if counterpart funds generated through increased foreign aid do not lead to a corresponding increase in government expenditure or any change in tax collection, for example due to a policy of cutting the budget deficit the consequent increase in government savings may result in a downward adjustment of aggregate demand and income.

It needs to be noted that the implied mechanism is quite different from substitution between domestic and foreign goods in a neoclassical sense, where substitution takes place with full employment of resources. In our Keynesian model, substitution against domestically produced consumption or investment goods provides only the initial impulse, that is, the first round of reduction in demand which then magnifies through successive rounds of the uaual multiplier process. Consequently, even if we make the neoclassical assumption that the economy starts at full employment, it is driven into a situation of underutilization of resources through deficient demand when foreign aid serves to substitute against domestically producible goods.

Nevertheless, the contractionary mechanism on output is unlikely to operate with full force. An exogenous increase in foreign aid would typically have a more complex impact. On the one hand, it would be used partly to substitute against domestically produced goods, resulting in downward demand and output adjustment through the multiplier. However, on the other hand, part of the aid may also be used to stimulate domestic expenditure, especially for investment purposes, leading to expansion of aggregate demand through the multiplier. This latter possibility is particularly strong if part of the aid is tied directly to investment projects by the donors : both because aid tied to specific investment projects would tend to stimulate investment directly, and often also indirectly through the local cost finding obligations on the recipient government.

Similarly, when aid makes a wider range of imported goods available, the demand effect may be positive, for example if it raises (lowers) the propensity to consume (save). On the other hand, if aid shifts the distribution of income in favour of a relatively rich class with privileged access to aid, its contractionary effect on demand may come into play through worsening income distribution, raising the propensity to save in the economy (Kaldor 1955-6). The possibilities are clearly numerous because aid inflow might influence both investment and consumption or saving. Therefore, in the general case we need to assume that both investment and savings are influenced not only by the level of income (that is, aggregate demand), but also by the level of aid. Form equation (15.3) this more general case is written as

$$I(Y^d,A) = S(Y^d, A) + A \tag{4}$$

On total differentiation and collection of terms, the local slope of the curve in the (A,Y^d) plane represents the value of the aid multiplier, that is, how aggregate demand and therefore income varies due to variation in the level of aid,

$$\frac{dY^d}{dA} = \frac{I_A - S_A - 1}{S_Y - I_Y} \tag{5}$$

where the subscripts denote the partial derivaties of the investment and savings function with respect to the relevant variables.

We may assume the usual Keynesian 'stability condition' for the income adjustment process to hold, that is,

$$1 > S_Y > I_Y > 0 \tag{6}$$

so that, the direction of the response of aggregate demand to aid depends only on the sign of the numerator on the right-hand side of equation (5).

In order to interpret the aid multiplier in Equation (5), note that it presumes an implicit functional relation between aggregate demand (=income) and aid as an exogenous parameter. Consequently, parametric variation in the level of aid affects the relevant macroeconomic variables of investment and savings (or consumption) not only directly, but also indirectly through variation in the level of income;[5] while income as the adjusting variable brings investment and savings plus aid into equality. This is shown graphically in Figure 15.1, where an exogenous increase in the volume of aid from A_1 to A_2 shifts upwards the investment schedule as a function of income from I_1 to I_2. If the effect of aid is also to depress savings (that is, increase consumption), so that the $(S + A)$ schedule shifts from $S_1 + A_1$ to $S_2 + A_2$, then income must necessarily increase from Y_1 to Y_2, and the aid multiplier is positive. However, if higher aid does not depress savings (that is, increase consumption) strongly enough, so that the $(S + A)$ schedule shifts upwards to $S_2 + A_2$, then the aid multiplier may turn out to be negative, with income reduced from Y_1 to Y_2. This was illustrated by our previous examples of higher aid-financed imports substituting domestically producible goods, or increased government saving due to counterpart funds revenue generated by increased aid inflow.

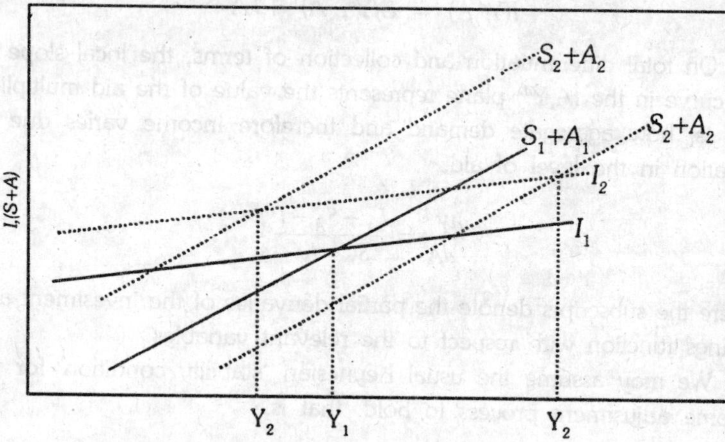

Figure 1 : The indeterminate direction of operation of the Foreign aid multiplier

In order to isolate how aid may affect income only through savings, assume $I_A = 0$ which implies that the investment schedule in Figure *1* would not shift when aid is incresed. While an increase in aid lifts upward the $(S + A)$ schedule initially, this may be counteracted subsequently by a corresponding reduction of savings to avoid a contractionary effect on aggregate demand. in this case, savings as a share of income would have to decline if a contractionary effect is to be avoided.

However, in general the interaction between investment and savings, both of which are influenced by aid, will determine the direction and magnitude of the multiplier. Because of tying of aid to specific investment projects by the donors in many developing countries and counterpart expenditure by the recipient government to cover the local component of investment costs, as well as easier availability of imported machinery, Figure 15.1 assumes that an increase in the level of aid would stimulate investment, that is $I_A > 0$, shifting the investment schedule upwards from I_1 to I_2 with higher aid inflow.

The effect of aid on saving is more difficult to predict a priori (Griffin 1970; Joshi 1970). As already pointed out, it may depress saving by stimulating total consumption through greater availability of imported goods. However, in some situations it may stimulate savings, for example by redistributing imcome in favour of richer classes with a higher savings propensity. Because of these various opposing tendencies at work, the net impact of aid on savings remains ambiguous, resulting in the possible ambiguity in the direction of operation of the foreign aid multiplier (see Figture 1). Nevertheless, in a liberalized import regime, where a significant proportion of total aid is given as general balance of payments support, the tendency would be rather strong to use aid to finance imports against domestically producible consumption goods.

Moreover, if most of the aid is spent on consumption goods, the investment effect of aid would also be weak, making I_A relatively small. As equation (5) shows, the aid multiplier could actually turn out to be negative in this case, with aid contracting aggregate demand in the home market in a liberalized import regime.[6] Note that from equation (15.5), given inequality (6), aid has this demand contractionary role if $S_A > (I_A - 1)$. For instance, if investment increases by half the increase in aid, that is, $I_A = 0.5$, whereas $S_A > -0.5$ (at constant income level), then aid has a contractionary effect on aggregate demand. Since this inequality is satisfied even for a range of negative values of S_A (smaller than half in absolute value), if follows that even if higher aid reduces savings, its overall impact may be to reduce demand owing to the relatively weak positive stimulus it provides to investment.

Turning to the supply side, we assume that supply in the short period depends on the degree of capacity utilization. However, the feasible degree of capacity utilization in the short run is determined by the ability of the economy to import the essential (that is, 'non-competitive') raw materials and intermediate inputs. If r units of imported inputs are directly and indirectly needed to produce one unit of domestic output, then aggregate supply Y^s is determined by the simple relation,

$$Y^s = \text{Min}\left[\frac{1}{r}M^r, \bar{Y}\right] \tag{7}$$

where Y = full capacity output in the short period and M^r = imported essential raw materials and intermediate inputs.

However, with exports exogenously determined in the short run by foreign demand conditions, the total import capacity of the economy depends on the level of aid already discussed in connection with equation (15.1). When this entire capacity to import is devoted exclusively to procuring only essential imported raw materials and intermediate inputs, euqation (15.7) can be used to define the short-run maximum production level of the economy from the supply side, that is,

$$Y^s_{max} = \text{Min}\left[\frac{E+A}{r}, \bar{Y}\right]$$

since, $M^r_{max} = E + A$ by assumption.

This way of viewing the short-run supply side helps to dramatize an economic tension in the use of limited foreign exchange which is often acute in a developing country. A higher utilization of existing capacities through increased imports of essential raw materials and intermediate goods also means a lower rate of new capacity creation through the import of final investment goods. In turn, this may slow down the pace of structural change, while maintaining a higher level of current production.

Without entering into the problem of how this tension between utilization of existing capacity and creation of new capacity is resolved in different regimes of foreign exchange management, it suffices for our limited purpose here to assume that a certain proportion of the total import capacity is devoted either administratively or through the operation of market forces to procuring intermediate inputs, and the remaining proportion to the purchase of final investment and consumption goods. If λ is the proportion of import capacity devoted to importing intermediate inputs and raw materials, then definitionally

$$\lambda = \frac{M^r}{E+A^2}, = 1 > \lambda > 0$$

so that equation (7) becomes,

$$Y^s = \text{Min}\left[\frac{\lambda(E+A)}{r}, \bar{y}\right], 1 > \lambda > 0. \tag{8}$$

The aggregate supply curve in equation (8) has a positive slope λ/r in the (A,Y) plane until full capacity is reached.[8] At that point, the supply curve becomes horizontal owing to capacity limitation, and more imports of intermediate inputs can no-longer raise production in the short period. This specification of the supply curve in (8) together with the specification of the aggregate demand curve in (4), whose slope is defined locally from (5), permits us to analyze how the level of economic activity is determined through the interaction between demand and supply in response to variations of the exogenous flow of foreign aid.

AID AND ECONOMIC ACTIVITY

It only remains to put together the considerations on the demand side as well as on the supply side to see how the level of economic activity may be affected by the level of aid in the short period. Since the binding constraint on the level of economic activity determining actual income would operate either from the demand or from the supply side, we write

$$Y = \text{Min } [Y^d, Y^s] \tag{9}$$

where, Y = level of actual output, and Y^d and Y^s are defined from equations (4) and (8), respectively. AS already pointed out, the supply curve Y^s is positively sloped in the (A,Y) plane until full capacity output is reached (at the level of foreign aid A_1 in Figure 2). Assuming exports and the proportion of import capacity devoted to imports of intermediate and raw materials to be given in the short term, this positively sloped Y^s curve can shift upwards only through a reduction of the import content in domestic production. However, this usually takes place only through structural change in the longer term.

Turning to the demand relation, the schedule for Y^d may be either positively or negatively sloped from equation (5). Consequently, demand and supply considerations together determine the actual output level Y at any exogenous level of foreign aid, in accordance with equation (9). This is shown in Figure 2 by the more heavily shaded line, when foreign aid is assumed to have the role of demand contraction.

Probably the most interesting aspect of Figure (2) is the emergence of an economic regime in the short period, in which a higher level of foreign aid beyond A^* turns out to be counter-productive insofar as it depresses rather than augments the levgel of income. The reason, as already argued, is the impact of a higher level of aid in depressing the level of aggregate demand through the multiplier mechanism, in situations where the demand constraint is already binding (that is, to the right of A^* in Figure 2). In other words, when domestic production is restricted by the size of the domestic market with exports given in the short period, an additional dose of foreign aid may actually reduce production by contracting domestic demand further through the multiplier process. This means that aggregate demand is reduced by an amount significantly greater than the initial magnitude of imports which substituted against domestically produced goods.[9] In this situation, an increase in foreign aid can stimulate output only if it is combined with an expansionary domestic demand policy, shifting the Y^d curve out to the right in Figure 2.

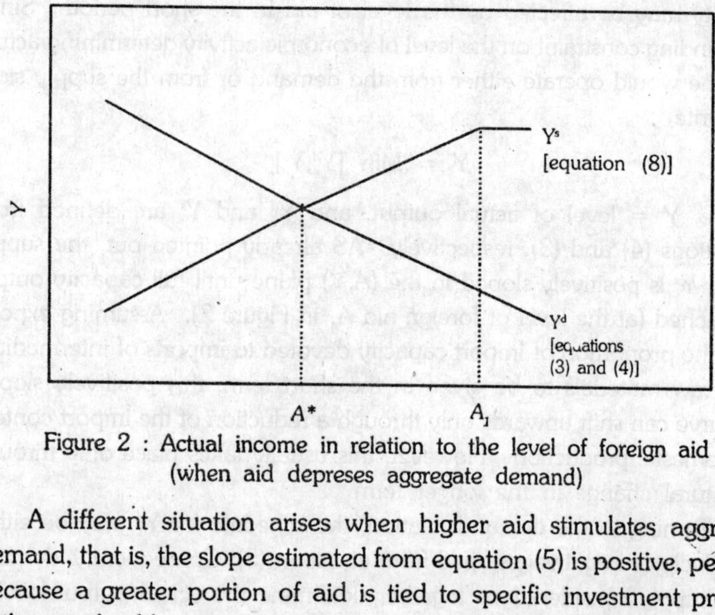

Figure 2 : Actual income in relation to the level of foreign aid (when aid depreses aggregate demand)

A different situation arises when higher aid stimulates aggregate demand, that is, the slope estimated from equation (5) is positive, perhaps because a greater portion of aid is tied to specific investment projects with considerable supporting local currency investment by the recipient government. As Figure 3 shows, the possibility of 'multiple equilibria' can no longer be ruled out, even when aggregate demand is simplistically assumed to be linear.

The emergence of multiple equilibria in Figure 3 is associated with the dual role of foreign aid in stimulating both supply and demand, but at different rates. Thus up to A_1, foreign aid has the more conventional role of relaxing short-period supply side constraints; but in the excess supply regime $A_1 - A_3$ the economy gains from additional foreign aid mainly through its less conventional role in simulating aggregate demand. However, when the stimulation of demand through standard methods like expansionary fiscal policy is available, more foreign aid seems an inappropriate instrument of policy to use. Thus, as Figure 15.3 shows, simply an expansionary or less austere economic policy, raising the aggregate demand schedule from Y_0^d to Y_1^d, may capture the demand side benefits of higher foreign aid, provided enough foreign exchange provision is also made for the procurement of essential imported inputs to raise supply along Y_s. However, with (or without) such expansionary economic policy, foreign aid would turn counter productive by adding simply to the level of excess demand and inflationary pressures in the short period, if carried beyond A_2 (or A_3).

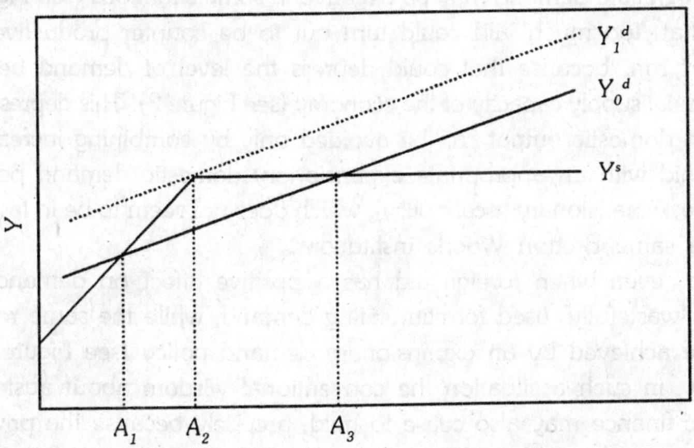

Figure 3 : Actual income in relation to the level of foreign aid (when aid stimulates aggregate demand)

Summary and Concluding Observations

This paper was motivated by the need to provide an analytical scheme for examining the short-term effects of foreign aid, not only on aggregate supply but also on aggregate demand in the recipient economy. Existing modes of thinking on this issue—exemplified by the Two Gap or the Dutch Disease model—pay insufficient attention to the problem of the impact of aid on domestic demand, because they assume either full employment of resources or the output level to be supply-constrained.

This preoccupation with the supply side analysis of foreign aid could be justified in the context of planning models, where the government is the main agent both for mobilizing saving and for investing it. Nevertheless, assigning such a powerful role to the government could be misleading when an independent economic role for the private sector is being so vigorously promoted by the policies of liberalization sponsored by the Bretton Woods institutions.

Analytically, this implies that private investment decisions independent of saving decisions have to be introduced in the model in the manner taught to us by Kalecki and Keynes, for deriving the aggregate demand constraint on the economy [equations (2-4)]. It is the influence of exogenous variations in foreign aid on this demand constraint which was the main focus of our enquiry. We argued that the effect of foreign aid on aggregate demand may be negative in some situations (see Figure 1), so that 'too much' aid could turn out to be counter productive in the short run, because that could depress the level of demand below the potential supply capacity of the economy (see Figure 2). This depressive effect on domestic output can be avoided only by combining increased foreign aid with an appropriate expansionary domestic demand policy (example, expansionary fiscal policy), which does not seem to be in favour with the same Bretton Woods institutions.

And, even when foreign aid has a positive effect on demand, it may be 'wastefully' used for stimulating demand, while the same result could be achieved by an expansionary demand policy (see Figure 3). Ironically, in such a situation the conventional wisdom about austerity in public finance may also cease to hold, precisely because the private sector has a more independent and important role to play as the major investor in a 'liberalized' economic environment!

We used a starkly schematized model to indicate the qualitatively different role that foreign aid might play when aggregate demand is incorporated into the analysis. Neither conventional trade theory nor conventional planning models have been up to this task, because they tend to underplay the domestic demand problem related to the inflow of foreign aid. Nevertheless, in this context a particular limitation of our model also deserves emphasis, Our starkly schematized analysis formulates the demand problem along conventional Keynesian lines, which presupposes a predominantly industrial economy. This ignores, for example, the structural problems that arise in the formation of domestic demand in an underdeveloped economy with an important agrarian sector (Taylor 1983). Thus, price rather than output may respond to change in demand insofar as the agricultural sector is concerned, and the analysis of aggregate demand through the multiplier mechanism will need to be modified accordingly to conform broadly to the particular structural characteristics of an aid recipient agrarian economy.[10] This is neither an easy task nor our purpose here (see Chapters 7 and 8). While the descriptive accuracy of the model could be easily challenged, our simple model will have served its purpose if it reminds the reader that the macroeconomic link between foreign aid and domestic demand needs more systematic exploration, especially in strategies of economic liberalization which emphasize the dominant role of the private sector. Current orthodox wisdom about either foreign assistance or fiscal austerity may well not survive when this macroeconomic link is fully explored.

NOTES :

1. The essential 'pre-Keynesian' bias of the analysis is implicit in the assumption that higher expenditure leads to price-rather than quantity-adjustment.
2. Consequently, the impact of foreign aid on the money supply base—the 'high-powered' money—is not the subject of our analysis either.
3. The relevant concept here is domestic savings out of domestic income and not 'national' savings out of disposable income including foreign aid. We are concerned with domestic savings, which together with total consumption expenditure add up to domestic income, because it is changes in domestic savings (and consumption), caused by changes in foreign aid as an exogenous variable, which bring about changes in domestic income and output through the multiplier process.
4. For expositional simplicity, we assume here that no wages and all profits are saved.
5. Assuming Y^d to be an implicit function of A, differentiation of the expenditure definition of Y^d in (2) yields.

$$(1 - C_A - I_A) = (C_Y + I_Y - 1)\frac{dY^d}{dA}$$

Note : $C_A+I_A \neq 1$ as an identity, but may be true as an equation only when $(C_Y+I_Y-1) = 0$ or $dY^d/dA = 0$. The latter may be formally true only for some values of Y^d, because it would otherwise contracdict the postulate of an implicit functional relation between y^d and A. Economically, if a part of aid is spent on imports of intermediate goods or raw materials, $C_A + I_A$ do not add up to unity.

6. This has some bearing on the question of 'incentive goods'. Our argument it that increased imports of 'incentive goods' financed by foreign aid implies increased consumption expenditure on foreign goods which may substitute against domestic production (we though of soap, beer, textiles in Tanzania). By contrast, the literature on "incentive goods" seems to take for granted that the economy is supply constrained. Hence, increased supply of 'incentive goods', especially consumer goods, can only come from imports, which in turn is expected to stimulate particularly the peasants to increase marketed production in order to buy more of these goods, resulting in incresed domestic agricultural supply (for example, Bevan et al. 1989, pp. 197-203). In this paper we do not discuss the question of supply side incentives, but point to the possible demand implications of the 'incentive goods' argument.
7. This can be computed, in principle, from the inverted Lneotief matrix, separating competing from non-competing imports in each cell.
8. λ/r may be contrasted against the foreign trade multiplier originally due to Harrod (1983, ch. 6). In our case, exports and aid are added together to determine the foreign exchange budget, a part λ of which is spent on intermediate imports for capacity utilization. In contrast, only net exports enter in the Harrod trade multiplier from the demand side, whereas the entire foreign exchange budget (or a proportion λ of it) is relevant for the analysis from the supply side.
9. Our argument should be distinguished from the possible disincentive effect of aid-financed imports which depress domestic prices, for example the probable disincentive of food aid on domestic farmers (Maxwell and Singer 1979). Such an aid-induced price disincentive operates on the supply side, whereas

our argument is concernd with the formation of aggregate demand in the short period.

10. For instance, by depressing the price of food grains and, therefore, the income received by the farmers, foods aid may reduce rural demand for industrial consumer goods. (See also footnote 9 in this context). On the other hand, a lower price of imported food, resulting in higher real wages, may increase urban workers' demand for industrial consumer goods according to Engel's Law. Thus, the net effect of food aid on the demand for industrial goods is ambiguous without quantitative estimates (Taylor 1983).

Reference :

Bevan, D., P. Collier, and J. W. Gunning (1989), *Peasants and Governments, An Economic analysis,* Clarendon, Oxford.

Bhaduri, A. (1986), *Macrosconomics : the Dynamics of Commodity Production,* Macmillan, London.

Chenery, H.B. and M. Bruno (1962) 'Development alternatives in an open economy : the case of Israel', *Economic Journal,* vol. 72, March.

Chenery, H. G. and A.M. Strout (1966), 'Foreign assistance and economic development', *American Economic Review,* vol. LVI, September.

Chenery, H. and I. Adelman (1966), 'Foreign aid and economic development : the case of Greece', *Review of Economic and Statistics,* February.

Corden, W.M. and J.P. Neary (1982), 'Booming sector and de-industrialization in a small open economy', *Economic Journal,* vol. 92, December.

Enders, K. and H. Herberg (1983), 'The Dutch Disease : causes, consequences, cures and calamities, *Weltwirtschafchilites Archiv,* vol. 119, no. 3.

Griffin, K. (1970), 'Foreign capital, domestic savings and economic development', *Bulletin of the Oxford Institute of Economics and Statistics,* May.

Harrod, Roy (1933), *International Economics,* Cambridge University Press, Cambridge.

Joshi, V. (1970), 'Saving and Foreign Exchange Constraints' in P.

Streeten (ed), *Unfashionable Economics,* Weidenfeld and Nicolson, London.

Kaldor, N. (1955-6), 'Alternative theories of distribution', (reprinted) in F. Targetti and A. P. Thirlwall (eds), *The Essential Kaldor,* Duckworth, London 1989.

Maxwell, S. J. and H. W. singer (1979), 'Food aid to developing countries : a survey', *World Development,* Vol. 7.

McKinnon, R. (1964), 'Foreign exchange constraints in economic development and efficient aid allocation', *Economic Journal,* vol. 74, June.

Robinson, J. (1978), 'Pre-Keynesian theory after Keynes' reprinted in J. Robinson *Contributions to Modern Economics,* Basil Blackwell, Oxford.

Salter, W. (1959), 'Internal and external balance : the role of price and expenditure effects', *Economic Record,* vol. 35, August.

Taylor, L. (1983) *Structuralist Macroeconomics, Applicable Models for the Third World,* Basic Books, New York.

Wijnbergen, S. van (1984s), 'The "Dutch Disease" : A disease after all?', *Economic Journal,* vol. 92. March.

—1984b), 'Inflation, employment, and the Dutch Disease in oil-exporting countries : a short-run disequilibrium analysis', *Quarterly Journal of Economics,* vol. 99, May.

—(1986), 'Macroeconomic aspects of the effectiveness of foreign aid : on the Two-Gap Model, home goods disequilibrium and real exchange rate misalignment', *Journal of International Economic,* vol. 21.

THE IMPACT OF GLOBALIZATION ON INDIAN ECONOMIC DEVELOPMENT

A dilemma faces the developing countries today as they find themselves in an awkward corner. The policy space left for the nation-state is shrinking gradually in the current phase of globalization, while that space is being occupied increasingly by the emerging rules of globalization. And yet, the global rules of the game are flawed, as they are biased strongly in favour of the richer countries, especially the Untied States. The dilemma arises because the developing countries tend to feel on the one hand that there is no alternative to accept globalisation in its present form, the so-called TINA syndrome in a uni-polar world dominated by the U.S. On the other hand, they know that they can rely hardly on the current rules of globalisation to further their developmental objectives. In many cases the dilemma is acute irrespective of how the government decides to present the case to the public. As a result, developmental problems are seldom faced from the standpoint of the developing countries,; instead solutions tend to be imposed on them in the name of globalization.

Let a couple of well-known examples illustrate the point. The issue of a fairer global trade in agricultural commodities, without subsidy to the farmers in richer countries, is required not merely for a freer trade regime it also affects the poorest one billion people in the world, as most of them are connected directly or indirectly with agricultural activities in the rural areas of developing countries. There is hardly any other trade-related example with greater compatibility between a more efficient international price mechanism operating through freer trade, and greater global equality. And yet, international negotiations governed by immediate and narrow national interests of the richer nations reduced global rule making recently to a 'tit-for-tat' strategy, that led to breakdown in negotiations, and the tendency to impose solutions by the richer and more powerful nations.

In a parallel vein, one could think of other examples of imposed rather than negotiated solutions. Both the Bretton Woods institutions, namely the IMF and the World Bank, make policy recommendations to the developing countries in financial difficulties through their standard pro-market 'conditionalities'. The voting systems in these institutions are heavily biased in favour of the richer countries especially the United States, because of their higher economic contributions to these institutions. The market principle of the rich have more votes than the poor because of their greater purchasing power holds blatantly in the voting system. As a justification of imposing pro-market conditionalities on developing countries, both these institutions often place a great deal of emphasis on the principle of accountability to the market. However, it is ironical that they themselves remain totally unaccountable for their performances and recommendations, no matter whether an economic collapse occurs in Argentina under their guidance, or an acute financial crisis erupts in east Asia (the only country to escape largely its adverse consequences was Malaysia, which went openly against the IMF prescriptions), or years of stagnation continues despite their recommended large scale IMF-World Bank sponsored liberalization in sub-Saharan Africa.

These are mere illustrations of the power, the rich nations have over the poor nations. It arises to a large extent from some structural asymmetries inherent in the current process of globalization. Until we identify them clearly, it would appear that this process of globalization led by the interests of the rich is a natural phenomenon like an earthquake or a drought. The consequences have to be simply accepted because they cannot be controlled. The analogy is misleading. As we begin to know more about the workings of nature, we start to exert control to varying extent over the fall out of natural phenomena. Similarly, we would be in a position to able to integrate strategically with the global economy to our advantage, instead of meekly submitting to the process of globalization, only if we understand better some of these asymmetries that are also the source of asymmetric global power relations.

First, and perhaps the most fundamental asymmetry in the world economy arises today from the freedom of movement of capital, especially financial capital on one hand, and the restrictions placed on the other, on the movement of labour,especially unskilled labour from developing countries. Despite vast improvements in travel and communications technology available estimates suggest that labour migration as a proportion of the total world population has been lower in the current phase (approximately 1973-to date) compared to the earlier phase of globalization (approximately, 1870-1913).On a rough reckoning, about one in six persons crossed national borders for employment or livelihood between 1860 and 1900. They went as indentured labour from China and India, or as colonial settlers from Europe to North, Central and South America and to Australia. Over a comparable period of nearly five decades of the current phase of globalization for which we have estimates suggesting that not more than one in eight persons has migrated despite vast improvements in transport and communication. Contrast this relatively sluggish movement of labour during the current phase of globalization with the movements of capital, especially financial capital. Rough estimates available from the Bank of International Settlements suggest that the daily volume of private trade in foreign exchange is over 1.2 trillion (10^{12}) U. S. dollars. Of this, less than 2 percent is accounted for by trade in goods and services, and even if one adds all direct foreign investment it would still be well below 4 percent. A few days of hostile private trade in the foreign exchange market can wipe out the entire foreign reserve of all the central banks in the world. The defining characteristic of the current phase of globalization has become this overwhelming supremacy of private financial capital. The world has not seen anything like this before.

The rise to ascendancy of international finance started with successive waves of liberalization of the major capital markets of the advanced capitalist countries starting from about the mid-1970s. It assumed irresistible momentum by early 1980s ushering in the current phase of economic globalisation dominated by international finance. Although little explicit note is taken of its implications in public discussions and government pronouncements, its imprint on the pace and pattern on Indian development too has been unmistakable. Economic policies are increasingly formulated by the government as never before with a view to the sensiments of the financial markets. The English language media, especially the electronic media that shape Indian middle class opinion, behave as if the daily fluctuations of the stock-market is an accurate barometer of the health of the real economy. However, underlying this is an uncomfortable fact that is overlooked willingly or unwillingly. The Indian stock-market is pathetically small in relation to the vast size of global private trade in foreign exchange mentioned earlier. The rupee and Indian stocks can easily be set into an uncontrollable downward spiral by a few large international players speculating against some Indian stocks or the rupee. This is not at all fanciful. Recall how the Dalal Street nose-dived immediately after the 2004 general elections results, because a few large, mostly foreign institutional investors began to withdraw from the Indian capital market under the fear that a coalition government supported by the Left will be unfriendly towards private businesses. However, as soon as the United Progressive Alliance government named its top economic team, a trio of the prime minister, the finance minister and the deputy chairman of the planning commission, all known for their extreme pro-market and corporate-friendly outlook, the stock-markets began to stabilise in no time. Nothing had changed about ground realities of the Indian economy in those few weeks, except international finance capital needed assuring political signals. In the process, the future course of economic policies for the country got set.

This story would remain incomplete for India (and for many other developing countries) without mentioning the critical role of the IMF and the World Bank. Since those two institutions are in a pivotal position to influence the perception of private foreign investors like multinational corporations, banks and other financial institutions about a country's investment climate, their role becomes critical. They shape to a significant extent at least in the short run, the sentiments of the financial markets. If the economic policies of a government are favourable to the corporations, it generally gets a favourable signal from the pro-market IMF and the World Bank, with the result capital tends to flow in to stabilise or even stimulate the stock market. On the other hand, with an unfavourable signal from the same institutions, the government runs the risk of destabilising capital flights. This is the core game under globalisation in so far as these two institutions are concerned, while academic research on themes like poverty and macroeconomic policies are mere sideshows. This has been part of the unwritten script of financial globalisation in so far as developing countries are concerned.

The major players in the financial markets as well as the IMF and the Bank with their pro-market, and pro-corporate philosophy are generally against the expansion of the economic role of the government. So we have in India a Fiscal Responsibility and Budget Management Act (FRBM), which prevents the government from spending additionally in areas like elementary education or expanding employment guarantee or strengthening decentralization of the panchayat system through adequate fiscal autonomy. Tribals and peasants are evicted from lands with little compensation to improve the 'investment climate' for the corporations. If we have the eyes to see, it becomes increasingly apparent that, in the name of development we are typically pursuing policies that might deliver high growth, but it is growth without a democratic content It does not reach the poorest citizens of India who need to benefit most urgently from the process of growth. However, this sort of pro-market reforms and high growth led by the corporations, might make the IMF, World Bank and some in government happy. It may even be accompanied by a rising trend in the stock-market to create the illusion of a healthy state of economic affairs, but all this will remain merely irrelevant statistics for the poor majority in this country. This is why each and every government that has been following this sort of policy gets showered with the approval of the corporate sector, of the IMF and the World Bank, and even of the upper middle class, but loses the general election. The Congress government under the then prime minister Narasimha Rao with Dr. Manmohan Singh as its finance minister spearheading economic reforms lost the general election. Dr. Singh himself personally failed to win a seat. The pattern got repeated. The BJP-led coalition crashed in the elections with its 'shining India' slogan; and, it did especially badly in Andhra which was said to have been shining under the glow of IT industries. There is no reason to believe that things would be any different next time, unless remedial interventions like employment guarantee and fair price and subsidies to farmers despite WTO become sufficiently strong counter-acting forces. However, this would require going against the hidden script of globalisation by upsetting the alliance between large multinational corporations and banks including the IMF and the WB, and a pliable domestic government.

Let me turn now to the second important asymmetry in the current phase of globalisation. It arises from the increasingly freer flow of trade in goods and services on the one hand, and the growing restriction on the transfer of knowledge and technology embodied in the production of those goods and services on the other. In the emerging regime of trade-related intellectual property rights (TRIPS), all developing countries including India find it increasingly difficult to learn and adopt the production technology involved in the goods and services they import. The asymmetry of the emerging trade regime has been characterised by freer trade in goods and services coupled with greater restrictions on the flow of productive knowledge. Thus, in the more liberalized trade regime of the World Trade Organisation, India come under increasing pressure to import goods and services rather than produce them at home, while it is conveniently forgotten that international trade has been the vehicle for learning the technology embodied in the traded goods and new products throughout industrial history. This learning process involved through international trade may well be the most important dynamic gains from freer trade, far outweighing the static gains of existing comparative advantage. By treating knowledge more and more as simply a privately tradable commodity, the current trade regime shows its bias towards corporations as the generator of knowledge who should be handsomely rewarded, but forgets the importance of other sources of knowledge. It has tended to underplay traditional community based knowledge to the detriment of many indigenous communities. Submitting blindly to such an asymmetric trade regime in the name of globalisation would serve the interests of the rich and powerful nations, but would leave the most vulnerable sections of our population especially in agriculture in even greater distress. The suicides of farmers in Maharastra, Andhra, Kerala and Punjab, adding to over 10 thousand in a year, foretell the kind of disaster that the commercialisation of agriculture under WTO regime might bring.

It is in this context that the inevitable consequence of globalization in terms of the increased relative importance of the external vis-a-vis the internal or domestic market needs to be examined. It has influenced thinking on macroeconomic policy in a way, which is seldom highlighted. It emphasises the importance of reducing the costs of production through more efficient supply side policies for increasing the international competitiveness of the national economy; but ignores the problem of creating adequate purchasing power and aggregate demand in the domestic market.

The shift in focus from the demand to the cost or supply side has had serious consequences. The most apparent consequence of this shift concerns labour market 'flexibility', i.e. some form of wage restraint. Lower wages tend to depress the unit cost of production, but also the consumption demand from wage income. Consequently, unless either higher investment or increased export surplus makes up for that reduction in consumption demand in a regime of investment or export-led growth, insufficient aggregate demand at home would be a drag on development.

Similarly, the emphasis on increasing output (value added) per worker or labour productivity to reduce labour cost of business, and use this as a tool for enhancing international competitiveness has a downside. Exclusive attention on productivity separates it from its consequences on total GDP, and the employment in the economy. For instance, total output would decrease despite an increase in productivity, if the percentage decrease in the level of employment exceeds the increase in labour productivity. Consequently, the corporate strategy of'down-sizing' the labour force to create a "lean and efficient corporation" for increasing market share, might turn out to be good for a particular corporation, but macro-economically counter-productive if either total supply, or the size of the domestic market shrinks.

Policies of reducing unit cost in search of greater efficiency, through down-sizing the labour force and restraining wages are encouraged under globalisation by the predominance of external market considerations. However, in many cases, these policies often turn out to be a macro-economically flawed. Because while they are efficient on the microeconomic scale of a single corporation or enterprise, such policies can also become counter-productive on the macroeconomic scale due to their effect of depressing demand.

The underlying problem is more general. The blurring of the distinction between micro and macro- efficiency has become a generic problem with many currently pursued economic policies. It stems from the influences of 'methodological individualism' in economics and, from 'neo-liberalism' in politics. It gives rise to many 'fallacies of composition' in macro-economic policy by assuming that the individual micro-economic 'parts' have the same properties as the 'whole' macro-economic system. To illustrate the point, an individual corporation restraining wage or shedding labour to raise productivity might raise the efficiency and profit of that corporation. But if many corporations follow this policy at the same time, total demand and employment in the economy will shrink, and even the profit of all corporations might be reduced. Similarly, one country might increase its export more than its imports, but all cannot achieve it because, one country's export surplus has to be matched by some other country's import surplus. It is a zero sum global game in which all cannot be winners at the same time. And, it would be foolish to rely entirely on the external market if only for this reason.

In the current phase of globalisation a third asymmetry arises from the role assigned to the state in monitoring and regulating economic activities. The market-oriented philosophy intends to curb the role of the state as an economic actor. This often gives rise to an almost schizophrenic view of the capabilities of the state. It is usually claimed that the state cannot be trusted with expansionary monetary and fiscal policies (e.g. FRBM Act mentioned earlier) because the state has an in-built tendency to be financially irresponsible. At the same time however, the same state is relied upon to undertake far more complex financial tasks like extending the scope of the market through privatisation, regulating the stock exchange etc. This schizophrenic view about the capabilities of the state is rooted in denying the state its developmental and welfare role, but using it to promote the reach of the multinational corporations through measures like privatization. The result often is greater corruption and lack of transparency in governance.

Finally, in India the most fundamental asymmetry is to be found in the uneasy relation between our political democracy and the market mechanism. The two have come to be treated as mutually reinforcing concepts in neo-liberal philosophy because both the free market and democracy extend the scope of individual choice and yet, the relationship between the two types of freedom granted by the market economy and, by political democracy often tends to be in conflict in developing countries. The democratic principle of 'one-adult-one-vote' coexists rather uneasily with the free market philosophy that the rich, with greater purchasing power, would have more 'votes' than the poor in the market place. This asymmetry becomes even more acute, the greater is the inequality in the distribution of income, and the larger is the proportion of the poor with political voting rights, but economically without a 'voice' in the market. In these circumstances, the democratic form of government comes under increasing strain if too much freedom is granted to the market. And yet, the forces unleashed by the process of globalisation tend to drive relentlessly towards a situation in which governments have little control over the free play of the global market forces.

As a matter of fact the history of the relation between economic development and democracy has been far more complex than the currently fashionable 'political correctness' would have us believe. Historically, the per capita income of the western countries had to reach some minimum of US dollars 2000 per capita per year. This was a high level compared to India's $200-250 around the time of our first general election in 1952 (measured in 1999 PPP calculation). It is an unparalleled achievement in the recorded political history that political democracy in India could be sustained at that level of poverty despite the tremendous diversity of the country. However, this should not blind us to the fact that democracy historically co-evolved with development without necessarily being either its cause or consequence. The challenge posed to our'democratic form of government is different today. It must control the excesses of globalisation and domination by corporations of the economy. Our democracy has to ensure that the process of growth is not corporate driven, but is decentralised and employment driven to allow for the widest participation of our citizens. Only then will the wealth created by growth be fairly shared, and growth itself will assume a democratic content. It will be wealth created by the people, for the people. The nature of globalisation must fit into this objective. This is the compulsion of our time.

References :

Bank of International Settlement(BIS).2001 Central Bank Survey of Foreign Exchange and Derivatives Market Activity in April, 2001; Global Data, Press Release.

Barro,R and Sala-I-Martin,X. 1995.Economic Growth, New York, McGrew Hill.

Bhaduri,A. 2002. 'Nationalism and economic policy in the era of globalisation, in D.Nayyar (edited), Governing Globalisation: Issues and Institutions, Oxford, Oxford University Press.

Bhaduri, A and Marglin, S. 1990. 'Unemployment and the real wage: the economic basis of contesting political ideologies', Cambridge Journal of Economics (14): 375-93.

Chang,H-J.2002.Kicking Away the Ladder: Development Strategies in Historical Perspective, London, Anthem Press.

Felix, D. 1998.'Asia and the crisis of globalisation' in D.Backer, G.Epstein and R.Pollin (edited), Globalisation and Progressive Economic Policies, Cambridge, Cambridge University Press.

Fischer, S.2003. 'Globalisation and its challenges', American Economic Review, Papers and Proceedings, 93(2).

Krugman,P. 1996.Pop Internationalism, Cambridge, Massachusetts, MIT Press.

Marglin, S and Bhaduri, A. 1990. ' Profit squeeze and Keynesian theory' in S. Marglin and J. Schor (edited), The Golden Age of Capitalism,Oxford, Clarendon Press; pp: 153-187.

Nayyar,D. 2002.'Cross-border movements of people', D.Nayyar edited Governing Globalisation, Oxford, Oxford University Press.

OECD. 1998.Trends in International Migration.' Annual Report, Paris, OECD.

Pasinetti,L.. 1981.Structural Change and Economic Growth, Cambridge, Cambridge University Press.

EXPANDED REPRODUCTION IN THE LIGHT OF MODERN GROWTH THEORY

In an all-purpose one commodity world, e.g. in the Recardian 'corn' model, no physical distinction can exist among the flows of consumption, saving and investment. The (annual) flow of production in excess of consumption of corn is the saving of the economy in terms of corn, which can be either consumed or invested directly, say as seed corn to augment further the future flow of corn output. This oversimplification of the one commodity model introduces a bias in the analysis in three distinct ways. **First,** the 'size' of the flow of production can be treated as independent of the distribution of the product, only because relative prices affecting, and affected by distribution in measuring the flow cannot matter in a one-commodity world. This underlined the search for an invariant 'standard of value'[1] in a world with many commodities with which Ricardo in particular grappled. Classical political economists, including Ricardo and Marx, were forced to short-circuit the problem by assuming 'labour value' as the standard of measure for different commodities which looked at the 'value' of a commodity in terms of directly and indirectly congealed labour in it. The measure is beset with many difficulties whose masterly analysis was provided by Piero Sraffa (1960).

Second, since both saving and investment must take place in terms of the same commodity in a one-commodity world, any distinction between saving and investment becomes hard to maintain. Both saving and investment appear as identical decisions, governed by simply the choice to optimize consumption over time. A subjective time rate of discount of the representative economic agent (which equals the interest rate in equilibrium), therefore emerges as the crucial psychological parameter even for the macroeconomic analysis of saving investment equality.

Finally, the all purpose one commodity world obscures the physical process underlying the transformation of saving in terms of consumables into investment or capital formation terms of non-consumables, e.g. machines', and the economic implications that follow from it.

The lasting significance of the schemes of reproduction — both 'simple' and 'extended' — introduced byMarx(1956) into macroeconomic analysis arises mostly on these counts. In particular, it broke the over-simplified habit of thinking of capital accumulation in terms of an all-purpose one commodity model, and for that reason, was able to anticipate some of the intellectual development associated with the 'Keynesian revolution' of the 1930s(Keynes, 1936).

A main focus of the Marxian reproduction scheme is to exhibit transparently the mechanism by which saving in terms of consumables is tranformed into non-consumable investment goods like 'machines' needed for expanding the future productive capacity. In order to achieve this, Marx himself used the 'labour theory of value' It emphasized on the one hand his central concern about the exploitation of labour, and on the other, it short-circuited (imperfectly) the problem finding an invarient standard of measurement in a multi-commodity world. However, Marx's achievement in setting out the scheme of reproduction, and its relation to modern growth theories, are easier to appreciate without the problematic detour through the labour theory of value.

To simpllify exposition, we assume that capitalists' consumption is negligible, while workers spend all their wage bill immediately on consumption. Moreover, the real wage rate per worker is assumed to be given in terms of 'corn', i.e. the composite consumption goods produced by Department II in Marx's scheme of reproduction. All intermediate goods needed either for the production of the consumption goods in Department II, or for the production of another composite investment goods in Department I can be abstracted from our exposition by assuming that both the departments are 'vertically integrated' (Pasinetti, 1981), i.e. they produce internally within the respective department all the intermediate inputs or variable capital directly and indirectly needed for the production of their final outputs. Thus, taking advantage of the subsequent important work by Leontief on input-output analysis(Leontief, 1966), we can get rid of the complications due to circulating capital which had complicated Marx's scheme of reproduction.

The significance of the distinction between simple and expanded reproduction lies in the level of 'economic surplus' that an economy is capable of generating for realization into monetary profit. Thus, if the given real wage rate per worker is 6 units of corn, but value added (i.e.output net of all intermediate inputs) per worker, i.e. net labour productivity is 10 units of corn in Department II, then each worker produces a surplus of (10-6), i.e. 4 units of corn. However two points should be noted in this connection. First, although both the level of absolute surplus per worker i.e. 4 units of corn, as well as the level of surplus relative to the wage rate, i.e. (4 - 6), i.e. 2/3 are given (roughly similar to Marx's notion of the absolute and the relative rates of exploitation) the level of surplus generated remains indeterminate without a theory to determine the total number of workers engaged in the consumption sector or Department II. Second, the surplus generated in terms of the composite consumption goods, corn is physical surplus. In a capitalist economy, where commodities are produced by definition with a view of selling in the market in exchange of money, the physical surplus of corn can become monetary profit, only if it finds an adequate market to sell that surplus corn. The Marxian scheme of reproduction exhibits clearly how these two aspects of determining the size of the surplus and its realization into monetary profit are interrelated. His analysis of this interrelation anticipated later developments in the theory of aggregate demand associated with the names of Kalecki(1971) and Keynes (1936).

The fundamental distinction between simple and expanded reproduction becomes relevant in this context. Suppose, the existing stock of fixed capital or machines used in the two Departments, but produced exclusively by the investment goods Department I, require the employment of exactly 12 workers in Department I to replace by new flow of machines, depreciated machines of each period. This keeps the capital stock intact in a stationary state. If these 12 workers engaged in the production of machines are also paid the wage rate of 6 units of corn, then their total consumption(=wage) bill would be 12x6 units of corn. As the scheme of reproduction exhibits, this provides the market for selling the surplus of corn of Department II, generated at the rate of 4 units of corn per worker. Thus, a determinate number of workers, has to be employed in the consumption sector to generate just enough surplus of corn to be realized into monetary profits through selling them in the market provided by the workers engaged in the investment sector. In our example, this is given by, $4X = 12 \times 6$, i.e. $X = 18$. If the number of workers engaged in the consumption goods Department II is more than 18, inventories of corn would accumulate without being realized into monetary profits; if $X < 18$, past stock of inventories would have to be run down. This also captures the essence of the equality between investment and savings as an 'equilibrium condition', where only at $X = 18$ workers in Department II, the sales expectations of the capitalists in Department II are realized because the market for the surplus corn is cleared. This results in equivalent realized monetary profits of the physical surplus corn without unplanned accumulation or decumulation of inventories of corn.

Note, in passing, that the proportion in which workers in the two departments are engaged is given by 12:18, i.e. 2:3 which is the same ratio as the surplus of corn to wage, 4:6, i.e. the relative surplus per worker. It is this proportion which maintains the balance between investment and saving to ensure that no problem of realization of surplus into monetary profit arises at the given real wage rate and labour productivity in terms of corn. In our particular arithmetical example, this proportion coincides exactly with the rate of relative surplus per worker in Department II (i.e. 2:3) because of the simplifying assumption that capitalist consume nothing out of their profits, while workers consume all their wages. Nevertheless, this is only a simplifying assumption in so far as a different such ratio would be entailed, so long as both the classes consume in fixed proportions out of their respective incomes (with workers having a higher consumption propensity) .

However, the scheme of simple reproduction can be misleading. Because, it specificies the investment requirement, i.e.number of workers required to be employed in Department I strictly in terms of maintaining the existing capital stock intact. The novelty of expanded reproduction lies in fact that investment is no longer specified. In other words, investment becomes an independent or exogenous variable decided by the capitalists in search of their profits, while, the rest the logic remains the same. Assume, for instance, that the capitalists in Department I decide, in search of their profit, to employ 20 workers so that, over and above the replacement of depreciated machines, new flow of machines are being added to the stock to expand the productive capacity of the economy. By our earlier logic, to sustain these 20 workers in Department I, $4X = 6 \times 20$, i.e. $X = 30$ workers now need to be employed in Department II. This would achieve the investment saving balance, maintaining again the same proportion of 2:3 as employment ratio between the two Departments.

Expanded reproduction exhibits the fundamental flaw in a modern version of the Say's Law, which is dressed in the guise of the proposition, that saving determines investment. Although the above arithmetic would have been the same, if saving governed investment, the economic causation would be different. We would specify independently, in the first place, the number of workers employed in the production of corn in Department II (at 30 in the above example). The surplus of corn or saving in terms of consumable generated by them i.e. 4 x 30 would now have to be absorbed by employing exactly (4 x 30 - 6) , i.e. 20 workers in Department I. Thus, starting with the number of workers in Department II as the independent variable, we specify surplus corn or savings exogenously which the capitalists must obligingly absorb with a matching level employment or investment in Department I. Over-production of corn is not possible in this scheme; nor is it possible to reckon with the driving force of capitalism which gives capitalists the power to decide independently how much they wish to invest in search of profits by choosing the employment level of Department I. Obversely, if the above version of the Say's Law were true, capitalists in Department II would find it profitable to employ an indefinitely large number of workers in Department. Because, each additional worker produces a surplus (of 4 units of 'corn') which can be further realized automatically into monetary profits by the obliging capitalists in Department I, absorbing that surplus through an exactly matching expansion of employment in Department I. With surplus (supply) creating its own demand in this sense, full employment and/or full capacity utilization becomes built into the model.

It is unfortunate that, despite the fact that Marx's scheme of expanded reproduction is more than a hundred years old, and its connection with the Keynes-Kalecki theory of effective demand is analytically established in the context of modern growth theory(especially Robinson, 1956), mainstream neo-classical economists of various persuations tend to ignore its fundamental insights in two ways. First, they assume that the economy operates always at full employment without any problem of profit realization through inadequate demand. In other words, the independent role of Department I in generating demand, which need not match necessarily the surplus of Department II, is ignored.Its extreme examples are growth models with intertemporal consumption optimization by the representative economic agent whose savings decisions from intertemporal optimization govern the investment level of the economy over time (e.g.

Romer, 1986). Even the well-known models of Swan(1956), Solow(1956) —apparently of 'Keynesian persuation' — suffer from their inability to deal with an independent investment function which Harrod's (1939) seminal essay so clearly pin-pointed as a source of instability of the capitalistic growth process. Second, given real wage and labour productivity the scheme of expanded reproduction exhibit the 'problem of proportionality'. Suppose each department requires a specific type of machine determining its capacity to produce which cannot be converted into another type of machine required by the other department, i.e. capital goods are 'non-shiftable' between sectors (e.e. Domar-Feldman 1957; Mahalanobis, 1953). Suppose the historically inherited stock of the two types of machines permit labour to be employed in the two departments in some arbitrary ratio of 1:2, but investment saving balance require labour to be employed in the different ratio of 2:3, as in our previous arithmetical example. Clearly, a 'problem of disproportionality' from the inherited capital stock would now arise. In subsequent works on multisector growth models (e.g. von Neumann, 1946; Leontief, 1966) similar requirements of proportionality in the stocks of goods also emerge for sustaining maximal, balanced growth (e.g. the von Neumann 'ray'). Nevertheless, this insight of Marx regarding disproportionality is ignored too by aggregative growth models relying on the assumption of malleable capital. In short, neither the problem of realization of profits nor the problem of proportionality — the two main insights of the scheme of expanded reproduction — has been integrated into modern, mainstream growth economics. This explains partly the unsatisfactory state of the subject.

References :

Domar.E. 1957. 'A Soviet model of growth'(A translation from the original Russian essay of 1928 by G. Fel'dman) in his *Essays in the Theory of Economic Growth*, New York, Oxford University Press.

Harrod, R. 1939 'An essay in dynamic theory', *Economic Journal*, vol.49, March pp 14-33.

Kalecki, M. 1971. *Selected Essays on the Dynamics of the Capitalist Economy*, Cambridge, Cambridge University Press.

Keynes, J.M. 1936. The General Theory of Employment, Interest and Money, London, Macmillan.

Leontief, W.W. 1966. Input-Output Economics, New York, Oxford University Press.

Mahalanobis, P. 1953. 'Some observations on the process of growth of national income' *Sankhya,* vol.12 pp. 307-312.

Marx, K (1956) Capital, vol. II. Chapter XX, 'Simple reproduction' and chapter XXI, 'Accumulation and reproduction on an extended scale[1] (translated from the original German edition, 1893 by I. Lasker), Moscow, Progress Publishers.

Pasinetti, L. 1981 *Structural Change and Economic Growth : A Theoretical Essay on the Dynamics of the Wealth of Nations,* Cambridge, Cambridge University Press.

Robinson, J. 1956. *The Accumulation of Capital,* London. Macmillan.

Romer, P. 'Increasing return and long run growth', *Journal of Political Economy,* vol.94, October.

Solow, R. 1956. 'A contribution to the theory of economic growth, *Quarterly Journal of Economics,* vol. 70, February, pp.65-94.

Sraffa, P. 1960. *Production of Commodities by Means of_Commodities: Prelude to a Critique of Economic Theory,* Cambridge, Cambridge University Press.

Swan, T. 1956.'Economic growth and capital accumulation', *Economic Record,* vol. 66, November, pp 334-361.

von Neumann, J. 1945-6. A model of general economic equilibrium' *Review of Economic Studies,* vol.13, pp.1-9.

CAPITALISTIC ACCUMULATION IN LOGICAL AND HISTORICAL TIME

INTRODUCTION

Despite its apparent mathematization, dynamic economic analysis has been singularly unsuccessful in dealing with the problem of time. Joan Robinson had been particularly insistent on this point. The very notion of 'equilibrium' in economic analysis, she argued, is counterproductive in dealing successfully with economic change as a historical process through time. The academic orthodoxy in economics, by and large, failed to appreciate the importance of this issue. It was either ignored as an index-number problem of'capital' measurement or simply avoided in the name of difficulties inherent in modelling uncertainty. Nevertheless, the problem is far too serious in nature to be wished away. Indeed, capitalistic accumulation as a historical process can never be analysed unless we learn to face seriously the problems caused by *historical* time. And yet, 'equilibrium' analysis by its very nature is simply unable to cope with this problem of historical time, despite all its heavy show of mathematics.

In Classical Mechanics (e.g. in Newton's equation and Kepler's law of planetary motion), no sharp distinction between movement *in space* and movement *in time* needs to be made. The fact that time is *irreversible* does not enter the analysis in any essential way,[1] Nevertheless, the problems posed by the irreversibility of time must be given a central place in the analysis of any *historical* process. As Joan Robinson puts it:

> In space, it is possible to go to and fro, but time goes only one way; there is no going back to correct a mistake; an equilibrium cannot be reached by a process of trial and error . . . today is an ever-moving break between the irrevocable past and the unknown future (Robinson, 1980, p. 8).

The analytical implication of this commonsense observation and the extent of damage it causes to orthodox 'equilibrium' analysis can best be illustrated by setting the problem of capitalistic accumulation against this uni-directional movement of time. It will be shown in this paper, following Joan Robinson's analysis, that typical neoclassical growth models become almost meaningless constructs once the problem of historical time is faced seriously.[2] In contrast, Marx's distinction—although often confused in his own writing on the subject—between the problems of *profit realization* and *historical proportionality* assumes great significance in characterizing capitalistic accumulation as a historical process. Indeed, one of the serious failures of many Keynesian-type growth models inspired by Harrod (1939) is their insufficient recognition of this proportionality problem as an essential aspect of historical analysis.[3]

Realization And Proportionality

In the Keynesian scheme, the macroeconomic condition for balance between *aggregate* expenditure and *aggregate* income is set out in terms of the familiar condition for equality between investment and saving (i.e. I = S). Although central to modern macroeconomic analysis, this condition was somewhat in the nature of a rediscovery. An equivalent condition was used much earlier by Marx in his two-department scheme to describe the condition for the *realization of surplus value into profit*. Without going into the unnecessary complications caused by measures in terms of labour value, the problem can be more simply stated by using the Ricardian notion of *surplus product* in terms of 'corn'. Given productivity per worker in the consumption sector producing 'corn', and given any *real* wage rate in 'corn', the *surplus per worker* in terms of corn is defined in the consumption sector. Unlike Ricardo and foreshadowing Keynes, Marx pointed out that the *total* level of surplus 'corn' that can be realized into monetary profits is indeterminate until the *size of the market*, where that surplus 'corn' can be sold as commodity, is determined. The size of the market, i.e. the level of effective demand for surplus 'corn', is determined in Marx's two department scheme (especially of expanded reproduction) by the wage bill of the investment sector (i.e. Department I) and by the level of capitalists' consumption. In other words, the level of *surplus* of the consumption sector realized into monetary profit is equal to the money expenditure on 'corn' (i.e. consumption goods) by workers engaged in the investment sector and by the capitalist class. Assuming all wage is consumed, we then have

Surplus of consumption goods[4] (Z_c)
= Monetary profits of the consumption sector (R_c)
= Money wage bill of the investment sector (W_i)
+ Money value of capitalists' consumption (C_p) (1)

The above condition for realization of surplus into profit underlies Kalecki's *profit realization equation* (Kalecki, 1971). Because, adding profit of the investment sector (π_I) to both sides of equation (1) above, we obtain[5]

$$\pi_c + \pi_i = \pi = (W_i + \pi_i) + C_p = I + C_p \quad (2)$$

where π = total/profit, I= value added by the investment sector (i.e. the *final* expenditure on investment goods), divided into profit (r,) and wage (W_i) in that sector.

As Kalecki pointed out, capitalists realize as profit (π) what they spend in terms of investment (I) and consumption (C_p), while, by assumption, workers spend what they get.

Equation (2) above is the same as the Keynesian condition for saving-investment equality. Because, by deducting capitalists' consumption (C_p) from both sides of equation (2), we obtain

$$I = \pi - C_p = S \quad (3)$$

where, π being capitalists' income (total profit) and C_p being their consumption, the difference between the two ($\pi - C_p$) is capitalists' savings. It is also the *total* savings of the economy (5), because by assumption, workers do not save.

If we assume capitalists' consumption to be a constant fraction ($1 - S_p$) of their profit, then (3) takes the special form

$$I = s_p \pi, \perp \geq s_p > 0. \quad (4)$$

We rewrite (4) in terms of sectoral shares of profit in value added as

$$I = S_p(h_i I + h_c C)$$

where $$h_i = \frac{\pi_i}{I} \text{ and } h_c = \frac{\pi_c}{C}$$

or $$(1 - S_p h_i)I = s_p h_c C. \quad (5)$$

The bracketed term on the left-hand side of (5) shows the *demand* generated *per unit* of value added by the investment sector and consists of ($1 - h_i$) as consumption demand out of wages *plus* ($1 - s_p)h_i$ as consumption demand out of profits. Similarly, the coefficient $S_p h_c$ on the right-hand side of (5) is the *surplus* of sumption goods *per unit* of value added by that sector. Therefore equation (5) balances demand for consumption goods *external* to the sector (i.e. generated by the investment sector) with the surplus of connsumption goods for realization of that surplus into monetary profits.

If P_i and P_c represent the price of investment- and consumption- goods, and x_i and x_c the respective labour productivity in physical terms in the two sectors, then the price-money-wage relations for the two sectors are given as

$$P_i x_i (1-h_i) = w$$

and $$P_c x_c (1-h_c) = w \tag{6}$$

where w = the uniform *money* wage rate.[6]

Since by definition, $I = P_i x_i L_i$ and $C = P_c x_c L_c$, we may simply use these definitions in (5) and substitute from (6) to obtain on simplification

$$\frac{L_c}{L_i} = \frac{(1-h_c)}{(1-h_i)} \cdot \frac{(1-s_p h_i)}{s_p h_c} = R \tag{7}$$

where L_i and L_c = number of workers in the investment- and the consumption sector, respectively.

Equation (7) explicitly shows the *realization proportion* shown by ray OR in Figure 1 between the two sectors. It is derived from the Keynesian investment-saving equality (see (3) and (4)) or the Marxian profit realization equation (see (1) reinterpreted by Kalecki (see (2)). It shows the number of workers that can be employed in the consumption sector *(L_c)* to produce just enough surplus to be realized as profit at any *given* level of employment in the investment sector *(Li),* assuming the sectoral income distribution h_i and h_c as well as the propensity to save out of profits *(s_p)* are given. Thus, when $s_p = 0.6$, $h_c = 0.3$, and $h_i = 0.25$, the realization proportion *R* is 4.41 (approximately) in (7), indicating that for each additional 100 Workers employed in the investment sector, about 441 workers have to be employed in the consumption sector to produce just enough surplus of consumption goods to be realized into monetary profits. If more than 441 workers are employed in the consumption sector, there would be unplanned accumulation of inventories of final consumption goods that could not be realized into profits; similarly, for $\Delta L_i = 100$ but $\Delta L_C < 441$, there would either be unplanned de-cumulation of past stocks of consumption goods or excess demand for it.

In contrast to the realization proportion (or ray OR) defined in (7), at every point of time, there is a *historical proportion* of existing capacities inherited from the past. In the two-departmental scheme, we may postulate X_i (0) and *X_c(0)* to be such historically inherited capacities, measured in terms of full-capacity outputs of the investment- and the consumption sector, respectively. Thus, full *utilization* of existing capacities in the investment sector would produce a flow of investment goods output

Figure 1
Realization and Proportionality

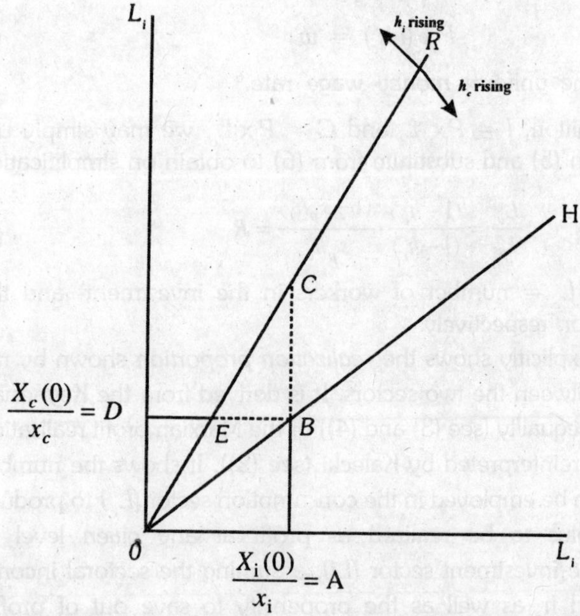

$0A = \frac{X_i(0)}{x_i} =$ employment level in the investment sector with full utilization of existing capacities in that sector.

$0D = \frac{X_c(0)}{x_c} =$ employment level in the consumption sector with full utilization of existing capacities in that sector.

Rays OR and OH are drawn in accordance with equations (7) and (8) respectively.

X_i (0) which would require, in turn, $X_i(0)/x_i = L_i$ (0) workers to be employed in the investment sector at the given labour productivity level x_i. Similarly, full utilization of existing capacities in the consumption sector would produce output flow $X_c(0)$ and employ $X_c(0)/x_c = L_c(0)$ workers. Therefore, the historically inherited proportion for distribution of labour between the two sectors is given as[7]

$$\frac{L_c(0)}{L_i(0)} = \frac{X_c(0)/x_c}{X_i(0)/x_i} = H \tag{8}$$

The proportion shown by ray OH in (8) characterizes the *arbitrary* initial condition of the economy. Since such an initial condition is arbitrarily inherited from the past evolution of the economy, there is no reason to expect OH to coincide with the realization proportion OR in (7). However, if slope OH ≠ slope OR, there must exist *structural* excess capacity or excess demand in one sector or the other. This is most easily seen in Figure 1.

It is evident from Figure 1 that if existing capacity is fully utilized in the investment sector, then OA number of workers would have to be employed in that sector. However, this creates demand for surplus consumption goods which can be met by employing AC number of workers in the consumption sector, while historically inherited capacity permits only AB workers at the most to be employed in the consumption sector. Thus, full utilization of capacity in the investment sector results in *structural excess demand* for consumption goods, equivalent to BC workers in the consumption sector multiplied by their constant labour productivity x_c. Obversely, full utilization of inherited capacity in the consumption sector with employment level OD in that sector, creates surplus of consumption goods which can be realized into profit only if the level of employment is DE in the investment sector. Consequently, there would result *structural excess capacity* in the investment sector, equivalent to foregone investment output i.e. EB multiplied by x_i. Consequently, there would either be structural excess demand or structural excess capacity in one sector or the other, as the realization and the historical proportions differ.

Any discrepancy between the realization proportion ray OR and the historical proportion ray OH arises due to a mismatch between investments made *in the past* which survive to the present and the *present* state of the economy. The present state of flow equilibrium in the economy is encapsuled in the realization proportion which is uniquely determined from (7), given the sectoral class distribution of income h_i and h_c as well as the propensity to save out of profits, s_p in the present situation. Nevertheless, because the values of these parameters were not correctly anticipated in the past, the historical proportion i.e. ray OH of existing capacities diverge from the realization proportion. In short, the inequality between OR and OH emphasizes some *falsified expectations* that must occur in historical time. The *arbitrariness of the initial condition* in terms of the historical proportion is simply an analytical way of capturing mistakes of the past in relation to the present state of the economy.

ADJUSTMENTS IN HISTORICAL TIMES

When the arbitrary *stock* of capital goods inherited from the past entailing arbitrary sectoral composition of existing capacities along ray OH differs from the current realization proportion along ray OR, the economy is out of equilibrium due to the persistence of past mistakes into the present. Since history or the initial condition is not malleable, only the current situation can change in response to such an out-of-equilibrium position. It is a typical feature of many post-Keynesian adjustment mechanisms to consider change in sectoral income distribution. Thus, h_i rises when the price level of investment goods P_i rises faster than the money wage rate w in percentage terms at a constant level of labour productivity x_i. Similiarly, h_c rises if the percentage rise in price of consumer goods P_c exceeds that of money wage rate w at constant x_c.[8] It is easy to check from (7) that,

$$\frac{\delta R}{\delta h_c} = -\frac{(1-s_p h_i)}{h_c^2 p(1-h_i)} < 0 \qquad (10)$$

and

$$\frac{\delta R}{\delta h_i} = -\frac{(1-h_c).(1-s_p)}{(1-h_i)^2.s_p h_c} > 0 \qquad (11)$$

Thus, from (10), h_c rises to rotate the realization ray OR *clockwise* and from (11), h_i rises to rotate OR *anti-clockwise*, as indicated in Figure 1.

Consider a situation where existing capacity of the investment sector is fully utilized and employment in the investment sector corresponds to OA in Figure 1. This entails excess demand for consumption goods, equivalent to BCx_c, in Figure I.[9] If such excess demand for consumption goods induces consumption goods prices to rise faster than money wage, h_c would be rising over time. At first sight, it would appear that the discrepancy between the realization ray OR and the historical proportion ray OH is gradually reduced over time to generate tendencies towards an 'equilibrium'. Obversely, the same story can be told with initial, full-capacity employment at OD in the consumption sector. It results in excess capacity in the investment sector, measured by foregone output BEx_i. If such excess capacity in the investment sector induces a fall in the profit margin on investment goods, then h_i *falls* through time to rotate OR clockwise to set up tendencies to eliminate the discrepancy between the two proportions R and H.

Nevertheless, as Joan Robinson warned us, any such *mechanical* analysis of equilibrating adjustment is likely to be misleading. This is because it is based on an implicit false analogy of movement in space which is reversible and movement in time which is not. As h_c rises or h_i falls in the above example (even assuming prices and money wages to be flexible in the required manner), this will set up fresh expectations about *the future.*[10] Such expectations about the future in turn must influence current investment decisions in creating *new* capacities in the two sectors. As a result, the historical proportion H would also be gradually altered through time through a process of investment and disinvestment in the two sectors. What we are then encountered with is a shift in both R and H through time against a background of *changing* expectations about the future. Under these circumstances, it is an elementary error to think of an 'equilibrium position' towards which the economy adjusts.

To give the story a longer run under the most favourable conditions for conventional equilibrium analysis, suppose the *real* wage rate in terms of consumption goods falls through time. This implies h_c is rising to induce OR to rotate *clockwise* in Figure 1. Also suppose, this rise in the profit margin on consumption goods due to rising h_c induces investors to expand capacities in the consumption sector at a faster rate than in the investment sector. This entails that the historical proportion OH is shifting in favour of the consumption sector to rotate OH upwards, i.e. anti-clockwise through time. To fix our ideas, this is roughly shown in Figure 2, using exactly the same notations as in Figure 1.

As Figure 2 shows, *even if* the two proportions OR and OH coincide along OP through contrary rotations, it would be misleading to think of OP as an 'equilibrium position' for at least two distinct reasons. First, OP cannot be assumed to be a sustainable position because it is only *momentarily* attained through a falling real wage (i.e. rising h_c) in *historical* time. Such a fall in the real wage rate through time must generate its own momentum of expectations about the future so that expectations cannot simply settle down at OP to make it sustainable. Thus, for instance, the investors may continue to expect h_c to rise through time and continue to invest in favour of the consumption sector. This would keep rotating the historical proportion OH anti-clockwise beyond OP and the economy would *overshoot* in that case. It would again be a mistake to think of position P as an 'unstable equilibrium', drawing an analogy from classical mechanics. The overshooting occurs because *expectations*

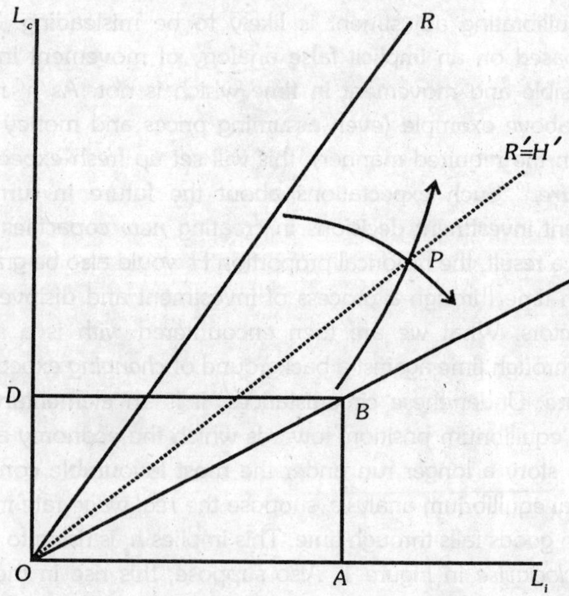

Figure 2

Hypothetical Adjustment in Realization and Proportionality Under Falling Real Wage Rate

Ray of historical proportion OH rotates anti-clockwise, starting from the initial configuration at B as investment shifts in favour of the consumpt.on sector. Rav of realization proportion Or rotates clockwise as h_c rises, implying falling *real* wage rate in terms of consumption goods.

are in an unsettled state through rising h_c in historical time; and, even if the 'physical' conditions for the 'equilibrium' are met at P through OR' = OH', *expectations* do *not* correspond to that 'equilibrium' position.[11] The influence of the future on the present through changing expectations (as h_c changes) makes any mechanical analogy in terms of 'stable' or 'unstable' equilibrium misleading in the context of the present analysis.

Secondly, there is a more conventional difficulty that needs to be mentioned. As the *real* wage rate falls through time (and k_c rises) in the above example, two *contradictory effects* arise : *potential* profit per unit of sale of consumption goods rises, but there is increasing difficulty in realizing profits as the level of effective demand tends to shrink through the falling real wage rate. Unless such fall in effective demand is continuously compensated by higher investment by the capitalists (due to rising *potential* profit per unit of sale of consumption goods), any equilibrium at P may also be vitiated by under-utilization of existing capacities. Without such 'right' assumptions about the investment behaviour of the firms, there would hardly be any sense in defining P as a 'position of equilibrium', even leaving out the earlier difficulties due to changing expectations through time.[12]

The upshot of all this can be summed up in a single proposition due to Joan Robinson. Since *neither* expectations are settled in a process of historical change (e.g. h_c falling through time in the above example) *nor* effective demand need be steadily maintained at the required level (due to autonomous investment behaviour of the firms') during an out-of-equilibrium traverse, 'approaching an equilibrium configuration' is a meaningless construct in analytical economics. The economy has to be in equilibrium already with expectations settled at that equilibrium level, if any such equilibrium is to be sustained. Among other things, it requires the initial stocks to be in the 'right' proportion. However, this means the initial conditions must *always* be 'right' rather than being *arbitrarily* inherited from history! But to rule out such arbitrary initial conditions is to banish historical time from the analysis of capitalistic accumulation. Problems of capital valuation apart, the malleable capital model, where capital goods can be costlessly and timelessly (i.e. with infinite speed of adjustment) shifted among sectors and the 'capital-labour' ratio can be instantaneously adjusted so that *all* existing techniques are always optimal in relation to the current wage-profit ratio, merely evades all the serious problems caused by the irreversibility of time in the analysis of capitalistic accumulation.

The tragedy of neoclassical economics is not simply that it makes such fantastically 'simplifying' assumptions. More sadly, it even fails to recognize that in the name of simplification, it has banished meaningful treatment of time altogether from economic analysis.

NOTES :

1. The conventional definition of dynamic analysis where time enters in an essential way is inadequate. Not only must time enter in

an essential way in defining the magnitudes of the relevant variable, but the irreversibility of time has to be ensured in dynamic economic analysis.

2. E.g. Swan (1956), Solow (1956), Meade (1961), to name a few of the typical neoclassical growth models.
3. In Harrod's definition of 'dynamic equilibrium', the two-sided role of investment was first emphasized. Increase in investment creates *additional demand* through the multiplier process which must be matched by *additional supply* created through (net) investment in creating new capacities. By emphasizing the requirement of matching additional demand with additional supply, Harrod concentrated on the *flow-equilibrium* of the system along his 'warranted growth path'. The problem of historical proportionality however relates to stock-equilibrium, as we shall see later in the text. Thus, in an otherwise exhaustive survey of growth theory, Hahn and Matthews (1964) fail to appreciate this very problem of the relation between stock-equilibrium and capital theoretic issues caused by the irreversibility of time.
4. The physical surplus of consumption goods is measured at the market price. Thus, this surplus would include unplanned accumulation of inventories as a part of (notional) gross profit measured by the accountants, if equality condition (1) fails to be satisfied.
5. Note (like in Marx) we leave out the problem of realization of profit (π_1) for the investment sector. To analyse profit realization in the production of investment goods, we need to introduce explicitly an investment function, showing the demand for investment goods.
6. These equations are also used in Bhaduri and Robinson (1980)—Mathematical Appendix, Note C—except that by choice of output units $x_c = 1$ and $x_i = 1$.
7. More exactly, the historical 'proportion' represents a point like B in Figure 1. We consider the ray OB through that point, more in analogy with Marx's analysis.
8. Kaldor (1955-6), Robinson (1956), and Kahn (1959) introduced such adjustment in the analysis of capitalistic accumulation. It also forms a central theme in Pasinetti's (1974) analysis of aggregate growth models.
9. Assuming no problem of realization in the investment sector. See also footnote 5.

10. On the other hand, an 'inflationary barrier' may prevent *real* wages from falling when money wages rise at least as fast as prices.
11. Such *unsettled* expectations are a characteristic of an arbitrary initial position. Only when the economy has already been in equilibrium for a sufficiently long time, do expectations settle down to correspond to that equilibrium position. In mechanics, we do not distinguish between movement towards an equilibrium starting from an arbitrary initial position and the perturbation of an equilibrium in discussing the property of stability. However, this distinction is crucial in economics because of the differing nature of expectations in the two cases. See also Robinson (1974) and Hicks (1965,1973).
12. This relates to the well-known 'wage-cut' controversy of the 1930s which was recently revived by Malinvaud (1982). The logical inadequacy of Malinvaud's formulation is pointed out by Bhaduri (1983) and a consideration of the analytical issues involved can be found in Rowthorn (1981) and in Bhaduri and Marglin (1990).

References :

Bhaduri, A. 1983. Multimarket classification of unemployment: a sceptical note. *Cambridge Journal of Economics,* December.

Bhaduri, A. and Robinson, J. 1980. Accumulation and exploitation: an analysis in the tradition of Marx, Sraffa and Kalecki. *Cambridge Journal of Economics,* June.

Bhaduri, A. and Marglin, S. 1990. Unemployment and the real wage: the economic basis for testing political ideologies. *Cambridge Journal of Economics,* December.

Hahn, F.H. and Matthews, R.C.O. 1964. The theory of economic growth: a survey. *Economic Journal,* December. Harrod, R. 1939. An essay in dynamic theory. *Economic Journal,* March.

Hicks, J. R. 1965. *Capital and Growth.* Oxford: Clarendon Press.-1973. *Hicks, Capital and Time.* Oxford: Clarendon Press.

Kahn, R.F. 1959. Exercises in the analysis of economic growth. *Oxford Economic Papers,* June.

Kaldor, N. 1955-56. Alternative theories of distribution. *Review of Economic Studies,* March.

Kalecki, M. 1971. Determinants of profits in *Selected Essays in the Dynamics of the Capitalist Economy.* Cambridge: Cambridge University Press.

Malinvaud. E. 1982. Wages and unemployment. *Economic Journal,* March.

Meade, J.E. 1961. *A Neo-Classical Theory of Economic Growth.* London: Allen and Unwin.

Pasinetti, L.L. 1974. *Growth and Income Distribution: Essays in Economic Theory.* Cambridge University Press.

Robinson, J. 1956. *The Accumulation of Capital.* London: Macmillan.—1974.

Robinson, History *versus* Equilibrium. *Thames Papers on Political Economy,* Autumn.-1980.

Robinson, Collected Economic Papers, vol. 5. Cambridge, Massachusetts : MIT Press.

Rowthorn, B. 1981. Demand, real wage and economic growth. *Thames Papers on Political Economy,* Autumn.

Solow, R.M. 1956. A contribution to the theory of economic growth. *Quarterly Journal of Economics,* March.

Swan, T.W. 1956. Economic growth and capital accumulation. *Economic Record,* November.

INCREASING RETURNS AND THE DIVISION OF LABOUR IN THE THEORY OF ECONOMIC DEVELOPMENT

Classical concern with economic growth and development was rekindled towards the end of the second world war, as reconstruction and decolonization became part of an international agenda. Thinking about development and underdevelopment, some economists pursued a suggestive line of enquiry to argue that countries develop through processes that reinforce themselves overtime. Thus, Rosenstein-Rodan (1943) argued in favour of a "big push", consisting of several complementary investment projects, needed to set in motion such a self-reinforcing process. Myrdal found that disparities between ethnic groups (1944) and countries (1957) tend to widen due to the operation of a similar "principle of circular and cumulative causation". Kaldor (1989) explained regional and international imbalances through the self-reinforcing process of increasing returns, and argued that standard "equilibrium economics" is incompatible with this framework of analysis.

Self-reinforcing mechanisms appear in different fields of enquiry, e.g. as auto-catalysis in bio-chemical reactions or, as positive feedback in engineering systems. Examples also abound in economics. Current price rise may lead to expectations of even greater price rise to generate "bubbles"; similarly, a self-reinforcing "herd instinct" of agents may produce patterns of collective behaviour to produce "mania, panics and crashes" in the financial markets (Kindleberger, 1978). Even some fundamental norms of the market culture like trust, and respect for commercial contracts may be reinforced through an increasing number of market participants accepting them.

Almost since the birth of political economy as a distinct branch of enquiry, the presence of such self-reinforcing positive feedback, especially in manufacturing has been known. Petty (1623-87) recognised not only the importance of agricultural surplus in sustaining the **social** division of labour between agriculture and manufacturing, he also pointed out the possibility of cheaper production through the **technical** division of labour and **spacial** agglomeration of manufacturing activities : "........for in so vast a city (like London), Manufactures will beget one another and each Manufacture will divide into as many parts as possible, whereby the work of each Artisan will be simple and easy. As for Example, in the making of a watch, if one Man shall make the Wheels, another the Spring, another shall engrave the Dial-Plate, and another shall make the Cases, then the Watch will be better and cheaper, than if the whole work be put upon any one man" (Petty, 1963:471-2; quoted in Groenwegen, 1998:219).

Social as well as technical division of labour in a competitive economy was assigned a central role in Adam Smith's "Inquiry into the Nature and the Causes of the Wealth of Nations" (1776). In the vision he presented, greater division of labour leads to higher labour productivity which, under the classical assumption of a constant real wage rate, generates larger surplus per worker[1] Competition plays a critical role in the continuous reinvestment of that surplus. As the costs of production get reduced through a greater division of labour, the long-run normal prices are lowered in a competitive economy which, in turn, put pressure on the capitalists to reduce costs further by taking recourse to even greater division of labour through the reinvestment of the surplus (cf. Kurz and Salvadori, 1998). Young revived this vision by pointing out that the division of labour operates on an economy-wide scale through continuous product differentiation, the emergence of new products, industries, production-methods and organisation which result in a self-reinforcing process of cumulative progress. He summed it up in ".....the theorem that the division of labour depends in large part upon the division of labour" (Young, 1928:233).

This grand Smithian vision of capitalistic development as a continuously self-reinforcing process, driven by the twin forces of competition and division of labour, raises many issues, some of which were more closely analysed by subsequent developments in economic theory. Ricardo (1817) brought into sharp focus the consequences of the obvious neglect of non-reproducible resources like land. It led him to the dismal view that economic development ends ultimately in a "stationary state" with zero profit; because profit tends to dwindle while the differential rent on land increases at its expense, as the economy expands bringing under cultivation less and less productive land at the margin yielding diminishing returns (cf. Pasinetti, 1959-60). Although 'capital' is a produced means of production, on the questionable assumption (Pasinetti, 2000) that it can be treated in a manner analogous to land, diminishing return to capital is postulated to occur in modern neo-classical theory as the capital-labour ratio rises, if capital accumulates through the reinvestment of saving at a pace faster than that of the exogenously growing labour force[2]. The Ricardian "stationary state" is then reinvented as an exogenously given "steady state" rate of growth, determined by the steady, exogenous growth rate of the labour force, which can be measured either in natural units without technical progress, or in efficiency units of labour if technical progress takes the specific form of augmenting only labour productivity (Solow, 1956; Swan, 1956).

For a return to the Smithian view that, the growth process is driven endogenously by the interacting forces of competition and division of labour without any exogenously binding constraint like labour, attention has recently been focused in the neo-classical tradition to interpret the division of labour in a manner that counteracts the marginal product of capital from diminishing. Currently available endogenous models of growth explore the general idea that the growing stock of capital, that the reinvestment of savings would generate by itself increasing division of labour through **social** 'learning by doing' (Arrow, 1962), embodied in a larger stock of 'human capital' (e.g. Romer, 1986; Lucas, 1988). In effect, it by-passes the role of labour as an exogenous constraint, by postulating that the increasing division of labour, brought about by the production of further human capital can be achieved through a larger stock of physical capital (e.g. Arrow, 1962; Romer, 1986) or, through the stock of human capital and the proportion of labour time allocated to acquir human capital through training (Usawa, 1965; Lucas, 1988). In either case, human capital is so defined as to augment the total stock of capital in efficiency units. When this efficiency effect is assumed to be sufficiently strong to neutralize the tendency of the marginal product of physical capital from falling, economic growth may be sustained endogenously, despite the exogenously given growth of the labour force.

The possibility of social learning creates a wedge between the private and the public view of economic optimality. For instance, if gross investment provides the route to social learning, private investors would fail to take this externality into account, and private optimization would result in under-investment from a social point of view. It has long been known that the so-called fundamental theorem of static welfare economics, namely that every competitive equilibrium is Pareto optimal and vice versa, runs into difficulties because of various externalities in production and consumption (cf. Chakravarty, 1973). Social learning through capital accumulation extends this argument to the dynamic context of economic growth. It also warns against the Smithian reliance on competition to do necessarily a satisfactory job of maintaining dynamic efficiency in the presence of social learning, or other forms of externalities driving the division of labour.

However, the argument goes deeper than non-optimal temporal or intertemporal resource allocation in the presence of increasing returns, because it might render the very market form of competition **structurally** unstable. Marshall (1920) hinted at it in his famous Appendix H (see also Bharadwaj, 1989), and the incompatibility between his partial equilibrium analysis and the assumption of increasing returns was made explicit by Sraffa (1926). To restate the problem of structural instability of the market form with a simple example, consider only two competitive firms identical in every respect, and both subject to exactly the same extent of decrease in average cost with expansion in output. A small, accidental perturbation in favour of the market share of one firm, by reducing its average cost gives it only a slight initial competitive advantage. However, this almost negligible initial advantage might magnify cumulatively over time in a self-reinforcing manner, as lower average cost leads to higher market share to even lower average cost and so on, perhaps until one firm emerges as the monopolist, and the competitive market structure is irrevocably changed. Similar reinforcing mechanisms might also operate in the spatial competition between two industrial locations (Arthur, 1994). As a more dramatic example from socio-biology, consider the social organization of insects. Ants or termites are known to practise so extensive a division of labour that the survival of the individual is practically impossible outside the group. In the construction of termites' nest, initially random deposits of building materials may occur in several places. When, by chance, one of these deposits become sufficiently large, a similar self-reinforcing process takes over, as termites begin to deposit preferentially materials on the larger heap, while the smaller deposits are abandoned altogether or joined by arch in particular cases (Nicolis and Prigogine, 1977: 452-6). Thus, the emergence of structures or orders in the formation of termites' nest, industrial districts, cities or monopolies share in common the same basic mechanism of self-reinforcement.

As these examples suggest, many self-reinforcing processes over time, including dynamic increasing returns and division of labour, have consequences that are not easily dealt with in standard economic analysis. **First,** temporary, even small disturbances, may have large, permanent consequences, at times incorporated in a new order as our previous example of the emergence of monopoly from competition suggests. Similarly, short-term macroeconomic stabilisation policies that depress output and investment temporarily, may affect adversely the long-run growth prospect of the economy, if, for example, they retard social 'learning by doing' and human capital formation which reduces long-run productivity growth (Blackburn, 1999).

Second, the cumulative processes through which initial small disturbances magnify, usually take time. In a probabilistic framework, if the initial disturbances are random, fluctuations would occur initially, before any cumulative process is able to gather sufficient momentum to dominate the long-run dynamics. In the previous monopoly example, the fortunes of the two competing firms would fluctuate initially, if both are subjected to random shocks. Again, in the termites' nest-building example, the prospect of the location fluctuates initially among alternative sites of deposits. Fluctuations give way to order, when the self-reinforcing process becomes sufficiently strong through successive positive feedbacks in favour of one particular firm or building location. "Order through fluctuations" (Haken, 1978; Nicolis and Prigogine, 1977) is therefore a common phenomenon in many self-organizing systems, including economic systems which self-organize through self-reinforcing mechanisms like increasing returns and division of labour.

Third, each successive, positive feedback tends to "lock in" the system more firmly, through its cumulative effect along a particular path or trajectory. In the monopoly example, as one particular firm cumulate the advantages of successive rounds of cost reduction through higher market share, a path-dependent outcome towards the industrial structure of monopoly becomes more probable. One could also think of two competiting technologies in the same manner. By chance, or even due to its initial superiority, as a particular technology gets adopted, the firm producing that technology might enjoy initially increasing returns to scale internal to the firm, due to the spreading out of some fixed overhead cost over a larger volume of sales. However, over time it might also have the advantages of the distributional network getting increasingly geared to spreading that particular technology, while social learning and training about it also become easier. Thus, under increasing returns technological trajectories have a tendency to get trapped in a particular path. However, had the initially left-out technology been adopted, it might have become more efficient over time than the one actually adopted. Paradoxically therefore, dynamic increasing returns and division of labour which have long been recognized as a main source of achieving efficiency in production might also turn out to be a source of inefficiency in terms of the comparative costs of foregone opportunities over time (Arthur, 1994; David, 1985).

Although path of dependence and locking-in seem fairly generic properties of many economic, social and political processes, the formalism required to capture them is only at an early stage of development. At each stage of such a process, usually several possibilities or choices exist. Its formalization calls for a non-linear probability schema, and in some interesting cases it may be captured by a "generalized Polya process" (due to Arthur, Ermolieu and Karniouski, 1983, 1987; reprinted in Arthur, 1994). To illustrate intuitively this process, consider the economic example of locating a new industry among alternative industrial districts. If the probability of its being located in a particular district is postulated to depend on the proportion of total industries located already in that district, then the self-reinforcing mechanism appears only probabilistically, because the location actually chosen for the next industry may still be any one of the districts. The generalized Polya process demonstrates that, as industrial development continues, the proportion of industries located in a district ultimately settles down to an equilibrium (of "fixed point" of the probability function), where the (ex ante) probability of locating a new industry in a particular district equals exactly the (ex post) proportion of total industries located already in the district. The chance element in deciding on industrial location ultimately has little influence. In general, however, several such (stable) equilibria or fixed points are possible, so that deterministic prediction of the equilibrium position may not be possible.

Contrary to Kaldor's view (1989) that the cumulative causation of dynamic increasing returns is incompatible in general with economic equilibrium, Polya-like processes exhibit the possibility of equilibrium or multiple equilibria, because the strength of positive feedbacks tend to decrease in each successive round. Thus, if the proportion of industries in a district initially is 1/5 or 20%, as the next industry is located there, it becomes [(1+1)/(5+1)] = 33%; with the next one [(2+1)/(6+1)] = 43% and so on; i.e. while the feedbacks remain positive and self-reinforcing, in percentage terms they decrease non-linearly in strength at each round[3]. Without this additional assumption of positive feedbacks of decreasing strength at each round, self-reinforcing processes of increasing returns may indeed rule out the existence of equilibrium.

From the macroeconomic point of view, however, a far more compelling reason limits the extent of the division of labour than the positive feedbacks of decreasing strength in a self-reinforcing process. Adam Smith had rightly observed that, "the extent of the division of labour is limited by the size of the market"; but he failed to analyse clearly what determines the size of the market. The interaction between the size of the market which is determined by aggregate demand, as the Keynes (1936) - Kalecki (1971) theory taught us, and the division of labour lies at the core of the macrodynamics of economic growth. And yet, post-war neo-classical growth models, exogenous or endogenous, share with the Ricardian model the unfortunate common characteristic of ignoring effective demand altogether. It is simply assumed instead, in a pre-Keynesian manner, that all savings are automatically reinvested in a world ruled by Say's law[4]. And yet, the matching between demand and supply is particularly problematic in the presence of increasing returns, as pointed out by Weitzman (1982). Because, suppliers inevitably become large under increasing returns, and they may fail to create adequate demand necessary to make continuous expansion of supply profitable.

Restated from a Keynesian perspective, the independence of investment from saving decisions forces us to recognise that the higher labour productivity and surplus per worker made possible by a greater division of labour need not be invested automatically by the firms. Because increasing returns exacerbate the tendency towards monopoly and market concentration, the share of profit in income may increase. How this impacts on the incentive to invest remains an open question. While Schumpeter (1942) emphasised "creative destruction" through rapid technical progress in an oligopolistic market structure, Steindl (1952) suggested that a higher profit share under greater market concentration might push the economy towards stagnation by depressing aggregate demand. However, insofar as a higher profit share lowers consumption demand but raises the profit margin per unit of sale to stimulate investment demand, the effect on aggregate demand remains ambiguous. Depending on which effect dominates, it might result in a lower-consumption induced stagnationist regime, or a higher-investment-led expansionist regime (Bhaduri and Marglin, 1990). Thus, the division of labour impacts in a complex way on the level of aggregate demand, and the size of the market. In the case of investment-led expansion with higher profit share, it can perhaps help the process of further division of labour in a self-reinforcing manner (cf. Young, 1928); but it might also hinder the same process in the consumption-induced stagnationist case. Without analysing these alternative patterns of interaction between the market size and the division of labour, we could end up telling the story of Hamlet without mentioning the Prince of Denmark !

NOTES :

1. Higher surplus per worker need not imply higher total surplus, because that depends also on the level of employment. Smith's (pre-Keynesian) discussion fails to explain how the levels of employment and output are determined.
2. Again, as in Ricardo's or Smith's discussion, the level of employment or output is not determined; instead, it is simply assumed that full-employment is maintained somehow, and that full-employment level of saving is automatically reinvested under the (pre-Keynesian) Say's law to drive the process of rising capital-labour ratio.
3. Obversely, if in successive rounds, the next industry is not located in that district, probability decreases from 20% to [1/(5+1)] = 17% to [1/(6+1)] = 14% etc. Intuitively speaking, the intersection(s) between the increasing and the decreasing probability defines one or more Polya fixed points, at probability less than or equal to unity.
4. See previous end notes 1 and 2, on this point.

REFERENCES :

Arthur, W.B. 1994. *Increasing Returns and Path Dependence in the Economy.* Michigan University Press, Ann Arbor.

Bhaduri, A. and Marglin, S. 1990. 'Unemployment and real wage : the economic basis for contesting political ideologies', *Cambridge Journal of Economics.* (14): 375-93

Bharadwaj, K. 1989. 'Marshall on Pigou's Wealth and Welfare' in her *Themes in Value and Distribution* : 159-75, Oxford University Press, Delhi.

Blackburn, K. 1999. 'Can stabilization policy reduce long-run growth?' *Economic Journal* (109): 67-77.

Chakravarthy, S. 1973. 'Theory of development planning : an appraisal' in H.C. Bos, H. Linneman and P. de Wolff (eds), *Economic Structure and Development.* North Holland, Amsterdam.

David, P.A. 1985. 'Clio and economics of QWERTY', *American Economic Review,* Papers and Proceedings 75 : 332-7

Groenweagen, P. 1998. 'Division of labour' in H.D. Kurz and N. Salvadori (eds). *The Elgar Companion to Classical Economics*_(A to K): 217-22, Edward Elgar, Chettenham, U.K.

Haken, H. 1978. *Synergetics,* Springer-Verlag, New York.

Kaldor, N. 1989. The case for regional policies' in F. Targetti and A.P. Thirlwall (eds) *The Essential Kaldor* : 311-26, Duckworth, London.

Kaldor, N. 1989 'The irrelevance of equilibrium economics, *op.cit:* 373-98.

Kaldor, N. 1989. 'The role of increasing returns, technical progress and cumulative causation in the theory of international trade and economic growth', *op.cit* 327-51.

Kaldor, N. 1989. 'What is wrong with economic theory', *op.cit* : 399-410.

Kalecki, M. 1971. 'Determinants of profits' in his, *Selected Essays on the Dynamics of the Capitalist Economy* : 78-92, Cambridge University Press, Cambridge.

Keynes, J.M. 1936. *The General Theory of Employment, Interest and Money,* Macmillan, London.

Kindleberger, C.P. 1978. *Mania. Panics and Crashes,* Basic Books, New York.

Kurz, H.D. and Salvadori, N. 1998 ' "Endogenous growth models and the "Classical" tradition', in H.D. Kurz and N. Salvadori, *Understanding 'Classical' Economics:* 66-89, Routledge, London.

Lucas, R. 1988. 'On the mechanics of economic development', *Journal of Monetary Economics,* 22 : 3-42.

Marshall, A. 1920. *Principles of Economics,* (8 edition), appendix H, Macmillan, London

Myrdal, G. 1944. *An American Dilemma : The Negro Problem and Modern Democracy,* (Carnegie Foundation Study), Harper and Row, New York.

Myrdal, G. 1957. *Economic Theory and Underdeveloped Regions.* Duckworth, London.

Nicolis, G and Prigogrine, I. 1977. *Self-Organization in Nonequilibrium Systems.* John Wiley and Sons, New York.

Pasinetti, L.L. 1959-60. 'A mathematical formulation of the Ricardian system', *Review of Economic Studies* (26): 78-98.

Pasinetti, L.L. 2000. 'Critique of neoclassical theory of growth and distribution', *Banca de Lavoro Quarterly Review* (53): 383-432.

Petty, W (original 1662). *A Treatise on Taxes and Contributions* in C.H. Hull (ed) *The Economic Writings of Sir William Petty*, Cambridge University Press, Cambridge, 1899; revised Augustins M. Kelly edition, New York, 1963.

Ricardo, D. (original 1817). *Principles of Political Economy and Taxation* in P. Sraffa (ed) *Works and Correspondence of David Ricardo*, Cambridge University Press, Cambridge, 1951, vol 1.

Romer, P. 1986. 'Increasing returns and long-run growth', *Journal of Political Economy* (94): 1002-37.

Rosenstein - Rodan, P.N. 1943. 'Problems of industrialization of Eastern and South-Eastern Europe', *Economic Journal* (53): 202-11

Schumpeter, J.A. 1942.*Capitalism, Socialism and Democracy,* (3rd edition). Harper Brothers, New York.

Smith, A. 1776. *An Inquiry into the Nature and Causes of the Wealth of Nations*, the Glasgow Edition of the Works and Correspondence of Adam Smith (vol 2), in R. H. Campbell, A.S. Skinner and W.B. Todd (eds), Oxford University Press, Oxford.

Solow, R. 1956 'A contribution to the theory of economic growth', *Quarterly Journal of Economics.* 70 : 65-94.

Sraffa, P. 1926. The Laws of returns under competitive conditions', *Economic Journal.* (36): 535-50.

Steindl, J. 1952. *Maturity and Stagnation in American Capitalism* (2nd edition), Monthly Review Press, New York.

Swan, T. 1956. 'Economic growth and capital accumulation', *Economic Record* 32 : 343 - 61

Usawa, H. 1965. 'Optimum technical change in an aggregative model of economic growth', *International Economic Review* (6): 18-31.

Weitzman, M. 1982. 'Increasing returns and the foundations of unemployment theory', *Economic Journal* (92): 787-804.

Young, A. 1928. 'Increasing returns and economic progress', *Economic Journal* (38): 527-42.

PREDATORY GROWTH

Over the last two decades or so, the two most populous large countries in the world, China and India, have been growing at rates considerably higher than the world average. In recent years the growth rate of national product of China has been about three times, and that of India approximately two times that of the world average. This has led to a clever defence of globalisation by a former chief economist of the International Monetary Fund (IMF) [Fisher 2003]. Although China and India feature as only two among some 150 countries for which data are available, he reminded us that together they account for the majority of the poor in the world. This means that even if the rich and the poor countries of the world are not converging in terms of per capita income, the well above the average world rate of growth of these two large countries implies that the current phase of globalisation is reducing global inequality and poverty at a rate as never before.

Statistical half truths can be more misleading at times than untruths. And this might be one of them, in so far as the experiences of ordinary Indians contradict such statistical artefacts. Since citizens in India can express reasonably freely their views at least at the time of elections, their electoral verdicts on the regime of high growth should be indicative. They have invariably been negative. Not only did the "shining India" image crash badly in the last general election, even the present prime minister, widely presented as the 'guru' of India's economic liberalisation in the media, could never personally win an election in his life. As a result, come election time, and all parties talk not of economic reform, liberalisation and globalisation, but of greater welfare measures to be initiated by the state. Gone election times, and the reform agenda is back; Something clearly needs to be deciphered from such predictable swings in political pronouncement.

LIVED EXPERIENCES

Politicians know that ordinary people are not persuaded by statistical mirages and numbers, but by their daily experiences. They do not accept high growth on its face value as unambiguously beneficial. If the distribution of income turns viciously against them and the opportunities for reasonable employment and livelihood do not expand with high growth, the purpose of higher growth would be widely questioned in a democracy. This is indeed what is happening, and it might even appear to some as paradoxical. The festive mood generated by high growth is marinated in popular dissent and despair, turning often into repressed anger. Like a malignant malaise, a sense of political unease is spreading insidiously along with the near double-digit growth. And, no major political party, irrespective of their right or left label, is escaping it because they all subscribe to an ideology of growth at any cost.

Unequal Growth

What exactly is the nature of this paradoxical growth that increases output and popular anger at the same time? India has long been accustomed to extensive poverty coexisting with growth, with or without its "socialist pattern". It continues to have anywhere between one-third and one-fourth of its population living in subhuman, absolute poverty. The number of people condemned to absolute poverty declined very slowly in India over the last two decades, leaving some 303 million people still in utter misery. In contrast China did better with the number of absolutely poor declining from 53 per cent to 8 per cent, i.e., a reduction of some 45 percentage points, quite an achievement compared to India's 17 percentage points. However, while China grew faster, inequality or relative poverty also grew faster in China than in India. Some claim that the increasing gap between the richer and the poorer sections in the Chinese society during the recent period has been one of the worst in recorded economic history, perhaps with the exception of some former socialist countries immediately after the collapse of the Soviet Union.

The share in national income of the poorest 20 percent of the population in contemporary China is 5.9 percent, compared to 8.2 percent in India [Radhakrishna 2008]. This implies that the lowest 20 percent income group in China and in India receives about 30 and 40 percent of the per capita average income of their respective countries. However, since China has over two times the average per capita income of India in terms of both purchasing power parity, and dollar income, the poorest 20 per cent in India are better off in relative terms, but worse off in absolute terms. The Gini coefficient, lying between zero and one, measures inequality, and increases in value with the degree of inequality. In China, it had a value close to 0.50 in 2006, one of the highests in the world. Inequality has grown also in India, but less sharply. Between 1993-94 and 2004-05, the coefficient rose from 0.25 to 0.27 in urban, and 0.31 to 0.35 in rural areas. Every dimension of inequality, among the regions, among the professions and sectors, and in particular between urban and rural areas has also grown rapidly in both countries, even faster in China than in India. In short, China has done better than India in reducing absolute poverty, but worse is allowing the gap to grow rapidly between the rich and the poor during the recent period of high growth.

A central fact stands out. Despite vast differences in the political systems of the two countries, the common factor has been increasing inequality accompanying higher growth. What is not usually realised is that the growth in output and in inequality are not two isolated phenomena. One frequently comes across the platitude that high growth will soon be trickling down to the poor, or that re-distributive action by the state through fiscal measures could decrease inequality while keeping up the growth rate. These statements are comfortable but unworkable, because they miss the main characteristic of the growth process underway. This pattern of growth is propelled by a powerful reinforcing mechanism, which the economist Gunner Myrdal had once described as "cumulative causation". The mechanism by which growing inequality drives growth, and growth fuels further inequality, has its origin in two different factors, both related to some-extent to globalisation.

Jobless Growth

First, in contrast to earlier times when less than 4 percent growth on an average was associated with 2 percent growth in employment, India is experiencing a growth rate of some 7-8 percent in recent years, but the growth in regular employment has hardly exceeded 1 percent. This means most of the growth, some 5-6 percent of the GDP, is the result not of employment expansion, but of higher output per worker. This high growth of output has its source in the growth of labour productivity. According to official statistics, between 1991 and 2004 employment fell in the organised public sector, and the organised private sector hardly compensated for it. In the corporate sector, and in some organised industries, productivity growth comes from mechanisation and longer hours of work. Edward Luce of *Financial Times* (London) reported that the Jamshedpur steel plant of the Tatas employed 85,000 workers in 1991 to produce one million tonnes of steel worth $ 0.8 million. In 2005, the production rose to five million tonnes, worth about $ five million, while employment fell to 44,000. In short, output increased approximately by a factor of five, employment dropped by a factor of half, implying an increase in labour productivity by a factor of 10.

Similarly, Tata Motors in Pune reduced the number of workers from 35,000 to 21,000 but increased the production of vehicles from 1,29,000 to 3,11,500 between 1999 and 2004, implying a labour productivity increase by a factor of four. Stephen Roach, chief economist of Morgan-Stanley, reports similar cases of Bajaj motor-cycle factory in Pune. In the mid-1990s the factory employed 24,000 workers to produce one million units of two-wheelers. Aided by Japanese robotics and Indian information technology, in 2004, 10,500 workers turned out 2.4 million units - more than double the output with less than half the labour force, an increase in labour productivity by a factor of nearly six.[1] One could multiply such examples, but this is broadly the name of the game everywhere in the private corporate sector.

Augmented Profit and Misery

The manifold increase in labour-productivity, without a corresponding increase in wages and salaries, becomes an enormous source of profit, and also a source of international price competitiveness in a globalising world. Nevertheless, this is not the entire story, perhaps not even the most important part of the story. The whole organised sector to which the corporate sector belongs, accounts for less than one-tenth of the labour force. Simply by the arithmetic of weighted average, a 5-6 percent annual growth in labour productivity in the entire economy is possible, only if the unorganised sector accounting for the remaining 90 percent of the labour force also contributes to the growth in labour productivity. Direct information is not available on this count, but several micro-studies and surveys show the broad pattern. Growth of labour productivity in the unorganised sector, which includes most of agriculture, comes from lengthening the hours of work to a significant extent, as this sector has no labour laws worth the name, or social security to protect workers. Subcontracting to the unorganised sector along with casualisation of labour on a large scale become convenient devices to ensure longer hours of work without higher pay. Self-employed workers, totalling "60 million, expanded fastest during the high growth regime, providing an invisible source of labour productivity growth [the data in Rangarajan et al 2007 could be interpreted this way]. Ruthless self-exploitation by many of these workers in a desperate attempt to survive by doing long hours of work with very little extra earning adds both to productivity growth, often augmenting corporate profit, and human misery.

However, inequality is increasing for another reason. Its ideology often described as neoliberalism is easily visible at one level; but the underlying deeper reason is seldom discussed. The increasing openness of the Indian economy to international finance and capital flows, rather than to trade in goods and services, has had the consequence of paralysing many pro-poor public policies. Despite the fact that we continue to import more than we export (unlike China), India's comfortable foreign-reserves position is mostly the result of accumulated portfolio investments and short-term capital inflows from various financial institutions. To keep the show-going in this way, the fiscal and the monetary policies of the government need to comply with the interests of the financial markers. That is the reason why successive Indian governments have willingly accepted the Fiscal Responsibility and Budget Management Act (2003) restricting deficit spending. Similarly, the idea has gained support that the government should raise resources through privatisation and so-called public-private partnership, but not through raising fiscal deficit, or not imposing a significant turnover tax on transactions of securities. These measures rattle the 'sentiment' of the financial markets, so governments remain wary of them.

The hidden agenda, vigorously pursued by governments of all colour, has been to keep the large private players in the financial markets in a happy mood. Since the private banks and financial institutions usually take their lead from the IMF and the World Bank, this bestows on these multilateral agencies considerable power over the formulation of government policies. However, the burden of such policies is borne largely by the poor of this country. This has had a crippling effect on policies for expanding public expenditure for the poor in the social sector. Inequality and distress grows as the state rolls back public expenditure in social services like basic health, education, and public distribution and neglects the poor, while the discipline imposed by the financial markets serves the rich and the corporations. This process of high growth traps roughly one in three citizens of India in extreme poverty with no possibility of escape through either regular employment growth or relief through state expenditure on social services. The high growth scene of India appears to them like a wasteland leading to the hell described by the great Italian poet Dante. On the gate of his imagined hell is written, "This is the land you enter after abandoning all hopes".

Extremely slow growth in employment and feeble public action exacerbates inequality, as a disproportionately large share of the increasing output and income from growth goes to the richer section of the population, not more than say the top 20 percent of the income receivers in India. At the extreme ends of income distribution the picture that emerges is one of striking contrasts. According to the *Forbes* magazine list for 2007, the number of Indian billionaires rose from 9 in 2004 to 40 in 2007: much richer countries like Japan had only 24, France 14 and Italy 14. Even China, despite its sharply increasing inequality, had only 17 billionaires. The combined wealth of Indian billionaires increased from $ 106 to $ 170 billion in the single year, 2006-07 [information from *Forbes* quoted in Jain and Gupta 2008]. This 60 percent increase in wealth would not have been possible, except through transfer on land from the state and central governments to the private corporations in the name of "public purpose", for mining, industrialisation and special economic zones (SEZS). Estimates based on corporate profits suggest that, since 2000-01 to date, each additional percent growth of GDP has led to an average of some 2.5 percent growth in corporate profits. India's high growth has certainly benefited, the corporations more than anyone else.

After several years of high growth along these lines, India of the 21st century has the distinction of being only second to the, US in terms of combined total wealth of its corporate billionaires coexisting' with the largest number of homeless, ill-fed and illiterates in the world. Not surprisingly, for ordinary Indians at the receiving end, this growth process is devoid of all hope for escape. Nearly half of Indian children under six years suffer from under-weight and malnutrition, nearly 80 percent from anaemia, while some 40 percent of Indian adults suffer from chronic energy deficit. Destitution, chronic hunger and poverty kill and cripple silently thousands, picking on systematically the more vulnerable. The problem is more acute in rural India, among small children, pregnant females, dalits and adivasis, especially in the poorer states [Radhakrishna 2008], while market-oriented policies and reforms continue to widen. the gap between the rich and the poor, as well as among regions.

Income Elasticities Of Demand

The growth dynamics in operation is being fed continuously by growing inequality. With their income rapidly growing, the richer group of Indians demand a set of goods, which lie outside the reach of the rest in the society (think of air-conditioned malls, luxury hotels, restaurants and apartments, private cars, world-class cities where the poor would be made invisible). The market for these goods expands rapidly. For instance, we are told that more than three in four Indians do not have a daily income of $2, equivalent about Rs. 20/- per day. They can hardly be a part of this growing market. However, the logic of the market now takes over, as the market is dictated by purchasing power. Its logic is to produce those goods for which there is enough demand backed by money, so that high prices can be charged and handsome profits can be made. As the income of the privileged grows rapidly, the market for the luxury goods they demand grows even faster through the operation of the "income elasticities of demand". These elasticities roughly measure the percent growth in the demand for particular goods due to 1 percent growth in income (at unchanged prices). Typically, goods consumed by the rich have income elasticities greater than unity, implying that the demand for a whole range of luxury goods consumed by the rich expands even faster than the growth in their income. Thus, the pattern of production is dictated by this process of growth through raising both the income of the rich faster than that of the rest of the society, and also because the income elasticities operate to increase even faster the demand for luxuries than income.

ANTI-POOR

The production structure resulting from this market-driven high growth is heavily biased against the poor. While demand expands rapidly for various up-market goods, demand for the basic necessities of life hardly expands. Not only is there little growth in the purchasing power of the poor, but the reduction in welfare expenditures by the state stunts the growth in demand for necessities. The rapid shift in the output composition in favour of services might be indicative of this process at the macro level [Rakshit 2007]. But specific examples abound. We have state-of-the-art corporate-run expensive hospitals, nursing homes and spas for the rich, but not enough money to control malaria and tuberculosis which require inexpensive treatment. So they continue to kill the largest numbers. Lack of sanitation and clean drinking water transmit deadly diseases especially to small children which could be prevented at little cost, while bottled water of various brands multiply for those who can afford. Private schools for rich kids often have monthly fees that are higher than the annual income of an average unskilled Indian worker, while the poor often have to be satisfied with schools without teachers, or class rooms.

Over time an increasingly irreversible production structure in favour of the rich begins to consolidate itself, because the investments embodied in the specific capital goods created to produce luxuries cannot easily be converted to producing basic necessities (the luxury hotel or spa cannot be converted easily to a primary health centre in a village, etc). And yet, it is the logic of the market to direct investments towards the most productive and profitable sectors for "the efficient allocation of resources". The price mechanism sends signals to guide this allocation, but the prices that rule are largely a consequence of the growing unequal distribution of income in the society. The market becomes a bad master when the distribution of income is bad.

Heightened Misery For The Poor

There are insidious consequences of such a composition of output biased in favour of the rich that our liberalised market system produces. It is highly energy, water and other non-reproducible resources intensive, and often does unacceptable violence to the environment. We only have to think of the energy and material content of air-conditioned malls, luxury hotels and apartments, air travels, or private cars as means of transport. These are no doubt symbols of "world class" cities in a poor country, by diverting resources from the country side where most live. It creates a black hole of urbanisation with a giant appetite for primary non-reproducible resources. Many are forced to migrate to cities as fertile land is diverted to non-agricultural use, water and electricity are taken away from farms in critical agricultural seasons to supply cities, and developmental piujecls displaces thousands. Hydroelectric power from the big dams is transmitted mostly to corporate industries, and a few posh urban localities, while the nearby villages are left in darkness. Peasants even close to the cities do not get electricity or water to irrigate their land as urban India increasingly gobbles up these resources. Take the pattern of water use. According to the Comptroller and Auditor General report released to the public on March 30, 2007, Gujarat increased the allocation of Narmada waters to industry fivefold during 2006, eating into the share of drought-affected villages. Despite many promises made to villagers, water allocation stagnated at 0.86 million acres feet (MAF), and even this is being cut.

Water companies and soft drink giants like Coca Cola sink deeper to take out pure groundwater as free raw material for their products. Peasants in surrounding areas pay, because they cannot match the technology or capital cost. Iron ore is mined out in Jharkhand, Chhattisgarh and Orissa leaving tribals without home or livelihood. Common lands which traditionally provided supplementary income to the poor in villages are encroached upon systematically by the local rich and the corporations with active connivance of the government. The manifest crisis engulfing Indian agriculture with more than a hundred thousand suicides by farmers over the last decade according to official statistics is a pointer to this process of pampering the rich who use their growing economic power to dominate increasingly the multitude of poor.

NO PLACE FOR THE POOREST

The composition of output demanded by the rich is hardly producible by village artisans or the small producers. They find no place either as producers or as consumers; instead, economic activities catering to the rich have to be handed over to large corporations who can now enter in a big way into the scene. The combination of accelerating growth and rising inequality begins to work in unison. Large corporations are needed to produce goods for the rich, and in the process they make their high profits and provide well-paid employment for the rich in a poor country who provide a part of the growing market. It becomes a process of destructive creation of corporate wealth, with a new coalition cutting across traditional right and left political divisions formed in the course of this road to high growth. The signboard of this road is "progress through industrialisation".

The middle class opinion makers and the media persons unite, and occasionally offer palliatives of "fair compensation" to the dispossessed. Yet, they are at a loss as to how to create alternative dignified livelihoods for those affected by large-scale dis. placement and destruction in the name of industrialisation. Talks of compensation tend to be one-sided, as they focus usually on ownership and, at best use rights to the landed. However, the multitude of the poor who teke out a living without any ownership or use right to landed property, like agricultural labourers, fishermen, or cart-drivers in rural areas, or illegal squatters and small hawkers in cities, seldom figure in this discussion about compensation. And yet, they are usually the poorest of the poor, outnumbering by far, perhaps in the ratio of 3 to 1, those who have some title to landed property. Ignoring them altogether, the state acquires with single-minded devotion land, water and resources for the private corporations for mining, industrialisation or SEZS in the name of public interest.

With some tribal land that can be acquired according to the PESA (1996) Act only through the consent of the community (gramsabha), consent is frequently manufactured at gun point by the law and order machinery of the state, if the money-power of the corporations to bribe and intimidate proves to be insufficient. The vocal supporters of industrialisation never stop to ask, why the very poor who are least able, should bear the burden of 'economic progress' of the rich?

It amounts to a process of internal colonisation of the poor, mostly dalits and adivasis and of other marginalised groups,through forcible dispossession and subjugation. It has set in motion a social process not altogether unknown between the imperialist "master race" and the colonised "natives". As the privileged thin layer of the society distance themselves from the poor, the speed at which the secession takes place comes to be celebrated as a measure of the rapid growth of the country. Thus, India is said to be poised to become a global power in the 21st century, with the largest number of homeless, undernourished, illiterate children coexisting with billionaires created by this rapid growth.

An unbridled market whose rules are fixed by the corporations aided by state-power shapes this process. The ideology of progress through dispossession of the poor, preached relentlessly by the united power of the rich, the middle class and the corporations colonise directly the poor, and indirectly it has begun to colonise our minds. The result is a sort of uniform industrialisation of the mind, a standardisation of thoughts which sees no other alternative. And yet, there is a fatal flaw. No matter how powerful this united campaign by the rich corporations, the media and the politicians is, even their combined power remains defenceless against the actual life experiences of the poor. If this process of growth continues for long, it would produce its own demons. No society, not even our malfunctioning democratic system, can withstand beyond a point the increasing inequality that nurtures this high growth. The rising dissent of the poor must either be suppressed with increasing state violence flouting every norm of democracy, and violence will be met with counter-violence to engulf the whole society. Or, an alternative path to development that depends on deepening our democracy with popular participation has to be found. Neither the rulers nor the ruled can escape for long this challenge thrown up by the recent high growth of India.

NOTE :

1. Data collected by Aseem Srivastava, 'Why This Growth Can Never Trickle Down'. Aseem can be reached at aseem62@yahoo.com.

REFERENCES :

Alternative Economic Survey, India (2006-07): by Alternative Survey Group, New Delhi, Dannish Books.

Dev, S Mahendra (2008): Inclusive *Growth in India,* Oxford University Press, New Delhi.

Fisher, S (2003): 'Globalisation and Its Challenges', American Economic Review, Papers and Proceedings, Vol 93, No 2.

Government of India, Economic *Survey* (2006-07): Ministry of Finance, New Delhi.

Green Left Weekly (2007): Issue No 710, May.

Rakshit, Mihir (2007): 'Service-led Growth', Money *and Finance,* February.

Radhakrishna, R (2008): *India Development Report,* (ed), Oxford University Press.

Rangarajan, C et al (2007): 'Revisiting Employment and Growth', Money and Finance, September.

Jain, Anil, Kumar and Parul Gupta (2008): 'Globalisation: The Indian Experience', *Mainstream,* Delhi, February 8-14.

A FAILED WORLD VIEW

A badly kept secret among economists should be shared with non-economists on this occasion. Economic theory, in so far as it consists of results derived logically from clearly stated premises, is mostly precautionary knowledge which warns against unfounded economic propositions. Very rarely, it is positive knowledge for guiding policies. There is an even more fuzzy area of economic knowledge which infers from quantitative data through statistical techniques and historical analogies. Such knowledge is even more tentative, yet essential in a subject like economics where controlled experiments are impossible. With data generated over time subject to observational error, bias, and random shocks, we would do well to remember the saying of the Greek philosopher Heraclitus, a rough contemporary of Buddha, "It is never possible to step twice into the same river."

As a body of inexact knowledge economics requires us to be intellectually modest, and that leaves little room for inflexible views. And yet, exactly the opposite happens. Driven by ideology or vested interests, politicians, captains on industry, media men, spokespersons of the chambers of commerce, labour-unions and even academic economists posture with absolute confidence, often to mislead the public for their own interest, and conveniently change suddenly, again to suit their interest in a changed situation. Flexibility in views is necessary in economic policy making, but only if one is willing to learn honestly also from one's past mistakes. The problem with most politicians changing suddenly their views is that they change only their posture, but not their ideology. Their interests remain the same. Otherwise, how can we explain our prime minister on his recent return flight from China telling his captive audience on board that, he foresaw the current financial crisis 18 months ago, while on March 18, 2006 he told a global audience that the Reserve Bank of India would prepare a road map on full capital account convertibility to integrate the Indian financial system completely with the global capital market, but now he talks of insulating India. And even now he talks of the rescuing role of the IMF and the World Bank (Times of India, 26.10.2008), while these two institutions with their continuous support for financial liberalization has all along been part of the problem. As a matter of fact, until the global financial crisis gripped the world, our 'dream team' of policy makers including the current prime minister, deputy chairman of the planning commission and the then finance minister insisted on speedier liberalization of the financial sector with measures like capital account convertibility, greater presence of foreign banks and insurance companies with freedom to shift funds. Now they want to take credit for being prudent and slow in introducing reforms, making the nationalised banks safer etc. Politicians may be right in believing that public memory is short, but perhaps would find that it is not that short! Women and men in practical affairs pretend to know and change posture to suit the situation, but it should be the job of economists to call the bluff. We have not done too well on that count. As a well-known economist once said, "Some knowledge of economics is useful, if only to guard against being fooled by other economists." Amidst the global financial crisis and the quick U-turn taken by our so-called economic technocrats in the government, I am often reminded of the intrinsic wisdom of this statement.

It is remarkable that despite the inexactitude of economics as a body of knowledge which should have left enough space for some if not several contesting economic ideologies, over the last twenty years or so all the major political parties in India cutting across the spectrum from the Left to the Right largely converged to a very similar point of view on economic management. While differentiating themselves mostly by rhetoric, they came to subscribe to the view that globalization, market based liberalization and corporate led industrialization are inevitable compulsions for economic development in India. Consequently, they all sought foreign investments and funds on whatever terms, accepted World Bank-IMF views of growth and equity, and engaged in a race to the bottom by offering competitively favourable terms to attract large corporate houses in the states where they were in power. In short the TINA syndrome that, There Is No Alternative gripped economic action as well as imagination. For the traditional Left, recent history explains part of it. The failure of Soviet style bureaucratic central planning, U- turn of officially socialist China and Vietnam in embracing capitalist style policies undermined confidence in old fashioned socialist ideas. Economic success stories of countries like South Korea, Singapore, Taiwan, Malaysia and Hong Kong pointed to attractive possibilities. Nevertheless, in the orchestrated celebration of the market economy, one tends to forget this story is onesided. It is inconvenient for a pro-market economist to remember that most countries of sub-Saharan Africa, of Latin America, of central Asia underwent dramatic economic stagnation or decline for several years by embracing the same principle of market based liberalization (Maddison, 2001).

With economic history seldom giving unambiguous answers, economic theory has to play a critical role in making our inexact knowledge appear more plausible in the service of economic ideology. The ideology of the self regulating free market that came to rule the world and is commonly known as neo-liberalism has its origin in the idea of perfect competition as the prototype market-form. We all know markets involve buying and selling, activities which are organized under certain rules that vary enormously, say from the weekly village market to the Stock Exchanges in Dalal Street or Wall Street. Economists study the properties of the market-organization by taking a perfectly competitive market as their point of reference. Under highly unrealistic assumptions, which rule out for instance all forms of uncertainty and banishes the unknown future from the analysis, some results are obtained. It is shown that an equilibrium set of prices exist which simultaneously clears all markets by equating demand and supply. The prices in equilibrium correspond to an efficient arrangement in the sense that the production of no commodity can be increased further without decreasing the production of some other, and no participant in the market can do better either as a producer or consumer, without someone else becoming worse off. The powerful ideological metaphor is that of the invisible hand of the self-regulating market leading the society of selfish individuals to an optimum. This is indeed a most spectacular case of self-organization, where neither any intervention of the state nor any concern for the collective expressed in social norms like trust and fellow feeling is needed to reach the optimum economic state. Margaret Thatcher, the former prime minister of Britain and a main architect of the neo-liberal world view famously echoed this sentiment by claiming that there is no society, only individuals.

However, even this mythical land of perfect competition is flawed on its own terms. The optimum equilibrium that is shown to exist under idealized conditions does not guarantee that the distribution of income in the society would be tolerably good. To appreciate its practical implications, remember demand depends on the purchasing power of individuals, so a grotesquely unequal distribution of income under competitive conditions might mean millions of children dying from easily treatable diseases like malaria and T.B, while most expensive hospitals in the metropolis provide state of the art treatment at a price which only the rich can afford. Villages go without sanitation and drinkable water, but selected areas of cities might pride themselves with world class luxury apartments and glittering malls. And yet, by the logic of the market any such equilibrium would still be considered optimum because it allocates resources efficiently, and the poor in the city slums or in the villages cannot be made better off without hurting the rich in the cities.

A deeper logical flaw is that the stability of the equilibrium in a competitive market is not guaranteed without imposing further stringent conditions, and it remains unspecified how long it would take to converge to it. This is a political catch. A decision maker in a democracy, say a prime minister, can always say that economic reforms are about to produce results without specifying the time horizon. Like a dictator, the competitive market can go on promising without delivering, as it is without accountability within any specified time period. In this sense the market as an institution has no accountability except for the largely make belief ideology of self-regulation. This is the fundamental difference between the market and democracy in so far as in a democracy, there is some reckoning at the time of elections. I need only to remind you that market-based reforms did badly in India on that count. The slogan of "shining India" crashed in the last general election, and the present Prime Minister, widely considered the guru of India's market-oriented reforms, could not personally win an election.

Enthusiastic reliance on the market mechanism as the main driving force of efficient resource allocation and growth by the government accentuated poverty to create rumblings outside the electoral process in the countryside which often spills over into desperate fury and despair. Over hundred thousand farmers have committed suicide over the last decade or so. According to government estimates, some 125 districts, spread over 12 states, and covering more than a quarter of the land mass mostly in the central part of India, is affected by extremist Naxalite activities. The Dalits (16 percent) and the Adivasis (8 percent), approximately one quarter of the population provide the main support to these movements, suggesting a combination of economic and socially oppressive factors as a major cause. Despite near double digit growth for more than a decade and a half, available estimates suggest that more than one third of the Indian population live in sub-human poverty (a recent World Bank estimate puts nearly 42 percent as absolutely poor by international standard), more than three fourths of the population has a daily purchasing power of less than rupees 20 a day, nearly half the children are undernourished and many crippled by undernourishment, anemia is on the increase among women, and food deprivation in the countryside has not decreased in the last two decades. And all along the logic of the market has been encouraged by government policies to work relentlessly against the poor majority through three major routes.

First, is the extraordinarily slow growth in regular employment. Regular employment in the organised sector over the last decade or so grew at only about 1 percent, while the rest of the average 6-7 percent growth in GDP came from the growth in output per worker or labour productivity. In contrast, during the earlier decades, when GDP grew on an average at less than 4 percent, regular employment grew at the annual rate of 2 percent. The recent drive to increase labour productivity is related to globalization. International trade means increasing the importance of the external compared to the internal market, while corporations compete in the export market mostly by cutting costs to increase their international competitiveness. This usually means shedding labour force through mechanization. For instance, if the labour force in a corporation is downsized to half at the same wage, labour cost per unit of output would also be halved. Let one example suffice to illustrate How this process is working in practice. Tata Motors in Pune reduced the number of workers from 35 to 21 thousand but increased the production of vehicles from 129 to almost 312 thousand between 1999 and 2004, implying labour productivity increase by a factor of 4. The aggregate picture broadly conforms to this. According to the Economic Survey of the Government of India (2006-07), total employment in the organised sector declined from 28.2 million in 1977 to 26.4 million in 2004, because the much talked about growth of the private organised sector under the reform policies of the government hardly compensated for the decline employment by the public sector. Another telling piece of evidence against the belief that, corporate-led industrialisation and greater direct foreign investment would promote more employment came from the headlines of 'The Times of India (7 July, 2008).

> Long hailed as most dynamic in these respects, a recent comparison of the various states of India suggested Gujrat and Maharastra, have

been among the slowest growing states in terms of creating either non-agricultural or manufacturing job."

With regular employment opportunities growing far too slowly compared the number of job seekers, more and more people are being pushed to the unorganised sector. Agriculture in particular has become even more over-crowded. According to the National Sample Survey (61st round), approximately 110 million agricultural workers (out of a total work force of 400 million) found employment for 209 days in 2004-05 compared to 220 days in 1999-2000. People desperate for a livelihood join the rank of the so called self-employed in the unorganised sector, the fastest growing category, marked by long hours of work with negligible earning, lack of any social security or labour protection and extensive use of child labour. More than half the hawkers of Kolkata, and more than one third the hawkers of Amhedabad belonging to this category of self employed are retrenched industrial workers, now threatened once more with the corporatisation of retail trade in this era of globalisation in the name of economic efficiency. This vast informal sector is increasingly becoming a refuge for people devoid of all hopes, and reminds one of the Hell imagined by the great Italian poet Dante. On its gate is written, "You enter this land after abandoning all hopes".

The **second** reason for growing inequality lies in the style of economic management pursued by the government. While opportunity for regular work is growing at a grossly insufficient pace despite a high growth rate of output, the government has become increasingly weary of spending more for social welfare like health, education, public distribution and social security for the poor. Government expenditure remained more or less steady around 22 percent of GDP throughout 2000-2007, with health receiving 1.4 and education receiving 2.9 percent of GDP on the average. The apparent reasons given are lack of 'money' and poor public delivery system for social services. However, these are superficial justifications, and there is a more compelling reason which has come out into the open due to the financial crisis. Globalisation of finance made the government highly sensitive to the moods of the stock market and the financial sentiments of major players in that market. India has a relatively large foreign exchange reserve (283 billion U.S dollars in February 2008), but unlike China which has been enjoying export surplus for several years, our reserve comes mostly from capital inflows exceeding balance of payments deficits, like deposits from NRIs, and portfolio investments by various international financial institutions. These are far more fickle in nature and can be withdrawn at relatively short notice if the mood of the financial market turns sour. A main thrust of the pro-market government policy has been to keep the financial market happy by being on the right side of the IMF and the World Bank in so far as they have a central role in shaping international financial opinion for banks, credit-rating agencies, and other financial institutions. This means following their economic guidelines in formulating policies. As a result the government minimised its welfare spending by letting it stagnate as percentage of GPD even during the years of high growth. The cost of this squeeze of expenditure on social security, education and health falls mainly on the poor who cannot turn to the market due to lack of purchasing power and job opportunities.

The **third** route is paved by the style of industrialisation the government has increasingly adopted. It amounts to extending various privileges to the large corporations by the federal and state governments irrespective of their professed political colour as incentives for promoting corporate-led industrialisation. Land acquisition by the states (land is a state subject under the constitution) for 'public purpose' has become its politically most visible aspect. The central government all along has provided the legal and logistical support for land acquisition, and the original '1894 Land Acquisition Act' proclaiming the 'eminent domain' status for the state, was significantly revised successively in 1952, 1963, and 1984 to give greater power to the government to acquire land for the defence sector, companies, co-operatives and public sector companies. The present government has brought two related bills (of land acquisition amendment act, and rehabilitation and resettlement act both under consideration of parliamentary standing committees) to extend in many ways further the reach of the government. They are all linked directly or indirectly to a view of the model of development for three major purposes, namely (a) mining, (b) land for industrial sites and (c) Special Economic Zones, SEZ. First consider the mineral rich usually forested land acquired mostly from the tribal populations, concentrated heavily in the states of Jharkhand, Bihar, Chhattisgarh and Orissa. As has often been pointed out, these are some of the richest lands in the country where the poorest live. A piece of revealing statistics shows, mining displaces typically the poorests in the country, the Adivasis or tribals who constitute some 8 percent of the population but account for nearly half of the people displaced in the name of development. The state apparatus takes recourse to silent violence in various ways. Forcible acquisition of land and dispossession is obtained often through manufactured consent of the Gram Sabhas at gunpoint to comply formally with the legal requirements of the PESA Act(1996) relating to tribal areas. The public purpose is granting possession to private corporations of the iron ore rich land in Chhasttisgarh, Jharkhand , Madhya Pradesh, bauxite rich land of Orissa, prospect of diamond mine in Bastar etc. MOUs (Memorendum of Understanding) between the large private corporations and the concerned state governments are seldom revealed despite applications under RTI (Right to Information) Act. The mining land taken from the locals at unilaterally announced low compensation price (that are frequently not paid) is handed over to large corporations and industrial houses often with supporting infrastructure provided by the government at public cost by displacing more people. A telling instance of public private partnership is the proposed SEZ comprising of 45 villages in Raigad district of Maharastra, which has been recently rejected almost unanimously in a referendum held in 22 villages. While the government had the area under notification for acquisition for a 'public purpose', in that very same area Ambani's agents were privately trying to acquire land illegally with direct help from the Maharastra government.

It must be left for you to infer whether this is done only to pursue a model of industrialisation, or large money also changes hand benefiting our political class and many bureaucrats in this process. This is at least a part of the story behind the phenomenal growth in corporate wealth and dollar billionares in the country in recent years. Available statistics show that in hardly 4 years, between 2003-04 and 2006-7 the market value of capital of the companies listed on Bombay Stock Exchange grew almost three hundred percent, while until the recent stock market crash (October, 2008) India with the majority of its population desperately poor could perversely boast of the highest number of dollar billionares after the United States. The logic of a liberalised market mechanism buttressed further by state power to help the private corporations is relentlessly creating unprecedented inequality in India along with high growth. Sub-human poverty for millions, and billions of dollars for a handful of citizens has become the name of this game called development.

For this growth process to remain economically viable over time, slow growth of domestic purchasing power of the majority of the population must be countered by a compensating expansion either of our exports or expenditure by the rich. However, because our export exceeds import and we buy more from the foreigners than we sell to them, the net contribution of the foreign-trade sector to the expansion of demand in our economy is negative. As a result, this anti-poor pattern of growth is being sustained by a rapid expansion of income and expenditure by the richer groups in the society (a maximum of top 20-25 percent). The increasing inequality entailed in such a process of high growth means that the corporations sell their products and realise handsome profits by concentrating mostly on the production of goods consumed by the richer sections of the population. As a result some 75 percent of Indians with a daily per capita purchasing power of less than 20 rupees have virtually no place in this corporate led modern economy as consumers. Their space as small rural producers or as small businesses in the unorganised sector also shrinks, as the goods produced for the high end of the market can mostly be produced only by corporations (e.g. cars, refrigerators, air-conditioned malls, state-of-the-art hospitals etc). Thus, growing inequality and lack of employment opportunities are coupled, and an output composition oriented towards a rich minority of this country, tend to exclude the majority of our fellow citizens and often destroy their livelihoods. Thus the big dams that we build, the electricity that we generate, the worldclass cities that we strive for divert even non-reproducible natural resources. The large corporate houses use them efficiently to produce and sell to the rich profitable products , but their efficient utilization of natural resources imply the exclusion of the poor both as producers and as consumers. The process of growth is sustained by growing inequality, and inequality reinforces growth in a mutually supportive manner. The Swedish economist Gunner Myrdal had called it "cumulative causation", somewhat similar to the engineer's system of strong positive feedbacks, the evolutionary biologist's symbiosis between two species, and perhaps the notion of autocatalysis in chemical reactions.

While all this has been happening around us for quite some time, most of us refused to see it. The mainstream English language media, largely owned and controlled by large corporate houses, condition us continuously to turn a blind eye and believe that the virtual economy of the hourly fluctuations in the stock-market is far more news-worthy than the growing inequality, despair and fury engulfing gradually the countryside. Most economists who should have known better fuelled this perception, and cheered politicians in power for the rapid emergence of India as a global economic power; and of course politicians in power never tire of congratulating themselves for their own achievements. When the market boomed they took credit for liberalising the market, then as the market crashed they took credit for not liberalising the market! They took credit for forcing labour market flexibity of 'hire and fire' rule, when the market crashed the Prime Minister begged with the captains of industry in a specially called meeting not to fire workers near the time of election! This hypocritical politics has been going on as business as usual until the recent global financial crisis shook deeply the confidence in self-regulating free-market capitalism with its global reach. The comfortable thought that more economic reform to deregulate the market and speedier integration with global market would lead us rapidly towards an optimal economic state is no longer fashionable. Like their counterparts in the U.S and Europe, pro-market reformers of yesterday are now looking for cover; they who had opposed now want more supervision and regulation of the market in India. However, this is only passing, because as an old English rhyme says: "Those who are convinced against their will/ Are of the same opinion still."

Neo-liberalism has merely gone out of sight, but not out of mind. Vested interests cryslallised around corporations are merely on the defensive at the moment.

We are still being misled to support a model of corporate led industrialisation. Financially helped by the state in difficult times as the way to our economic development, without questioning its relevance in the Indian context. A deep-seated habit of thinking inculcated by the globalisation, privatisation and liberalisation rhetoric still wants us to believe that this market-fundamentalism, practising developmental terrorism selectively on the poor, will ultimately help them as high corporate growth trickles down. To keep our conscience comfortable, it claims that the market can substitute for social ethics by deciding what is profitable to produce, and who should be in charge of production. So we no longer question how without extensive public action and state intervention in favour of the poor, in this country of overwhelming poverty the logic of political democracy of one adult one vote can be compatible with the logic of the market dictat6ed by the rich with many more votes with their higher purchasing power than the poor. These are almost subversive questions; and yet, the ability to pose them is the first step to liberate ourselves from the ruling system of conventional economic wisdom that has failed us so badloy despite the big show of producing precise technocratic economic knowledge, helped by various vested interests including the distribution of a disproportionately large number of Nobel Prizes to make market-oriented economic conservatism academically respectable. Long ago in the introduction of his famous allegorical novel. The Animal Farm George Orwell had wa5rned us that British democracy is not very different from the totalitarian monster he was describing in his book. Unpopular ideas, he said, can be suppressed without the use of force with two methods. First, the press is owned by wealthy men (read corporations these days!) who have every reason not to want certain ideas to be expressed. And the second reason, Orwell said, is a good education. If you have gone to the best schools (read specially the top management and economics schools), it has been instilled in you that, there are certain things it would not do to express or even to think. Aided by the media, our educated middle class showed its excellent education until recently by banishing all skeptical thoughts about the efficiency and intrinsic wisdom of the market, and the virtues of corporate led high growth under financial globalization. Would this global financial crisis give us the courage necessary to reeducate ourselves to view the 'logic of the market' more logically? For, at times the unintended effects of history can be beneficial.